Fire in the Dark

Studies in Applied Anthropology

General Editor: **Sarah Pink**, University of Loughborough
Reflecting the contemporary growing interest in Applied Anthropology this
series publishes volumes that examine the ethnographic, methodological and
theoretical contribution of applied anthropology to the discipline and the role of
anthropologists outside academia.

Volume 1
Anthropology and Consultancy:
Issues and Debates
Edited by Pamela Stewart and Andrew Strathern

Volume 2
Applications of Anthropology:
Professional Anthropology in the Twenty-First Century
Edited by Sarah Pink

Volume 3
Fire in the Dark:
Telling Gypsiness in North East England
Sarah Buckler

Fire in the Dark

Telling Gypsiness in North East England

Sarah Buckler

Berghahn Books
New York • Oxford

First published in 2007 by
Berghahn Books
www.berghahnbooks.com

© 2007, 2011 Sal Buckler
First paperback edition published in 2011

Library of Congress Cataloging-in-Publication Data

Buckler, Sarah.
Fire in the dark : telling Gypsiness in North East England / Sarah Buckler.
    p. cm. -- (Studies in applied anthropology ; v. 3)
Includes bibliographical references.
ISBN 978-1-84545-230-8 (hbk) -- ISBN 978-0-85745-147-7 (pbk)
1. Romanies--England, North East. I. Title.

DX213.B83 2006
305.891'4970428--dc22

                                                                    2006028128

British Library Cataloguing in Publication Data

A catalogue record for this book is available from the British Library

Printed in the United States on acid-free paper

ISBN 978-1-84545-230-8 (hardback)
ISBN 978-0-85745-147-7 (paperback)
ISBN 978-0-85745-317-4 (ebook)

CONTENTS

LIST OF ILLUSTRATIONS

ACKNOWLEDGEMENTS

I would like to thank the following people without whom this book could never have been written:

The Gypsies and Travellers of Teesside, for your help, instruction, stories, teasing, interest, encouragement, challenges and so on, not to mention your friendship and the good times we have had.

The council workers, school teachers and other colleagues, for your advice, assistance, interest and friendship. I hope this book contributes in some way to our ongoing quest to find ways of working and living together effectively and constructively.

Professor Michael Carrithers and Dr Bob Simpson, my Ph.D. supervisors from the Anthropology Department at Durham, and all those who participated in the Work in Progress Seminars and discussed my work with such interest, your contributions really helped.

My children, Emma and Haarland, for making sure I kept a sense of perspective, and all my friends who have been there for me.

Many thanks also to the Harold Hyam Wingate Foundation, which awarded me a Wingate Scholarship for the years 2000-2002, without which I could not have afforded to embark on this project.

Thanks also to the Workers' Educational Association, who employed me as a development worker and allowed me to conduct this research as part of my job.

The years of research and study that have resulted in the production of this book have been an experiment, an adventure and a challenge for me. I have been given an opportunity that is given to very few people and I am enormously grateful for it. It is an opportunity that I could not have had were it not for all those I thank above and I am more grateful and happy for that than I can say. I hope you like the result.

Sal Buckler, 2005

Introduction

Beginning of February 2002: I was sitting in a poorly lit council chamber, around a large square of tables with approximately twenty other people. Sitting alongside me were two Romany Gypsies, Janey and Robert, whom I had worked with for almost four years – I was a development officer for a local charity. Also present were representatives of various departments of the council and other service providers: health workers, education workers, police and so on. We were all there with the same purpose in mind – to decide upon a course of action for the council regarding the presence of an unauthorised camp of Gypsies in the area. It was expected that the adoption of a particular response would also outline how the council should deal with complaints it had received from housed residents and local business owners in the area where the camp had set up.

For two hours or so we talked around the various issues, explored different options, sought clarification, made suggestions and so on. At the end of the two hours no definite decisions had been made and everybody was left with a shared sense of frustration – we had got precisely nowhere. To me (and to others I spoke to after the meeting) it felt like the meeting had achieved nothing at all. What was all the more frustrating was that it had achieved nothing at all despite the fact that for the first time not only had some members of the Gypsy Traveller population been invited along, but two had actually shown up. Before the meeting it was thought that asking Gypsies and Travellers about what they wanted and what they might suggest as possible courses of action would help the process – in the end it seemed as if it had simply muddied the water and that even less had been achieved than usual.

At the end of the meeting – after I had said goodbye to Janey and Robert – I went to speak to Mark, a council officer I knew quite well. Mark asked if I thought there would ever be a solution to the problems involved in trying to provide for Gypsies and Travellers. My response was 'No, it's not about solutions – it's all about how well you dance.' Mark and I both laughed at this – he understood what I meant and responded with a small turn across the council chamber – nonetheless, it wasn't a satisfactory explanation although there was a grain of metaphorical truth in it. I still could not really understand how it was that a group of people could come together with a shared intention to achieve an agreed end, and yet could go away, after two hours of what had seemed to be reasonably constructive talk, having achieved nothing – not even a greater understanding upon which to base any future decisions. It did feel as though we had simply been dancing around the crucial issues.

This book is the result of my desire to try and untangle exactly what was going on at the meeting, why no resolution could be reached – and why we were all left with a dull sense of frustration.

Book Structure

Metaphors are things we think with (Quinn 1991: 68) and this book is informed by those metaphors I find particularly useful and illuminating. For the most part I have ditched the dance metaphor and those that are most apparent in the text are visual metaphors – perhaps especially the major, organising image of the wasteland wherein burns a fire surrounded by darkness. This image is an echo of a favourite image of the Gypsies I worked with – a campfire burning on ground where Gypsies are camped – and with it I structure the work into three sections: 'The Wasteland', 'The Fire' and 'The Dark'. The first section deals with the theoretical and background information upon which the study rests, setting out the context in which the research was carried out and in which the book was written. The first chapter deals specifically with the theoretical background to the study, the ideas that place the following ethnography in the context of anthropological and other academic trains of enquiry. This chapter is specifically concerned with two issues that crop up repeatedly in the following chapters. The first is the concept of boundaries – a metaphor used repeatedly in anthropology and ethnography but which is nevertheless simply that, a metaphor. The second theme is that of the socially constituted and distributed nature of what might be termed 'identity'.

The second chapter of the first section elaborates upon the ideas introduced in the first chapter, examining what it means to view some metaphors as useful or illuminating or appropriate and others as less so. This chapter also sets the study within a methodological frame, focusing on ethical issues, particularly those tied up with issues of representation.

The final chapter of the first section places the study within a geographical, historical and political context. The people that this book is about lived and worked in a specific place at a specific time and the events I describe take place against a particular visual and political backdrop. It is my hope that describing some of the history and appearance of the area will bring it more to life in your mind's eye and by making it more easily imaginable make it more easily enjoyable.

In the second section, 'The Fire', the main grounds of my argument – my analysis of why the meeting described above could not reach a resolution – are outlined. In 'Stories and Teaching Gypsiness' I explore the role of stories in the intersubjective process of socialisation, describing in detail some of the ways this process is played out amongst the Gypsies I worked with.[1] Anthropologists have noted the various practices of child rearing in different cultures (e.g. Mead 1931; Mead and Macgregor 1951; Schieffelin and Ochs 1986; Schieffelin 1990) and have shown how the ways in which we are brought into this world and the ways we are cared for have a significant impact upon the ways we learn to behave and the ways we understand others. In this chapter I examine these arguments specifically with reference to ways of using and thinking about language and speaking and even more specifically how these processes become evident in the ways that stories are told and used both by Gypsies and by non-Gypsies I have worked with.

Having laid out my general perspective I go on to examine in greater detail one aspect of Gypsy life – namely, that of 'family' – hence the second chapter of 'The Fire' is called 'Stories and the Telling of Family'. In this chapter I explore ways in which stories weave together various 'cultural scenarios' (Schieffelin 1976: 3) and combine to form a cultural landscape in which the enactment and interpretation of such cultural scenarios takes place.

In many ways ideas about 'home' and 'family' go hand in hand, and, as much of my development and advocacy work with Gypsies concerned issues to do with finding places for Gypsies to set up their homes, an exploration of the notion of 'home' in Gypsies' talk provides a useful expansion of the issues discussed in the preceding chapters and a link to issues discussed later. In 'Home is Where the Heart is' I show how the making and telling of stories together builds a sense of home that is situated in a network of relationships rather than in a place and how stories are used in the continual recreation and maintenance of this web of relationships.

In the final chapter of 'The Fire' I stay with the face-to-face world of the Gypsies' families but turn towards the non-Gypsy world to see how Gypsies learn to deal with being both part of and apart from the non-Gypsy world. This chapter examines how the processes described in the preceding chapters are played out in interactions between Gypsies and non-Gypsies, keeping the notion of 'family' as a reference point.

Having described 'The Fire' – i.e. the face-to-face world of Gypsies' families – I then go on to describe 'The Dark' – the non-Gypsy world in which 'The Fire' burns. I explore how ideas about Gypsiness and non-Gypsiness affect the interactions of people who go about their daily lives inhabiting worlds that are apparently the same but that are also worlds apart.

The first chapter, 'The Mediated Moral Imagination', shifts the perspective to look less at how Gypsies make sense of and to themselves and more at how they are made sense of by non-Gypsies. I show how a 'typical' understanding of Gypsies and Gypsiness is established through the practice of telling stories about Gypsies. As a focus I look specifically at the stories – their telling and their enactment – that appeared in a local newspaper as the events took place that led to the meeting described at the start.

I then close in upon the interactions of people behind the story – and specifically the interactions that took place at a meeting the November before the crucial February meeting. By focusing in more detail on the interactions of people in a meeting context we can begin to see the ways in which 'story seeds' (Carrithers 2003) – the potential to make one sort of sense or another of the situation in hand – are proposed, used, discarded and so on.

In the final chapter of 'The Dark' I return to the meeting described at the beginning – now more fully equipped to examine in detail what was going on, what was achieved in that meeting, and why what had been intended could not come about. We see how the ability to engage in intersubjective interactions enables people to try to build a shared sense of purpose – a shared storyline. We also see how coming from different traditions of practice can make this process difficult as different understandings and expectations are drawn upon.

Applying Anthropology

The final point I would like to raise in this introduction concerns the relationship between applied and academic anthropology. Throughout my research the boundaries that distinguish one thing from another (Gypsies and non-Gypsies, settled and travelling people, the 'field' from the 'academy') became blurred and often seemed irrelevant or misleading. This was equally so in the distinction between different ways of putting the kinds of knowledge and understanding that ethnographic research can generate into use. Perhaps inevitably, because of the multiple roles I had throughout the project (student, development worker, advocate, friend and so on), my understanding and use of anthropology emerged as simultaneously theoretical and applied. This book is an illustration of one way in which apparently different kinds of anthropology can work together to provide understandings that are meaningful and useful for multiple audiences. Perhaps also, and I very much hope, this work can demonstrate the enormous usefulness of carrying out long-term, engaged, ethnographic work – not just for the academic discipline of anthropology but also for those engaged in policy and development work. The understandings reached and written about in this work could not have come about other than through such long-term and involved research, nor could they have come about without being engaged in both the theoretical work of anthropology and the applied work involved in development and advocacy. That this has been a productive and useful relationship is, I hope, demonstrated in the pages that follow.

Note

1. See Trevarthen and Aitken (2001) for a useful review of research into the intersubjective processes involved in human cognitive development.

PART I

THE WASTELAND

1.1 Horses at Bankside

What are the roots that clutch, what branches grow
Out of this stony rubbish? Son of man,
You cannot say, or guess, for you know only
A heap of broken images, where the sun beats,
And the dead tree gives no shelter, the cricket no relief,
And the dry stone no sound of water. Only
There is shadow under this red rock
(Come in under the shadow of this red rock),
And I will show you something different from either
Your shadow at morning striding behind you
Or your shadow at evening rising to meet you;
I will show you fear in a handful of dust.

From T.S. Eliot, *The Waste Land*

1.2 Entrance to the Stockton Site

hungry and homeless,
old, weary travellers:
they who have buried
their innermost hopes.
In the pores of a woman,
living and breathing,
lies the burden of sorrows
endured by her ancestors
as they march down centuries
along the turbulent river.

In her lies the place
Where reality meets
With a new beginning,
Down a dirt road
Towards a horizon
that ever recedes.

From Alija Krasnići, *We did not break our century-old drums*
reprinted in Hancock et al. 1998: 142

Chapter 1

DEFINING THE FIELD
People and Practice in an Indeterminate Place

―――∞∞∞―――

Early in 1998 I wandered on to a semi-deserted Gypsy site in Bankside to meet a man called Charlie Oldham and his wife, Jane.[1] Until then I had never visited a Gypsy camp, instead I did as most others seemed to and looked on from a distance, wondering about the people who lived in the caravans that would park around the area from time to time. As I walked on to the site I had a number of voices running around in my head, voices that repeated the well-meaning concerns of friends and family – 'Take care,' 'Will you be all right?' 'Do you want me to come with you?' 'Rather you than me.' When they had been voiced I had shrugged off all these remarks – I had phoned Charlie and arranged to meet him, he seemed friendly enough and it felt like going on an adventure. In fact, I was more concerned about the distance I would have to cover in the walk from the populated, built-up areas of Bankside to the site, which is tucked away down near the docks. The route to the site is surrounded by derelict land and scrapyards, apparently empty of people but patrolled by tired and hungry-looking dogs. It was a place you just didn't go to.

I walked on to the site that February day in 1998 as a candidate for a development post with a local charity. Charlie seemed reasonably happy to see me, he greeted me in the brusque offhand manner I have since come to expect from Gypsy men and ushered me towards his caravan. The silence was broken by the persistent barking of a collection of dogs chained to their respective kennels and struggling to get free – it was clear they weren't happy about having a stranger in their midst. Charlie introduced me to his wife and then showed me into another caravan – one that didn't seem to be lived in as it was bare of any of the paraphernalia of everyday life. We spoke for some time about the problems that Gypsies had in Bankside and what could be done about them, about the way that the council had asked Gypsies' opinions and then ignored them, about the way that most people didn't understand anything about Gypsies.

When I returned from that first meeting my perspective on the world had changed. I could now answer the voices in my head – 'See, it was fine

– I haven't been kidnapped or robbed or raped.' Not only could I respond to the voices in my head, I could also begin to answer the new questions people started to throw at me: 'What's it like?' 'Were they OK about you going down there?' 'Where exactly is the site?' and so on. I felt like a traveller returning from a foreign land with tales of a mythical people. In fact, I'd spent an hour or so sitting in a caravan on a concrete plot less than a couple of minutes' walk from the main drive to work of most of the people who were questioning me.

Some years after my first visit to the site in Bankside I could be found regularly walking the distances between the settled residential areas of the industrial towns of Teesside and the Gypsy sites where I carried out most of my work (I did get the job). These spaces came to hold a significance for me that reached beyond the simple journey to and from work. They were (and are) wastelands and they are both margin and meeting point between Gypsies and non-Gypsies; they still feel dangerously uncertain.

Whilst carrying out my work as a development officer I was also conducting research into interactions between Gypsies and non-Gypsies. Through this research project I have come to understand these wastelands as the products of multiple layers of interaction incorporating conflicts, dichotomies and ambivalences. This understanding is influenced by studies that stress the interactive and contextual nature of identity (e.g. Drury and Reicher 2000: 581). Such a perspective encourages me to view the wastelands as sites of interaction rather than as boundaries marking out a different world inhabited by Gypsies.

Gypsies on Teesside occupy a number of different and sometimes conflicting social positions simultaneously, creating multiple layers of overlapping social identities. These multiple layers of interaction demonstrate the complexity of being 'Gypsy' – a complexity that cannot be contained within any neat and singular model of identity and that requires the existence of ill-defined spaces (material and metaphorical wastelands) where conflicts and contradictions can be worked through or left unresolved. This study shows how these conflicts arise in everyday interactions between Gypsies and non-Gypsies in the Tees Valley, and how they are creatively worked with in order to create and maintain a cohesive sense of what it is to be a Gypsy or non-Gypsy.

Boundaries and Meeting Places

From the perspective of ethnography the participants in the research, including myself, are engaged in the production of culture and identity. My understanding of the process we engaged in during the research is influenced by F. Barth (1969), who depicts cultures as dynamic and as changing over time in ways that are not always predictable. Barth's conclusion is that the boundaries that divide one culture from another are themselves not fixed entities but are also liable to change. He claims that, in order to understand the mutable and complex nature of ethnicity and its relationship to social structure as continually reconstructed through interactions, it is necessary to look at the boundaries that divide one ethnic group from another rather than analyse what is inside those boundaries. In a later piece Barth develops the idea of the boundary as evidence of a shared and socially constructed cognitive device, arguing that what is worthy of examination is the way that interaction takes place across, and sometimes enabled by, our ideas about boundaries and social distinctions (Barth 2000: 17).

The social emphasis of Barth's view of boundaries differs from that developed by Anthony Cohen – boundaries as symbolic constructions (Cohen 1985: 13). Whilst Cohen's work also proposes a theory of boundaries that are both mutable and manipulable, and also metaphorical, Barth's more recent work moves away from the idea that boundaries are *symbolic* of difference, as Cohen proposed, towards the idea that boundaries are realms of material and social action and production. The implications of Barth's approach are profound – the suggestion is that boundaries are marginal places where we can investigate the social actions of people in terms of what they produce or create; there is something discernible going on. This differs from the implications of Cohen's view, which places the significance of boundaries within the ultimately inaccessible depths of individual minds (Cohen 2000: 15).

Both Barth and Cohen agree that boundaries mean different things to different people depending upon their orientation to whatever boundary is in question. Given this variability it is useful to view the notion of boundary as a focal point (rather than delimiting an area) around which people negotiate their relationships. Discernible actions and interactions as the object of study suggest that 'boundaries' are viewed as enabling interaction (Barth 2000: 30) rather than representative of differences of consciousness as suggested by Cohen (2000: 2).

Translated to my own research the suggestion of Barth's approach is that the wastelands between towns and sites, and their social corollaries between Gypsy and gorgio[2] (non-Gypsy) peoples, are not fixed representations or symbols of difference but are, rather, the products of our interactions. The subject of research becomes what we produce through our relationships and how we orient ourselves towards one another, rather than an examination of what it is to be either Gypsy or gorgio per se.

Boundaries and Gypsy Identity

Nevertheless, the notion of boundaries still implies a certain symmetry – there is the suggestion that even if the boundary is shifting and vague it is still something that is recognised by people who find themselves on either one side of it or the other. However, issues concerning ethnicity and ethnic boundaries take on a particularly challenging flavour when applied to people who make no territorial claims, e.g. Gypsies or Celts (Fernandez 2000), and who live amongst members of other ethnic groups rather than separate from them. Arising from such complexities is a debate about the bound versus the unbound nature of identity, which is pivotal in analyses of Gypsy identity, the multiple nature of which has been dealt with in many ways that nevertheless all make use of the metaphorical notion of boundary. For instance, Sutherland represented a duality of identity as metaphorically recreated in a series of boundaries (Sutherland 1977: 377). Okely concentrated on the boundary separating Gypsy from gorgio (Okely 1983), creating a notion of Gypsiness that, because of its dependence upon the non-Gypsy world as an oppositional contrast, appears to perpetuate an idea of Gypsiness that is fixed in terms of its characterising cosmology (ibid.: 76, 77ff.).

Stewart has taken a more relativist and contextual approach, noting the degrees of difference in Gypsiness recognised by Hungarian Roma (Stewart 1997a, b: 28), an approach reflected in Okely's later work (Okely 1997: 195). All these approaches have in common the recognition of a particular space within which Gypsies identify themselves as Gypsies, and outside which people are identified as non-Gypsies. Stewart's work introduces an increased complexity to this notion, showing how this space is rarely rigidly defined and how it shifts according to context and who is involved in any interaction. A major focus of Stewart's work is on the performance of Gypsiness, an approach adopted in various analyses of Gypsy identity that pull Gypsiness away from the essentialising, prescriptive assertions of folklorists. Gay-y-Blasco's work amongst Gitanos in Madrid (1997, 1999, 2000, 2001) explores the performed nature of identity locating ideas about Gypsiness in webs of relationships as much as in any specifically Gypsy (or Gitano) practices. Recent work by Lemon develops similar themes; drawing heavily on the work of Erving Goffman (1981, 1986) Lemon describes how ideas about identity amongst Russian Roma continually shift, not only amongst Gypsy groups but also between Gypsies and non-Gypsies (Lemon 2000: 23, 80, 201).

In structuring this book I have used a metaphor that is used by the Gypsies I worked with. Not to do that, and to use metaphors to describe Gypsy culture that Gypsies themselves do not usually use, risks reproducing an understanding of Gypsiness that accepts the descriptions and definitions of the non-Gypsy world. So, for instance, to adopt too easily Goffman's metaphors, which draw upon binary oppositions (front stage/backstage, public/private), risks denying the paradoxical experience of Gypsiness, where one is not simply able to move through a more or less 'porous' boundary (Goffman 1986: 126) but where one is always and inescapably on both sides of any boundary – so 'boundary' needs to be seen as a defining tool of the non-Gypsy world, not a feature of the experience of being Gypsy.

Attitudes that draw upon the metaphor of a boundary separating Gypsies from gorgios are repeated throughout the popular mythology of contemporary British society, which holds particular ideas about what constitutes a 'true Gypsy'. This problem is recognised and dealt with in various ways by Gypsies themselves – Livia Járóka (2000) writes her own personal response to some of the challenges that confining and defining Gypsies within a particular conceptual space create for the people who actually live their lives affected by that experience. Nor is this problem only encountered by asylum seekers – it is continually endured and dealt with by British Gypsies as I know from my own experience of being asked (almost every time I told someone what my job was) whether I worked with 'real' Gypsies.

One common conception of Gypsies is that there were, at some point in the past, Gypsies who were a pure breed and who originated from somewhere in the East (e.g. Sampson, 1923; Trigg, 1973; Gropper, 1975; Liegeois, 1986; Fraser, 1995). The suggestion that sometimes accompanies this view is that each time a border or boundary was crossed there was a dilution of the original race until the Gypsies we see in the UK today are no longer pure Gypsies. Whilst this idea has been challenged by anthropologists as far as genetic and racial factors are concerned (see especially Okely 1983: 15ff.), there has been less attention paid to the very similar arguments made about their ethnic or cultural identity. Many studies (e.g. Hancock et al. 1998: 26; Kenrick and Clark 1999: 24) have tracked the 'journey of the Gypsies' from northern India, through the European land mass and into the UK. These studies bolster the view that Gypsies have accreted various aspects of the cultures and languages of the countries they have passed through and the boundaries they have crossed, a view adopted particularly by specialists in Romani language (Friedman 1985, 1991, 1995; Lapage 1997; Matras 1995, 2002; Matras et al. 1997). Again, the implication is that there was once a pure culture that was wholly Gypsy and that this pure culture has become gradually added to and detracted from – a process of syncretisation – and what is really interesting are the aspects of Gypsies' original culture (including their language) that still remain.

Drawbacks of this approach are pointed out by academics involved in lobbying for legal and political change (see Morris and Clements 1999). One of the major problems of this position is that it denies relevance to the current, dynamic, lived and experienced cultures of Gypsies today – it places them in a past over which they have no control and in which they have lost their place. In this way the boundary between Gypsy and non-Gypsy is imposed in time as well as in material and social space. It also illustrates how 'boundary' may be an appropriate term only when looked at from the perspective of those who impose it (in this case non-Gypsies), as Barth has noted (2000: 19).

An alternative way to look at Gypsies' culture draws on the idea of 'polytropy' (Carrithers, 2000). Polytropy, unlike syncretism, posits no notion of a pre-existing, pure cultural form, nor does it imply any process of corruption or decay. More importantly, polytropy is defined as 'a wholly and thoroughly social concept' (ibid.: 834), whereby cultural practices are performed through a vast spectrum of relationships. The role of culture is not to define and categorise the individuals who belong to any given culture, rather it is a means whereby relationships can be continuously reaffirmed and maintained. From this perspective the natural productivity and creativity of culture are in our relationships rather than in our replication of past forms and actions – it is a dynamic process rather than a habitual performance, and one that naturally lends itself to change (ibid.: 835). So, rather than there being some pure, original Gypsy culture from which all deviations are a form of corruption, the mutability and multiplicity of Gypsy identity are always an inherent aspect of their living and lived culture.

Anthropologists who have carried out research amongst Gypsy groups in Eastern Europe have noted the significance of 'the Gypsy way of doing things' (Stewart 1997b: 92; Lemon 2000: 205); these works show how Gypsies define their 'Gypsiness' through the kind and quality of their interactions with others. These interactions form connections that link people to people across space and time and allow an understanding of 'being a Gypsy' that is not rigidly defined in any way.

Such views have been developed most especially in the context of discussions concerning authenticity – a particularly salient theme in discussions of Gypsy culture and identity that have increasingly focused on paradoxical representations of Gypsies. Gypsies come to understand themselves as being simultaneously on both sides of a number of boundaries (e.g. between 'true' Gypsy and 'tinker'; Gypsy and Traveller; honest and dishonest; poor and rich). Such a position is in itself paradoxical and demands that the idea of a boundary is dispensed with and identity focuses on a process of shifting alignments and ways of interacting – the site of the paradox also becomes a site of creativity.

Conflicting representations are an aspect of Gypsy life across the world and suggest a commonality of experience if not a shared culture. In this commonality of experience might be found something that can be called 'Gypsy' – but if this is the case it will not be a label for definable cultural structures and practices, such as purity taboos and the Romany language. Rather, it would be a reference to strategies for reconciling or living with conflicting identities.

As noted above, ethnographers have generally represented the perpetual shifting of identity and perspective amongst the Gypsies they work with as a continual crossing back and forth across boundaries. The image is an especially potent one because of the actual physical places where Gypsies live – marginalized spaces on the boundaries of mainstream society (Sibley 1981: 31, 1995: 49; Smith 1991: 2; Kendall 1997). One difficulty with this image is that it does not allow for the perpetual shifting and realigning of identity that goes on amongst Gypsies themselves. An alternative to the boundary metaphor, and perhaps an equally potent image, can be found with Machin and Carrithers's idea of landmarks (1996). This idea suggests that we move away from bounding people's identity – situating them inside categories from which they then have to free themselves to cross boundaries and stretch our, and their, ideas about who they are. Instead, we are invited to look at the significant and widely recognised cultural 'landmarks' or conceptual points towards and around which people orient themselves. This returns us to the point made above regarding an analysis of relationships and focal points around which we produce our identity through our interactions with others and the world around us.

Recent approaches, such as that adopted by Lemon, tend towards this view of culture, as it more faithfully reflects their research experience and findings. The implications of this perspective become more apparent when we view the many peoples that comprise today's multicultural societies – including Gypsies. In the UK today, on Teesside as much as anywhere, there are groups of people living together in close proximity whose families have come from diverse ethnic backgrounds. In multicultural Britain ethnicity has become divorced from territory and demands another way of talking about culture and identity. Whilst people from many diverse backgrounds all live alongside one another, there is a recognition of their differing cultural origins – that there are aspects of experience they share, and aspects of experience that are unique to only a few of them. These communities are difficult to describe if we try to draw lines and erect boundaries to divide one group from another – even given that such boundaries would be flexible. Hence it becomes more productive to look at the ways people orient themselves both to one another and to other significant conceptual points – whether these be ideas about ways of talking, ways of acting, shopping, work, religion and so on.

Schematic Understandings

In the preceding discussion of Barth's work on ethnic boundaries, the concern focused upon the discernible aspects of culture and identity as it is lived – as it is performed, as Carrithers, Stewart and Lemon might put it. Barth also states a need for a way of making evident the interface between the individual and society – between the actor and the performance. Barth puts this as a need for a cognitive theory of culture (Barth 2000: 20) noting that it is not sufficient to be able to describe people's actions but that it is also important to 'lay bare the concepts that people are actually using, and the connections that people themselves make, when they perform such actions' (ibid.: 20)

Much work that has been carried out in the area of cognitive anthropology has focused on ways of speaking – discourse and conversation analysis (e.g. Holland and Quinn 1987; Gumperz 1992; Tannen 1993; Strauss and Quinn 1997). Many of these studies draw upon notions such as 'schemas' and 'frames' (Goffman 1981, 1986) in order to show the connections between speech acts and culturally distributed ideas and images. Such approaches are a valuable resource when looking at the processes of constructing and maintaining ideas about identity despite conflicting representations of self, and this is especially pertinent as regards ideas about Gypsy identity – whether they be ideas held by Gypsies or non-Gypsies.

As noted above, some of the conflicts that are present in the formation of Gypsy identity become evident in the portrayal of Gypsies by mainstream society. According to the popular press, Gypsies are de facto an elusive and magical people, somehow in touch with the mysterious side of life and able to see things that ordinary people don't. They have their own rules and ways of doing things and their own families and ways of recognising one another. These are the 'real' Gypsies, who occupy a mythical space and time, unaffected by the mundane requirements of survival in the 'real' world. There are also the 'tinkers' and other 'pretend' Gypsies – interlopers who have no connection with the wild and mysterious world of the real Gypsies (Romanies) and who give those real Gypsies a bad name (for more on this see, for example, Acton 1994; Kendall 1997: 82; Morris 2000). These are representations that every Gypsy has to adopt some sort of orientation towards, and they can seem to demand a choice between, for instance, being either a 'true Gypsy' or living in the contemporary world. These are also the ideas I was familiar with when I first began to work with Gypsies – and although I knew better than to take what newspapers say at face value there were still a lot of ideas that I had to disentangle in order to see the people I was working with as people and not as representative examples of either real or not real Gypsies.

Common conceptions about Gypsies are summed up in the comments that were being repeated in my head as I walked down to the Bankside site for that first meeting with Charlie, they include ideas about their criminal tendencies, their unfriendliness and the squalor in which they live. In fact, Gypsies are something of a mystery as far as mainstream society is concerned – for many people in this country, the most contact they will ever knowingly have with Gypsies is when somebody comes knocking at their door selling tea towels and trinkets or approaches them in the street selling lucky charms. To most, Gypsies are still those mysterious people that they were to me when I first began to work with them.

Gypsies, however, do not live in their own mysterious world, cut off from the rest of society – they interact with the same institutions as we do, go to the same shops, watch the same TV programmes, and so on. Similarly, all the non-Gypsies they interact with are individuals and cannot be lumped together into a single category of 'gorgio' towards whom all

Gypsies behave in the same way. What we do – Gypsy and gorgio alike – is continually reinvent our relationships, using ideas such as Gypsy and gorgio as points of reference rather than as determining qualities.

Disentangling common conceptions of identity has been a crucial part of the research process; there are various possible identities – Gypsy, gorgio, bureaucrat, researcher, council officer, etc. – and these are, effectively, 'landmarks' and form part of the wider social landscape through which we move and conduct our relationships. The issue is our changing orientation to these landmarks depending on context and how to figure out both what those changing perspectives entail and how to represent this in anthropological terms.

This focus on context relates to notions of schemas[3] – a notion that can also be related to ideas about schemes of expression and interpretation (see, for example, Schutz 1944, 1970, 1972; Bourdieu 1977, 1979; Bourdieu & Wacquant 1992). Various identities are given their sense through our understanding of what they connote – what it is we know about Gypsies, gorgios, bureaucrats, etc. as types (Schutz 1944, 1970, 1972; Carrithers 2001). The possible identities are fixed (as labels), but their attributes and relations to one another, as expressed through individual characters and interactions, are variable. So, for instance, two people might identify themselves as Travellers rather than Gypsies to a schoolteacher, but when I ask about their families they insist that they're not Travellers because they are Gypsies, and in talk between themselves one is a Gypsy and the other is a gorgio because she wasn't born into a Gypsy family, she married into it. The nature of what a Gypsy 'is' is different depending on whether you talk to a schoolteacher, a researcher, or a Gypsy. However, the notion of 'Gypsy' as a possible type is constant and, what is more, we all assume we know what we mean when we use the term 'Gypsy'.

What is at stake is not only the unearthing of schematic understandings but also the extent to which those schematic understandings and the types they connote are or are not shared between us and what happens when such understandings and the ensuing actions are 'asymmetrical' (Drury and Reicher 2000: 599). My research concerned identifying and analysing these schematic understandings and how they inform our everyday interactions and our production of identity, including times and ways in which they come into conflict and so challenge notions of coherence and unified identity. As the research progressed, we (myself and those I worked with) became increasingly aware of one another as particular and individual people – not simply representatives of types. We also became more sensitive to the schematic understandings of one another and through this process we began to explore the ways in which identity can be reconstructed according to our individual experience of one another as personalities rather than as objects that are made to fit into preconceived conceptual categories. Nevertheless, this process is always complicated by the conflicts that we encounter in the spaces where one conceptual 'landmark' seems to transform into another – sometimes even its opposite.

Take the case of Deborah, a woman from the Gypsy community whom I have known for some time. I was initially introduced to Deborah by one of the older women who lived on Riverside[4] when she had come along to a meeting about facilities on the site. Deborah had been very quiet and went away soon after the meeting started. When I commented on this, it was shrugged off: 'Well, it's Gypsies for you – they don't understand this sort of thing, it goes over their heads.' About six months later, the local council's community development team came down to the site and spoke to Deborah, asking her to help with a youth group – they said that they would train her and pay her a sessional rate as an unqualified youth worker. I had nothing to do with this arrangement but I was pleased for Deborah as she had wanted to do something along these lines for a while; she would often comment that there was nothing for the young people to do on the site. Unfortunately, the promised payments and training never materialised. Deborah ended up putting in many hours of voluntary work, only to be left without even any expenses – the community development workers never returned to the site after that initial visit. Deborah's husband's reaction to this was, 'I told you – you've been had by the gorgios.' The implication was that Gypsies should not trust gorgios as they would always 'pull a fast one'. It was not until many months later that I found out that Deborah had not been born into a Gypsy family herself and that she considered herself, and was considered to be, simultaneously inside and outside the Gypsy community.

The fact that people can hold conflicting ideas has been recognised (e.g. Strauss and Quinn 1997; Mackie and Smith 1998), and again the ideas can be useful when applied to concepts of ethnicity and identity. In her research about Americans' conceptions of marriage, Quinn noted how apparently conflicting ideas were reconciled by coming up with a new idea. In her research, Strauss also noted conflicts and showed how people can compartmentalise conflict where they cannot find a creative reconciliation (Strauss and Quinn 1997: 188ff.). Similarly Linde (1993: 6, 7) has shown how various aspects of a person's life story can be retold in different ways depending on the interactive context of the telling. These retellings sometimes indicate conflicting notions of identity, which have been compartmentalised or even forgotten in order to maintain a coherent sense of self. This idea was developed further by Bluck and Habermas (2000), who posit the idea of a life-story schema that incorporates various interpretations and tellings without necessarily implying a contradiction.

With reference to Gypsies, Lemon has noted how Russian Roma frequently shift the terms of their identity depending on context, in a way that suggests a compartmentalisation similar to that shown by the participants in Quinn's study (Lemon 2000: 202). Lemon also shows how aspects of Roma life histories are changed depending on context (ibid.: 225), thus suggesting the idea of a life-history schema, as suggested by Bluck and Habermas. Taking on board such an idea, 'schematic understandings', as I use the term, relate to both schemas (which are conceived as located in an individual, as illustrated in the life-story schema above) and interpretative and expressive schemes (which are conceived as being socially distributed and generated). The 'voices' in my mind as I went to the Gypsy site the first time are evidence of schematic understandings about Gypsies and as such they formed the basis of how I decided to act and also how I understood and interpreted the actions of myself and others.

Framing Interactions

The orientation we adopt around various types informs the nature of the 'interactive frame' (Tannen and Wallat 1993) of any particular interaction and hence our understanding of what it is the interaction is doing. As with different schematic understandings about the nature of the various types, there can be conflicts and asymmetries between the participants' understandings of what the interactive frame is. For instance, when a teacher talks to Gypsy parents about school attendance, there may be an agreement about the nature of the interactive frame: that they are talking about education and the welfare of a child. Alternatively, whilst the teacher may be acting within the idea of such an interactive frame, the parents may perceive the frame as being about the relationships between Gypsies and gorgios and associated power issues. Such differences of interactional perspective can lead to dissonance between the expected and actual behaviour of those engaged in the interaction (Watanabe, 1993), hence leading to further conflicts regarding identity and social position.

As with schematic understandings and potential misunderstandings, this research project is concerned with ascertaining the various frames underlying an interaction (and specifically, ultimately, those involved in the meeting described in the introduction) and the extent to which they are shared by all participants in that interaction.

Becoming a Person – Embodiedness

Conflicting identities, whether resolved or compartmentalised, are loosely bound together in one physical body, the mediator between mind and society (Mauss 1979). What the various approaches to the notion of boundaries have in common is an understanding of the mutually constituted nature of culture, a mutuality embodied and performed in our physical actions and in our interactions with one another. Ingold (1993) and Barth attempt to lift anthropological understanding out of the unknowable reaches of the individual human mind and into a tangible and mutually experienced world – a world of acting and interacting bodies in a sensual environment. This perspective is also reflected in the work of Drury and Reicher (2000: 596), who demonstrate that there is a real and enacted link between the possibilities and constraints upon action that inhere in any social position or relationship and the actor's sense of identity.

Research concerning identity formation in social contexts, such as that by Drury and Reicher, emphasises its mutual and social nature, stressing the role of social interaction as productive of identity; this echoes Carrithers's notion of polytropy, as it is dynamically embodied and performed through the practice of puja, thus bringing us back to the notion of culture as a creative and ever changing process. Drury and Reicher's research focuses on what happens when there is an asymmetrical relationship between perceived identities and associated expected actions. Whilst their research focused on interactions between police and road protesters, their findings are usefully applied to interactions between Gypsies and non-Gypsies and ways of dealing with conflicting representations and self-perceptions. As they note, 'when understandings become asymmetrical, it becomes apparent that our understandings of ourselves depend upon how others understand and treat us' (Drury and Reicher 2000: 599). The crucial point in Drury and Reicher's research is the focus on the way others treat us; this keeps identity firmly within the social sphere and within the realm of discernible actions and behaviour.

Focusing upon interactions between people and groups and across shifting boundaries leads to an interest in the extent to which culture is borne through demeanour, gesture and so on – the culture-bearing nature of 'habitus', as described by Mauss (1979) and developed by Bourdieu (1977, 1979). As Mauss states, 'we are everywhere faced with physio-psycho-sociological assemblages of series of actions. These actions are more or less habitual and more or less ancient in the life of the individual and the history of the society. (Mauss 1979: 120).

Here the significance of actors' personal histories again enters our understanding of how people from different backgrounds can engage in communicative and generative projects – the way we behave towards one another is informed by learned 'physio-psycho-sociological' actions. As Bourdieu states, habitus is comprised of 'systems of objective relations' not 'totalities already constituted outside of individual history and group history' (Bourdieu 1977: 72). Hence, in our physical actions, we embody psycho-sociological aspects of both the society we have grown up in and our own personal experiences. When these actions conflict with those that are expected of us, then we and those we are interacting with are challenged to shift our conceptions of who we are and associated permissible or appropriate behaviour.

Embodiedness can become apparent in quite formalised ways through an understanding of standards of politeness and social aesthetics – as has become clear in the time since that first visit to a Gypsy site three years ago. The first visits were always tinged with the curiosity of the outsider looking in – I was a visitor in a different place, with a different people, in a different culture and, as such, I was very self-conscious about how I should or should not behave. I read up as much as I could find about Gypsy culture – I learned about their taboos and customs, their history, their language. I was always painfully aware that I might cause offence or do something that would cause me to be rejected by the people I was supposed to work with. Nowadays that initial curiosity about an alien people has become a curiosity about personalities and characters whom I have a great affection for. I am curious about them in the same way that I am curious about friends and colleagues – not because we are different but because we are both the same and different. Similarly I am on the receiving end of their curiosity, but when I am asked questions about my family or my home it is not because these are realms of different experience, but because we have an emotional interest in one another's well-being – in other words, we are friends where once we were strangers.

This awareness of ourselves as friends has a physical aspect as much as an emotional one through the ways in which our relationships are materialised in the physical world. This aspect of research has been noted by a number of ethnographers concerned with the interactive nature of ethnographic research and the creation of the ethnographic product (Blacking 1977: 6; Jackson 1983, 1998; Desjarlais 1992: 66; Gay-y-Blasco 1997: 530). In my experience, this physical aspect of the project shows itself in the ways that we become easy together – I know better how to behave now, what is polite and what doesn't really matter. I worry less about offending, partly as a result of having caused offence and having worked through it. For instance, cleanliness taboos are much talked about in the literature concerning Gypsies (see, for example, Sutherland 1977; Okely 1983; Fonseca 1995) – I knew that Gypsies kept separate cups for gorgios to drink out of and that they used separate bowls for washing up, for washing themselves, for washing clothes and so on. I also knew that it was supposed to be quite common for Gypsies not to offer visitors cups of tea or food because of the associated risks of pollution.

In fact, it was a number of months before I was offered my first cup of tea. I was visiting an unauthorised site with a couple of caravans with families who had pulled off the official site because of violence and inter-family fighting. As I sat in the trailer talking about some of the issues and whether the Council was going to do anything about what was going on, Eileen, whose trailer it was, made a cup of tea. Once I had drunk the tea I placed the mug out of the way by my feet while we carried on talking. It was some months later that I found out that the cup had had to be thrown out – 'You never put a cup on the floor,' I was told in no uncertain terms by Annie, Eileen's aunt. 'If you do it'll be thrown out – nobody will say anything but they'll know you're a dirty gorgio who doesn't know any better. The cup will be thrown away because it's been made dirty.' Some months later still, I was having a cup of tea with a Gypsy woman in Darlington – one of Annie's cousins; when I had finished my tea I stood up and placed the cup on the mantelpiece (she was living in a house at that time), only to notice that she had put her cup on the floor beside her!

Since then I have learned more and more about the right ways of doing things – I cross that space between ways of behaving with Gypsies (I wouldn't drink out of a cup with cracks or chips in it) and ways of behaving with non-Gypsies (I wouldn't demand a different cup if the one I had been given had a small crack or a chip in it) as often as I walk the routes from towns to sites. Nowadays it is strange for me not to be offered a cup of tea, as it is strange for me to be given a cup that is reserved for gorgios. I also know that these 'right ways of doing things' do not refer to rigid rules, they refer to ways of marking out relationships and are subject to change and the whims of individual people, depending upon mood and circumstance. Learning these informal, embodied ways of doing things through the experience of working with Gypsies has been a vital part of the research process, and one that could only come about through being together in the same space. At times, the effect of sharing space has become very clear; for instance, my field notes contain the following comments:

> Sitting in a trailer on Riverside Site with Susan, Johnny, Charlie and Robert. Annie is here too – matriarchal grandmother figure. Outside it is grey and drizzly, cold as well. I am struck by the way the children are confined by the space.

> This is the site of socialisation, it is the location of habitus, of learning 'body techniques'. It seems obvious to me that this has so much to do with social aesthetics and the way people learn to carry themselves, the reason why they run wild when they do get out, the reason why houses feel so wrong, the reason why the children won't sit at school and why schools find them so difficult to handle. (Field notes 30/01/01)

The above passage illustrates how culture becomes embodied through interacting and sharing the same social spaces, a point made by Bourdieu (1979: 175). A familiarity with Gypsies and with appropriate ways of behaving has been accompanied by an increasing familiarity with the spaces that people live in. Whilst the routes from town to site might still feel dangerous and uncertain, being on site is familiar and welcome. This was brought home to me one day late in 1999 when I took my daughter, Emma, on to the Riverside site in Middlesbrough. As we walked over the A66 towards the site I was regaled with a series of questions about where we were going, how long it would take to get there and why there weren't any buses that would take us from town. Once we arrived on site, Emma was impressed at the way children would come up to me and talk, calling after me and asking who Emma was. She was also impressed by how friendly people were and the way she could go from one trailer to another and feel much safer than if she was visiting her friends' houses. I was happy with this – as far as I was concerned, my daughter was indeed safer wandering from trailer to trailer on site than she was walking anywhere at home.

For Gypsies, in order to become persons who are recognisable as Gypsies – 'proper people', as Gypsies often refer to themselves – there is a need to build up networks of relationships, orientations and ways of doing things that maintain those connections. Sometimes this necessitates holding on to a sense of self, despite also holding on to contradictory notions of what and who that self is. There is a process to be worked through of integrating or compartmentalising conflicting relationships and identities into an apparently singular whole. This sense of self is then maintained through continuously recreating and reconfiguring identities and relationships through 'meaningful' behaviour – through performing interactions according to a 'Gypsy way of doing things'.

Speaking and the Embodiment of Language

Concepts such as the 'schemas' and 'frames' discussed above have links to literary and critical theory, where, in association with ideas about scripts, they have been used as a means of analysing texts (Cook 1994). Indeed, there has been a fruitful sharing of perspectives between the various kinds of discourse, conversation and textual analysis, which in the work of many ethnographers has led to an interest in the way that language is performed (Bauman 1984, 1986; Bauman and Briggs 1990; Feld and Fox 1994; Farnell 1995, 2000; Ahearn 2001; Berger and Del Negro 2002). Running through many of these studies is the recognition of a further area of potential conflict and dissonance rooted in the work of Mikhail Bakhtin. Bakhtin (1981) postulated the notion of two forces at work in any utterance – a centrifugal force (heteroglossia) and a centripetal force (monologia) – a metaphor that has been adopted by Strauss and Quinn (1997: 85) and used to illuminate their theory of cultural meaning as both socially distributed and individually embodied. An awareness of these tendencies in spoken interactions adds to ideas about performance discussed above and provides an important backdrop to the analyses of spoken interactions that form a significant part of the body of this study.[5]

Summation

We need undefined regions – both metaphorical and material – in order to be able to negotiate conflicts. These regions are often regarded as boundaries or borders – I prefer to refer to them as wastelands as that is a more appropriate metaphor in terms of the physical and social environment in which the research was carried out. The significance of wastelands is not singular but multiple and frequently contradictory – hence the need to 'negotiate' relationships within and around them. These wastelands are not lines of separation as might be suggested by the term boundary, rather they are common points of reference and mutual creative interaction and so can as easily be seen as enabling the production of identities as limiting it.

All participants in the research – Gypsy and gorgio alike – have multiple and frequently contradictory orientations to these wastelands. These orientations are reflected in and often produce contradictory identities, which are worked through and resolved or compartmentalised in our interactions with others and with the environment – so reproducing the multilayered orientations. The study examines the process of becoming a Gypsy – as they might say, a 'proper person' rather than 'just an animal' – exploring the ways in which conflicting identities are resolved or compartmentalised. To do this, I examine the ways in which interactions with others and the environment are organised, reorganised and interpreted in order to help maintain a coherent sense of self despite conflict and contradiction. Such strategies include those that enable us to manage our awareness of the different realms of human consciousness – the present realm of consociates and intersubjectivity and the distant realm of contemporaries and ideal types.

1.3 The walk to my office

1.4 The walk to my office

Notes

1. Names have been changed throughout the text to preserve the anonymity of those involved. Place names have not been changed, a decision taken following the decision to include the newspaper cuttings (appendix II), which clearly identify a specific place.
2. Non-Gypsy, pronounced 'gorja' and spelt variously as gorja, gorgio, gauje gaudje and many similar variations. I shall use gorgio throughout, non-capitalised as the term does not apply to a singular ethnic minority.
3. An idea coined by psychologist Bartlett (1932), who has inspired the ensuing psychological leaning of its use in cognitive anthropology and linguistics but which can also take on an analogy with European ideas about schemes of expression and interpretation developed by, for example, Schutz and Bourdieu. As the theoretical underpinning of my approach is drawn from both traditions I prefer to use the term 'schematic understandings', using either 'schema' or 'scheme' only when referring to specific work where such a term is used.
4. The official site in Middlesbrough, which is described in more detail in chapter 3.
5. I have opted to analyse spoken interactions because of the enormous richness of the data and because of the relative ease with which it could be collected.

Chapter 2

REACHING AN UNDERSTANDING
Methods and Analysis

━━━━━━━━ ⊂❀⊃ ━━━━━━━━

In the following description and discussion of my chosen methods, I refer to the methods involved in gathering information and also to the methods used in the production of the book. I show how the research process has not been separated from the writing-up process in any clear way: how writing up and researching simultaneously make the book what it is and are again evidence of the inappropriateness of the boundary metaphor.

If the metaphor of a boundary creates an inappropriate framework to contextualise my work with Gypsies and the ethnographic description I endeavour to give in this work, it is also inappropriate as a metaphor to describe the research process itself. Ideas about boundaries – and the associated fragmenting and separating that go on when this metaphor is used to think with – have been common in much academic research and have led to the development of separate fields of investigation and study – for instance, anthropology, psychology, sociology, linguistics, geography, history and so on. This separating is not an accurate or 'true' reflection of the world we live in and that we investigate, and theoretical and disciplinary boundaries are being challenged just as much as geographical and cultural ones. A blurring of disciplinary boundaries does not, however, mean that this study could equally be considered history or geography or linguistics – it is rooted in a tradition of practice that is distinctively anthropological and ethnographic but that draws from other disciplines in order to illuminate the research findings and, hopefully, to add to the body of anthropological knowledge.

Boundaries and the Research Process

If culture and identity are produced through interaction, as explored in the previous chapter, this begs the question of the role of the anthropologist; if I am interacting with those I am researching, then there is an impact upon both my and their identity.[1] The need to locate the anthropologist in ethnographic research and also the need to consider the assumed boundary between researcher and researched are recurrent themes in the work of, for instance, Myerhoff and Ruby (1982), Clifford and Marcus (1986), Renato Rosaldo (1989) and others concerned with adopting a more reflexive perspective. Through such approaches it has become easier to see culture as a process in which the anthropologist is engaged rather than a thing that the anthropologist researches, hence necessitating a more reflexive perspective and challenging the assumed boundaries of the ethnographic exercise. Furthermore, such developments in anthropological understanding have also widened the field of anthropological and ethnographic investigation to incorporate an appreciation of the dynamic and creative processes of culture and cultural production, a point perhaps made most famously by Renato Rosaldo (1989: 207–8).

At their most extreme, these perspectives have developed into the heavily postmodern views of writers such as Aaron Turner (2000). According to Turner's vision of culture, taken together as a group we (Teesside Gypsies, council officers, myself and other colleagues) form a 'socially constituting configuration' (ibid.: 57), in that we jointly create the conditions of our interaction rather than wholly conform to a single set (or even multiple sets) of culturally predetermined rules and roles. We do this in a place where we can see that 'socially constituting configuration as the context of the constitution of culture and social relationships'. Turner, however, suggests a kind of extreme relativism, in which 'the idea and concept of community become problematic' (ibid.: 57) especially as regards any ethnographic research project. Turner's suggestion is that groups of people continually create anew the cultural terms of their being together in a way that denies the relevance of the personal histories and experiences of the actors involved – what is important is what we do together, not where we have come from. Such approaches reject the significance of those 'voices' that I was aware of when I first walked on to the site to meet Charlie. My memory of what my friends and family had said to me and the meaning of what they had said show that we are not 'blank slates' who somehow come together and create new and transient communities and groups in a way that is both serendipitous and ultimately inconsequential, as Turner might put it.

The inability to account for the influence of 'where we have come from' is not only a criticism of postmodernism in anthropology, it is a criticism that has been widely and effectively directed towards phenomenological approaches in the social sciences (see, for instance, Dolgin et al. 1977: 106; Demeritt 2002). It is a weakness that needs to be addressed in order to account for the significance – indeed, the existence – of those 'voices in my head' as I walked on to a Gypsy site that morning in February 1998. The need to take into account differences of origin that result in differences in both behaviour and expectation has been recognised by many social theorists and ethnographers (e.g. Besnier 1995: 6; Clifford 1997: 209; Berdahl 1999: 5) and points towards a way of combining the insights of postmodernism as regards the dynamic and constantly and mutually recreated nature of culture with a sense of culture as a process that has deep roots in a past that stretches beyond the immediate histories of those present at any particular time or event.

People, Culture and Organisations

Such studies as those noted above acknowledge the importance of institutions and power structures in the creation and maintenance of culture, as does much work examining the nature of contested identities. For instance, Paine (2000) analyses the role of the concept of authenticity as promoted by the white colonial culture of Australia in forming contemporary notions of aboriginality. Taking a slightly different though clearly related tack, Fernandez (2000) examines the interrelationship between ideas about the nation in forming a counterpart to non-national identities such as Celt. Clearly such ideas have an important bearing when considering ideas about Gypsiness – a notion that is commonly subjected to ideas about authenticity and that also reaches beyond the boundaries of any nation.

As regards my own research, these studies highlight the fact that I am not placed on one side of a set of relationships – me on one side, Gypsies on the other. I am situated within a whole web of relationships and these include my relationships with people I work with – the officers and councillors of local authorities, education workers, planners, housing officers and so on, as well as Gypsies. In the course of my research, I participated in the activities of organisations and their representatives, as well as in the everyday lives of the Gypsies I was working with. This participation needs to be recognised and viewed as a valid area of investigation – indeed, it is this aspect of my research that raised the crucial question with which this study is concerned – the difficulties of reaching a resolution to the meeting in February 2002.

Like me, though each in their own way, all those I have worked with cross that space between town and site, Gypsy and non-Gypsy. In this way they are also characters in the landscape I describe, a landscape of negotiated and continuously recreated relationships. Just as my developing relationship with Gypsies has led to changes of perspective that accompany a developing trust, so a similar process has taken place between me and other people I have worked with, the officers and representatives of various institutions and organisations.

Navigating the uncertain territory of these developing relationships – the places at which our various 'webs' merge – has not been easy, and at times I have felt as if I were caught in a space between two worlds, unsure of what to do or which way to move. The first time I really felt the inconsistencies and contradictions in my position came approximately eighteen months into my job. My role was to be an independent advocate for Gypsies and Travellers on Teesside, to increase the level of appropriate service provision for them and so enhance their quality of life. For almost a year I had been working with a number of local Gypsy families to try and sort out some issues concerning one of the authorised sites and why it was closed. We had been trying to find a solution to problems of extreme vandalism and inter-group violence – such a solution would involve finding someone who could be the warden of the site and ward off such problems in the future. I had in fact been approached by somebody who all the potential residents agreed was a good candidate – he was a bit of a 'hard man' but, bearing in mind the violent history of the site and the infighting that had been going on, being a 'hard man' was probably a necessary quality for the job. At first, Paul, an officer of the local authority, seemed quite pleased about this development and I arranged for local Gypsies, including the potential warden, to meet with him and say what they wanted to see on the site. It was also an opportunity for Paul, as the representative of the council, to meet the prospective warden.

At this point, things took something of a peculiar turn – Paul, in his role as representative of 'the council', decided that before he would meet the residents he would have to run a police check on the potential warden. This seemed strange to me – I had never heard of the council carrying out police checks on people before they would even agree to meet them. The whole situation began to spiral out of control, with both Paul and other representatives of the council refusing to meet the Gypsies until they had been allowed to carry out police checks. On the other hand, the Gypsies were accusing the council of being prejudiced and treating them differently from other people just because they were Gypsies. Up until this point, I had been clear about my views – I thought that Paul and the council had acted unfairly and I told them so. Eventually, however, I found myself sitting in a room with ten very unhappy Gypsies wanting to know exactly who had ordered the police checks and which police officer had advised the council to do this. I wasn't comfortable answering these requests – I didn't mind joining the Gypsies in their complaints about officers of the council as representatives of an institution, but I wasn't happy about using my 'inside' knowledge to give out names of individual council or police officers. My reluctance to share such specific information, however, was not good enough; Janey, the informal spokesperson for the Gypsies, said, 'I look at it this way – you either tell us or you don't and if you don't we'll know you're not really with us. We'll know where we stand.'

Here the ambiguity of my position is commented upon and turned into a point of negotiation by others involved in the process. There is a struggle for power that suggests conflicting notions of what my role is and my position relative to merging webs of relationships: for a start there are those of the council, on the one hand, and the Gypsies, on the other, and then there are my own ideas and expectations about my role. I am drawn into the situation in a way that denies the possibility of maintaining a pretence at being a distanced observer. The personal views and feelings of all characters involved, including myself, impose themselves at every turn, thus challenging any notional boundary that might be thought to exist between the observer and the observed. The implications of this both for the fieldwork and the writing up involved in creating this book, are that the subject matter of the study needs to acknowledge the involved and participatory nature of the research process. Throughout the research process, I did not experience myself as an 'outsider' coming into contact with another culture to which I do not and cannot belong: I was engaged in webs of understandings, some aspects of which were more and some less familiar to me. In writing this book, I try to convey some of these senses of familiarity and unfamiliarity and the ways in which we learned to work with our understandings.

Ethnography at Home

A further aspect of the ethnographic tradition is the expectation that eventually the ethnographer 'goes home' – and home is the academic institution within which the final work is produced (Clifford 1997: 211); the point of departure from the field marks the boundary between fieldwork and writing up. However, the role of the academic institution, in the case of my work, became involved in the web of relations that is the subject of the study. I studied, worked, wrote, visited, talked to supervisors and students and then went to discuss the same issues with Gypsies and with colleagues at work. Furthermore, people came to visit me – there was a great deal of curiosity about the 'place where I go and write', as it was referred to by some of the people I worked with.[2] The following passage describes an example of this kind of boundary crossing by the people who, in a more traditional ethnographic context, would be expected to stay firmly within the confines of their place and culture – as pointed out above, the research came to me as often as I went to it.

Being a sometimes disorganised sort of person, I don't always keep bits of paper and documents neatly filed and in the 'right' place. This trait has created openings that have been quickly pounced upon by some people curious about aspects of my life and work that they wouldn't normally get to see. For instance, I had been given the accounts of one of the Gypsy and Traveller Residents' Associations as they needed to be sent in for auditing. Before I had a chance to send them in, Annie and Mary realised that they needed the chequebook – urgently. Whilst I walked in the 'near-wasteland' from the Riverside site to Middlesbrough, a car drew up. Mary got out and said that she wanted the chequebook there and then. I explained that I had left it in my desk in the anthropology department at Durham and that I would have to get it to her the next day. This was not soon enough! It was decided that Mary, her husband Jim, her daughter Vicky and her sister Annie would all drive me to Durham to collect the chequebook. We did, and while I went to retrieve the required article from the desk in the postgrad room Mary, Vicky and Annie decided to take themselves on a tour of the place 'where I go to write about them', while Jim stayed outside to have a smoke. There was a sense of equality being demanded here – I go to their places – they expect to be able to go to mine. They expect to be able to wander around the department and look at it, just as I wander around their sites and look at them.

This illustrates how, unlike the expected scenario of the wandering academic returning home to write, the academic institution became drawn into the field and the field became drawn into academia, challenging the traditional boundaries of the academic project (for a fuller discussion of this, see Peirano 1998). In this process, everywhere becomes as alien and as familiar as anywhere else and the question becomes where is home and how do we get there – or how do I get there – in order to create some distance and so to write? In terms of practice, this issue has been addressed largely by ethnographers concerned with 'native anthropologists' (Narayan 1993; Clifford 1997). Similar issues have also been looked at as regards the disjointed nature of such research practices and the writing exercise (Brown 1991: 11–13; Edwards 1994: 346). Useful though these perspectives are for understanding the at times difficult position I found myself in whilst carrying out the research, what is little touched upon is how to deal with the conflicting roles of the anthropologist who is also something else (however, see Rose 1990). After all, I was spending time working with Gypsies and council officers and so on not primarily because I was conducting anthropological fieldwork but because I was expected to be a development worker – I was there to do something other than research. This casts a somewhat different light on the practice of research as it introduces a number of possible perspectives that are not often available to the anthropological researcher. These issues need to be addressed in the selection of the subject matter of the study and I have tried to address them through the use of the shifting perspectives referred to above.

The Search for the Subject Matter

The need to situate the researcher within the context of the research is a need central to much recent anthropological work dealing with the nature of ethnicity, a need that arises from an understanding of the relationship between the researcher and researched. Building upon this perspective has also opened up the suggestion that anthropological or ethnographic work is the product of such relationships rather than simply a representation of a world that exists somehow outside the researcher and the relationships they make whilst in the field (Ingold 1993: 218).

What is proposed here is that anthropology, presented as a discipline in need of a subject matter, has tended to explore the differences and separations between people. Ingold's suggestion is that what anthropology also needs to do is develop a way of exploring those aspects of the anthropological experience that are encounters with sameness and connectedness, i.e. those aspects that allow us to connect with one another rather than maintain an absolute and intractable separation. This has been a concern of anthropologists when faced with the prospect of writing up their fieldwork – a concern with the ways in which the discipline of anthropology creates its objects (Fabian 1983: 143 and *passim*). I have tried to deal with these issues in my own work through the selection of the subject matter: this study is not about Gypsy culture as opposed to non-Gypsy culture, it is about what happens when Gypsies and non-Gypsies come together in a context that brings an expectation of reaching some sort of mutual understanding. It is the processes of finding some ground of understanding that I am concerned with – and I was very much involved in those processes for all the time that I worked with Gypsies: I was most definitely 'there' (Geertz 1988: chapter 1) in such a way that neither questions nor validates any 'truth' in what I describe, but rather underlines what qualifies me to describe it.

Epistemological issues raised in the theoretical separation of researcher and researched are by no means limited to the process of writing and representing, as Ingold (1993: 230) notes when discussing the nature of the fieldwork experience. Here Ingold is concerned to situate culture in the realm of discernible actions, rather than 'inside' individual human beings. However, even in this way of describing the anthropological project, there is still room for a separation of anthropologist from object – note how Ingold refers to the ways in which he learns to attend to the world, but not how others in the world attend to him nor how he is taught how to do this attending; but if culture is something learned it is equally something taught. The difference between the approach I adopt and that suggested by Ingold is in the representation of a joint process – not only do I learn new ways of attending to the world, I am taught those new ways. This work is the product of what and how and by whom I have been taught, not simply what I have learned, and so my perspective will shift depending upon what particular teaching and learning process I am focusing on. For instance, in the section titled 'The Fire' I focus specifically upon what I have been taught and what I have learned as it relates to Gypsies; hence in this section the work has something of a traditional ethnographic perspective as I describe what to most readers would be seen, at least at first, as my interactions with people who have a quite different way of life from my own. In the section entitled 'The Dark' however, that perspective changes as I describe what is both to me and to my anticipated readership something of a more familiar world but acknowledging the point of view of people who find it strange and unfamiliar.

Self and Other – More Assumed Boundaries

Generally presented as an epistemological concern (Geertz 1988: 9), i.e. a concern about the methods of information gathering, the issue of self and Other, insider and outsider, has largely been discussed as it relates to the veracity or appositeness of the ethnographic product. In other words, the problem of self and Other is presented as a problem connected to the content of what is being told – as reflected in the issues surrounding the search for the subject matter discussed above. Dichotomising the self and the Other also has implications from a 'narratological' perspective (Geertz 1988: 9), i.e. a concern with the methods of writing up and representation – or who is telling who and how are they telling it, rather than what is being told (Clifford and Marcus 1986: 25; Pratt 1986: 27–29; Abu-Lughod 1991). Here a designation of 'self' can locate the ethnographer within a context whereby the reader can identify with them – they originate from the same place – the 'Others' are those who are unlike the self (and therefore, by implication, unlike the reader). The suggestion is that my expected readership is aligned with my position as ethnographer – thus placing us on one side of a divide across which we view the Other that is written about. Again, however, such a construct is unsatisfactory and inappropriate – I do not write about a singular 'Other' (for instance, Gypsies), nor do I expect you readers to be a homogeneous group. The fact that I have various roles suggests a bundle of possible identities that can be adopted, depending upon the context; my perspective or view of the social world shifts as the adoption of identities moves from one to another. This means that when viewing the words of Gypsies spoken to me as a worker or when viewing the words of council workers spoken to me as part of the Gypsy 'interest group', the points of origin and intended target for those words also shift. So should I choose one identity and write from there, portraying all my other identities as 'Others'? Indeed, this is a stance that has been hinted at by people concerned with the anthropology, the experience and the representation of the 'self' and its changing faces in changing social situations (see Ochs and Capps 1996: 28–29), albeit with reference to the anthropological object rather than the anthropologist. The point is, were I to adopt such a position, I would need to 'Other' myself in such a way as to misrepresent my experience of myself – I do not experience myself as a different person in different contexts, I do not feel myself to be fragmented in that way – I do experience myself as a whole and coherent person (maybe comprised of contradictions, but nonetheless these are all my contradictions – they do not belong to an Other).

From all these perspectives, the frequently assumed divide between the self and the Other turns out to be another unsatisfactory metaphor, a way of thinking, talking and writing about the world that might well be useful and illuminating sometimes, but for my purposes is obfuscating rather than illuminating. Blurring the distinction between self and Other gives an intimacy to the ethnographic approach that brings both rewards and problems, specifically between a greater depth of understanding and expressive potential and an awareness of the real significance of the differences between people who come from different places with different histories and learned ways of behaving. Karen McCarthy Brown also recognises this in her ethnographic study of a Vodou priestess called Alourdes who lived in Brooklyn (Brown 1991: 11). Brown brings this understanding into her work, stating that she wants, through her study, to combine the effectiveness of anthropology in showing the diversity of human social worlds and experience whilst also acknowledging the significance of the personal relationships she built up during research and that contribute to the overall power of the work (ibid.: 13).

In my own work I illustrate the complexities of Gypsy identity and the challenges faced at the interstice between Gypsy culture and 'mainstream' culture as it is lived. This is, I feel, best done through the lives of the people who live within that liminal space (Bhabha 1994: 139ff.) wherein cultures mix, merge and are continually reinvented as dynamic and enacted aspects of people's lives. This is the space that is metaphorically represented in the near-wastelands between town and site; in this familiar yet uncomfortable landscape, the traditional divisions of self and Other dissolve – we meet on neutral territory and as equal, though different, participants.

Engagement in the Field

Maintaining a stable sense of self might seem to be a difficult task for an anthropologist – it is often the ability to dismantle our sense of who we are and reconstruct it in a different way that allows for some of the greatest insights. Conversely, it is often in the strength of the individual anthropologist's sense of self that the clear contrasts between ways of thinking and being become apparent. Either way, the various expectations and associated behaviours that accompanied my various roles throughout the research process meant that a sense of a singular identity was challenged – my 'identity' became part of my analytic toolkit, my means of understanding the world and of now conveying that understanding to you. For five years I lived my life as the meeting point of a number of different ways of looking at the world. I was not situated at the meeting place – I was it; with Gypsies I was one person, with the council members and officers I worked with I was another, and I assumed yet other roles and associated identities in the academic establishment and with my family. The dismantling and reviewing of identity that anthropologists frequently adopt as a matter of course became something that I was expected to do many times a day. In many ways I could say that I was directly experiencing different modes of subjectivation and correlating different technologies of the self (Foucault 1979: 90, 119). In doing this, however, I must point out that I never felt myself to be in a position of subjection – I was never a passive victim of circumstance or a pawn of forces beyond my ability to influence; however, I was aware of myself as the subject of (rather than subject to) different understandings of how to be, again reminding us of the significance of processes of teaching as well as those of learning.

Near the time this book was nearing completion, I volunteered to be made redundant, partly because the demands of juggling a full-time job with part-time teaching, being a mother and writing a book had become quite exhausting, partly because I needed time to concentrate on the writing up – and by this time it had become something of an obsession. For five years the whole of my life had been permeated by Gypsies, Gypsiness, those who work with Gypsies and so on – it was more than I had ever understood 'participant observation' to be; my 'fieldwork' had reached into my family, my home, everything I understood myself to be. In many ways my research came to me and in the end it proved difficult for me to get away from it – I couldn't simply leave the field because the field was not a different or distant place – it was my life, it was me.

From the point of view of ethnographic research, the result of such ongoing, long-term fieldwork is a building of relationships that are more than either friendship or the relationship between ethnographer and informant. I have developed an intimate and sustained interest in the lives and well-being of the people I have been taught by, underlined by the fact that I worked for them. The work sometimes made it difficult for me to remain distanced as a scholar; similarly, the research sometimes made it difficult for me to remain impartial as a worker. The depth of understanding gained through being engaged in the ethnographic/anthropological process – the sometimes successful attempt to learn how to understand others in their own terms – increases the frustration when faced with policies and bureaucracies that are unable to take people (personalities, characters and their personal histories and learned ways of doing things) into account. This frustration also influenced the choice of subject matter as I felt a need to explore the ways in which the teaching and learning process did not always work; the points at which something fails are just as illuminating as the points at which it succeeds – perhaps even more so, because when it fails we are even more painfully aware that we are trying to achieve something. In exploring one particular site of such frustrated attempts to reach an understanding and a plan of action (the meeting referred to in the introduction), I also hope that others who might find themselves in a similar position (were they ever to read this book) would find a way of understanding the difficulties involved and the near impossibility of achieving a solution to those difficulties without planning an extended period of trying to achieve a solution – a period extended over many years, rather than a few short hours or even a few months.

Genealogies and Kinship Charts

Perhaps understandably, given my concern with webs of relationships and the socially situated and constructed nature of identity, much of the data collected centred around the relationships that people felt were important to them. In the case of Gypsies, this was more often than not information about family. My original intentions were not to collect kinship charts and genealogies; as mentioned above, I had intended to carry out unstructured or semi-structured interviews, to draw maps and to make tape and video recordings, to record information in a way that was as close as possible to the way it was given to me. In the traditional history of anthropology, the recording of kinship through genealogical charts had been first one of its major strengths and innovations (Royal Anthropological Institute 1951: 50ff.). It later became one of its perceived weaknesses, against which a major criticism was levelled in that kinship charts presented information in a way that was unrepresentative of people's experience (see, for example, Schneider 1984: 119ff.). Formal kinship diagrams could be viewed as either irrelevant or dangerously misrepresentative in a way that echoes debates about representation through the written word discussed below. It was with some surprise, then, that I found that the people I was working with seemed to respond naturally to the notion of 'family trees', whilst they proved resistant to any other form of recording our conversations. So it was that I started collecting 'family trees' and I continued because of the enormous amount of information the collecting generated.

One danger that is unavoidable when drawing diagrams of kinship is that it appears fixed and static – it presents structures that differentiate and define one culture as separable (and separate) from any other. In an attempt to minimize this problem, I view the charts I have as mnemonic devices; they are ways of recording and remembering whole patterns and connections of information of many different kinds, as will be explored in detail in chapters 5 and 6. For now I want to put the information in context; it is not my intention to give here a history of kinship studies in anthropology – that has been done very effectively elsewhere, for instance in Carsten's (2000) introduction to *Cultures of Relatedness*. I merely wish to lay out some intellectual coordinates from which to embark, in 'The Fire' section, on a discussion of kinship as it relates to my work with Gypsies and the people and institutions they come into contact with in the northeast of England.

Recently, kinship studies have begun to focus less on fixed structures and more upon the processes of making kinship and making kinship meaningful. Such studies frequently refer to ideas about belonging (Borneman 1992; 2001) rather than descent, metaphor rather than substance (Schneider 1984), choice rather than predestiny (Bargach 2001; Karim 2001). These studies often begin with a consideration of particular individuals and a discussion of types of people (brothers, mothers, children, etc.) comes after the introduction of specific, named people. Kinship is, then, one of the ways in which we can start to analyse strategies for dealing with the different realms of consciousness – the realms of consociates and contemporaries discussed above.

The processes involved in forming and maintaining kinship relations have been explored as potential ground from which to develop cognitive approaches to issues of culture and culture change (see especially Strauss and Quinn (1997) and their studies of the notion of marriage in the United States), potentially leading to the cognitive theory of culture that Barth suggested was necessary for anthropology to bridge the theoretical gap between the individual person and the notion of culture. In the first chapter, I noted how Strauss and Quinn developed a version of the schema theory as a 'cognitive theory of cultural meaning', in an attempt to deliver the kind of theory that Barth has maintained is necessary. In this book I draw upon such an approach, using ideas about narrative thought – and more specifically the teaching and learning of stories and ways of telling stories – as a cognitive process that includes ideas about culture and addresses notions of kinship and belonging.

From this perspective, kinship becomes a site of contested meanings – a field of study where once again boundaries are not easy to draw. In such a fluid environment, some anthropologists have become more concerned with kinship as one description of the ways in which we relate to one another – not through fixed rules and pregiven relationship structures, but through the actions of our everyday lives (Faubion 2001: 3). To leave it at that, however, is not enough. There is something more than this to kinship; it is a special kind of relating that is under discussion, the kind of relating that gives us a sense of belonging, of coming from somewhere, of being rooted in a culture, of emerging from a tradition of practice. It is this sense of belonging that provides the background to my own exploration of the meanings tied up in ideas about kinship amongst the Gypsies I have worked with. It also informs the later analysis of relations in a local government setting, as it is through this sense of belonging and the struggle to achieve and maintain such a sense that some of the difficulties of cross-cultural communication become highlighted.

Tales of Everyday Life and Conflicting Moral Frames

At the same time as collecting the genealogies, I also collected stories about people's everyday lives – indeed, the two go together quite naturally, as people would tell me about how the various characters they were talking about figured in their life, what they meant to them, how they had been influenced by them and so on. Sometimes such tales would take the form of life stories, although I never explicitly asked people to tell me the story of their life. As Linde has pointed out, the telling of a life story owes much to the context in which it is told, and when a life story is told in different contexts and for different reasons then it may well generate what appear to be contradictions and conflicts (Linde 1993). This point has also been addressed by Bluck and Habermas (2000) in their development of the idea of a life-story schema rather than a life story as a singular and coherent entity. Indeed, the likelihood of people holding different and possibly conflicting views has long been recognised (Schutz 1944: 500) and is less a problem than a fruitful area of investigation. As I spoke to people and gathered information about their everyday lives, I hoped to collect information that would show just where some of these conflicts arose – both amongst Gypsies and amongst council workers.

The Significance of Stories

In fact, it was just this listening to people and collecting what they had to say that eventually persuaded me to adopt the particular analytical approach that I have done. I originally intended to collect various kinds of data, much of it visual – maps and pictures especially. Had I persisted with this approach, I might well have come up with an alternative analysis of the construction of Gypsiness. Perhaps the visual data would have lent themselves more to an approach examining the manipulation of symbols in space, an approach that might have had more in common with Sibley's (1981, 1995, 2001) or Sutherland's (1977) work. Alternatively, such visual data might have been effectively interpreted by drawing heavily on the way objects signified social relationships, as Bourdieu has shown so effectively (Bourdieu 1979).

If I had collected many visual data and combined them with the masses of kinship charts I did manage to collect, I might well have been tempted to adopt a more structuralist approach similar to that adopted by Okely (1983). Alternatively, such data might have lent themselves to the interpretative approach, in which the underlying patterns of culture (see Benedict 1935) are presented and analysed (e.g. Geertz and Geertz 1975). As it was, I did none of these. I did not feel comfortable asking people for information they tried to avoid giving me. Nor would I feel comfortable describing their 'culture' in terms of patterns or behaviour that insisted on the presence of underlying structures or patterns that Gypsies themselves did not introduce or suggest to me. In the end, it was stories that won the day; when Gypsies tried to explain to me what it meant to them to be a Gypsy, they would always tell me a story – they didn't draw a picture or a map or pull out photographs or an object or recite their ancestry. Gypsies always began with a story: stories had pride of place in their telling of themselves and they have pride of place in this book as well.

The Ethics of Representation

In this odyssey of engagement and alienation I need to situate the work somewhere in order to write about my experiences – in order for there to be something for you to read – hence the adoption of the 'wasteland' both as a metaphor and as a material reference point. I need to provide a field of study that affords some sort of context for my actions, interactions and interpretations and for those of all the others who populate and move through this wasteland alongside me. My intention is to give voice to those people who struggle daily with issues of self, belonging, family, community and individuality in a way that gives full respect both to their own personal sense of being and also to our relationships with one another. I do not want to try and set the Gypsy people with whom I work within an abstract context, such as 'the Gypsy culture' or 'the Romany people', and, as Lemon points out, there never actually lived an abstract Gypsy (Lemon 2000: 4). Nor do I want to represent members of institutions as faceless and characterless servants of whichever institution they work for. However, there are differences and I do want to show what some of those differences are and what their implications might be. All the people involved, as individuals and as people who come from different traditions of practice, have their own voices, their own understandings, their own perspectives.

This issue becomes particularly pertinent when reproducing the spoken words of those who appear between these pages. As Richard Bauman has pointed out (1986: ix–x), it is easy to fall into the trap of representing the spoken word in such a way as to make the people who originally spoke them seem inarticulate and incoherent – a problem further emphasised in a culture that often portrays Gypsies as illiterate and ill-educated. I have tried to avoid this by adopting an approach similar to that of Bauman's – I have not produced transcripts exactly as spoken, with all the various pronunciations, hesitations and associated symbols; I have instead reproduced the sense of what was said. This inevitably affects the ways in which I can analyse the data I present – I cannot, for instance, adopt a rigorous conversation or discourse analysis approach, as I have not reproduced the discourse in sufficient detail to do this. Instead, I have adopted a narrative approach, combined with the analysis of tropes, including metaphor and irony. Such approaches can be effectively combined with the politically sensitive representation of the spoken word, as Bauman shows very effectively. Following Bauman's approach also underlines the active and dynamic aspect of the research process, as he outlined in *Verbal Art as Performance* (1984). This approach lends itself to a related representational approach of adopting metaphors and the like that more faithfully reflect those used by people involved in the research; hence the book is structured according to a favourite trope of Gypsies – that of a fire burning in a wasteland in the dark – as it helps to construct a different idea about the world than if I had structured the book according to ideas about boundaries and separations and how I went into the field and then came out again.

Nevertheless, this is my book: I have written it, I have chosen what to write about and I have chosen to represent people in one way rather than another way. As such, I run the risk of manipulating the voices and integrity of those I write about in order to serve my own purpose; I run the risk of co-opting and misrepresenting people's voices and constructing a picture of them they would neither recognise nor feel comfortable with if they did recognise it. This will always be a risk in carrying out what is essentially a solitary exercise such as writing a book. I have, however, tried to remain aware of and sensitive to this possibility and have requested that some of those that are written about read the book and agree that they are happy with it. This has not, however, been possible with everyone, mostly because some of those with whom I have worked have difficulty reading and writing and would certainly feel uncomfortable with the kind of writing that is necessary to produce an academic text.

Notes

1. Identity understood as the complex social interstice of attitudes, behaviours, expectations, contexts and so on outlined in the previous chapter.
2. In fact, I still do work with them – I couldn't simply cut myself off from them having been so involved for so long. Instead, I volunteered to help, advising on an unpaid basis and doing whatever I could – but without the expectations, pressures and, needless to say, the paperwork that go with being employed to do these things full-time.

Chapter 3

THE PAST AND PRESENT MAKING OF TEESSIDE
Building a Place in the World, Finding a Place amongst People

—— ∞∞∞ ——

Arriving

When I first arrived in Teesside I approached from the west. I have vivid memories of that first arrival, memories that are built upon each time I make the same journey. I left the A1(m) to follow the Tees Valley eastwards, heading towards the North Sea. As the land I travelled through became flatter, the horizons behind me and to my right took on the character of distant walls. The plateaux of the Yorkshire Dales (behind me) and the North Yorkshire Moors (off to my right) seemed to force my journey on towards the sea. In front of me stretched the plain of the Tees Estuary and the urban-industrial sprawl in which the events I describe are set.

In 1989, the year I came to the area, Teesside was one of the biggest industrial complexes in Europe – by day, it was frighteningly ugly, belching multicoloured smokes and steams, accompanied by an assortment of stomach-turning smells. By night, it was disturbingly beautiful – a strange, outlandish city of lights where lines of mysterious structures marked out areas of intense darkness. I have been told that Ridley Scott, film director and native of the Tees Valley, stood on top of Eston Nab, a prominent landmark, and was so struck by what he saw that it became the inspiration behind the set of the film *Bladerunner*. 'Bladerunner Country' is my preferred portrayal of the Tees Valley when I describe it to people who have never visited the area, or when I try to prepare visitors for what they will encounter. Perhaps these days, following the effects of increased industrial decline and dereliction, it would be more accurate to describe it as Bladerunner meets Mad Max.

Once a marshy and sparsely populated region, laid waste by William the Conqueror in his 'harrying of the north', contemporary Teesside has its roots in the forces of the nineteenth century industrial revolution. Home of the first commercial railway (the Stockton to Darlington Line), Teesside's huge urban expansion was generated by industry's appetite for coal; land on the banks of the navigable river was bought by industrialists such as Henry Pease, founder of Middlesbrough, with the intention of building ports for the export of coal. Increasing demand for iron encouraged the new landowners to parcel up and sell smaller pockets of land to those who wanted to produce iron. The area's fate as a bubble of urban, industrial production was sealed with the discovery of ironstone in the Eston Hills in 1850.[1]

Inevitably, along with industrial growth came increases of population; behind all these developments there were people. The sparseness of the population when the expansion began meant that labour had to be brought in from elsewhere and so industrial Teesside became populated with a variety of migrants and immigrants (Beynon et al. 1994: 19; Harrison 2001). Writing at the turn of the nineteenth/twentieth centuries, having witnessed the expansion of Middlesbrough since her marriage to a local industrialist in 1876, Florence Bell commented:

> The genesis of an ironmaking town which follows such a discovery (as that of iron) is breathless and tumultuous, and the onslaught of industry which attends the discovery of mineral wealth, whether ironstone or coal mines, has certain characteristics unlike any other form of commercial enterprise. The unexpectedness of it, the change in the condition of the district, which suddenly becomes swamped under a great rush from all parts of the country of people often of the roughest kind, who are going to swell the ranks of unskilled labour; the need for housing these people; all this means that there springs, and too rapidly, into existence a community of a pre-ordained inevitable kind ... A town arising in this way cannot wait to consider anything else than time and space: and none of either must be wasted on what is merely agreeable to the eye, or even on what is merely sanitary. (Bell 1985: 2–3)

You can still see the traces of industrial Teesside's birth as the child of visionary industrialists: from derelict blast furnaces that loom over townships and bear their names (Dorman Long), to the townships themselves (Dormanstown), the streets (Vaughan Street, Bolckow Road) and the social club that bears its founder's inspirational slogan 'Erimus' or 'We Shall Be'.

Judging from contemporary accounts, if you were to arrive on Teesside in those boom-town times you would find yourself in the middle of a moral quagmire. Concerned at the conditions in which people were living and feeling that they needed some sort of moral direction in their lives, many churches were established – almost on every corner of every street (Cleveland and Teesside Local History Society 1994; Orde 2000). The association between those early Teesside workers and questionable morality was also commented on by Florence Bell:

The boy of the ironworking district, when he leaves school, at the age of fourteen at latest, is in a part of the world where the principal industry offers hardly any occupation for boys. He is therefore, between the ages of thirteen and sixteen – that is, at the age of all others when, if he is to be a worthy man, a boy ought to be under supervision, under direction, when he ought to be given occupation and exposed to good influences – simply turned loose, either to do nothing, or else to take on one odd job after another of a temporary kind leading to nothing … He is mostly, as far as moral training is concerned, left to himself … No doubt a certain proportion of these boys are happily made of the stuff which, in spite of all adverse circumstances, will turn into worthy men … but, as a rule, I fear it is incontestable that most of the children who are playing about the streets of Middlesbrough are destined to grow up into a generation which will bring down the average of the deserving and efficient. This immense population of workers is growing up among physical and moral influences which are bound to be unfavourable. (Bell 1985: 138–9)

As you might expect, the bubble burst – the recession of the 1920s and 1930s hit Teesside as everywhere else. Unemployment rocketed as industry struggled to provide jobs not only for those they already employed but also for the still-growing numbers of incomers looking for a way to earn a living. Teesside, however, was luckier than most – rich in natural resources and with a ready workforce, the recession was a temporary setback. Next came plastics and chemicals[2] and the significant arrival of Imperial Chemical Industries.

Teesside remained an important manufacturing base for Britain throughout the Second World War and into the 1950s. As one industry died (coal mining, for instance), another started up (oil refineries and, with them, the expanding petrochemical industries). However, things had changed since the war and there was now a growing awareness that the workers who powered these industries were living in less than acceptable conditions – both materially and morally. Local authorities embarked on a programme of slum clearance, the intention being to provide new, affordable social housing. The overriding aim was to clear whole neighbourhoods of the material and moral decrepitude that was referred to as 'social blight' (Glass 1948: 48; Rutherser 1999: 323). However, the ingrained degradation of the area was not so easy to shake off. As Glass commented, 'slum clearance has been piecemeal. Many of the cleared sites have remained vacant, and thus the derelict appearance of the northern neighbourhoods is accentuated' (Glass 1948: 48), and a little further on, 'many of these families could not easily shake off the habits engendered by their former environment' (ibid.: 50).

It seemed as if the physical, social and economic environment had begun to settle itself into the landscape and the people of Teesside – in fact, as you drive through Teesside today the derelict appearance of many of the neighbourhoods is accentuated by the plots of vacant land that have been left behind following the clearance of old factory sites. In some ways, little has changed – though this is not for want of trying. Aware of a need to address these issues as the country began to look forward to the promise of the twenty-first century, the local authorities on Teesside launched an ambitious plan of modernisation. Teesside was to be propelled into the future on a wave of new building and investment in the manufacturing industries and communications infrastructure. So it was that on top of the originally unplanned and capital-driven emergence of urban Teesside, with its blithe disregard for anything 'merely agreeable to the eye', as Bell put it, was constructed a new vision of Teesside's future. This future was signalled by the spartan, functionalist architecture of Teesside's public buildings, the shape of things to come.

Whatever the intention, the outcome was once again a clash between the immediate and capital-driven needs of industry and the longer-term, human needs of local people (Durham University 1975). The promised prosperity that modernisation was supposed to herald never materialised; instead, Teesside felt the full force of the industrial downturn of the 1980s. Wave after wave of factory closures and job losses could no longer be compensated for by new openings and investments. The new 'clean' industries of the late twentieth century brave new world did not want to come to Teesside, a place stigmatised by its industrial past (Bush et al. 2001).

Now here today is Teesside – a place where, it seems, individuals always did take second place to policy (Durham University 1975; Beynon et al. 1994) and yet, at the same time, a place that has been formed by the visions and will of particular individuals and through the actions and willingness of countless others. Contemporary Teesside is a place that some 600,000 people call home[3] and, as Beynon et al. point out, it is a place where they have built up social networks and cultural contexts that give sense to their experience of being human, of being people and not simply bearers of labour power and producers of capital (Beynon et al. 1994: 5).

Many of these people are the descendants of those whom Florence Bell suggested would 'grow up into a generation which will bring down the average of the deserving and efficient'. They live with their past, they live amongst their past, it is they who form the main part of the local authorities' councillors, who appoint the officers who will implement policy, who live with and try to materialise their vision of what Teesside might become – who want, as Beynon et al. put it, 'what is best for Teesside' (1994: 184). Clearly inscribed, right across the Teesside landscape, are social relationships and social values made concrete: the space that industry saw as an opportunity has become a place where people live, a place where people learn to live.

It has frequently been pointed out that landscapes are invested with meaning (Lawrence and Low 1990; Ucko and Layton 1999) and also that the notion of landscape is a useful metaphor with which to explore some of the moral values in operation in a society (Helgason and Palsson 1997). It has also been noted that the urban environment, being an environment deliberately produced by human beings, reflects their values in material terms and can be read in the same way as a text can be read.[4] The landscape of Teesside seen in such a way is riddled with conflict and contradiction, ambiguity and ambivalence. As one of the local authority advertising brochures put it when I first moved to the area, it is a 'county of contrasts'. Industrial structures lining the Tees Estuary speak of dirt and decline, they also speak of a once promising past and of a place where people have come together and built a sense of community. Housing estates, with their boarded-up houses and unkempt gardens, speak of poverty and unemployment; yet sparkling windows, net curtains and neat flower beds that are mixed with the abandoned houses also speak of a fierce sense of pride, a recognition that some of the old houses were worse, combined with a sense of loss – the places where people grew up have been bulldozed to make way for patches of grass where dogs are walked. But how do these changes come about? Who decides what will happen where? What are these social relationships that become concretised in the landscape? And, importantly for my purposes, where are Gypsies in all of this?

Gypsies on Teesside

Gypsies were intimately involved with the building of Teesside: as the industries flourished, so also did opportunities for people to make a living recycling scrap, working on the growing road and rail network, selling household items to the residents of the rapidly growing townships. Whilst casual farm work was still the mainstay of Gypsies' livelihood in the summer (older members of the Gypsy population fondly remember their times in the strawberry fields and orchards, and they less fondly remember their toil in the potato fields), the industries provided some security of income in the winter months, whether through recycling scrap metal and rags or selling items such as pegs and artificial flowers to the workers and their families.

Davey made this point to me one day when I went on to the Bankside site to see him and his wife. Davey is a Gypsy of English and Irish background – he speaks with an Irish accent and has an Irish surname; he insists he is a Gypsy and not an Irish Traveller and he is related to many of the other Gypsies (English and Irish) on Teesside. We got talking, and I got scribbling:

> Davey's family were local people – Davey was brought up by (I think) his mother's cousin – one Robert O'Brien, his father had died. Robert was a good friend of Charlie Smith (from Annie and Janey's family), who owned lots of the scrapyards in Bankside – got the job of dismantling Dorman Long …

Davey says he has some good pictures of Skippers Lane as it was in the old days – pictures of the Travelling families living in tents on the side of the road. (field notes)

Some sense of the extent to which people from Gypsy backgrounds populated the growing industrial townships around Teesside can be seen by a look at the kinship diagrams (in appendix I), where I have marked those who are living on Teesside, including both those living in trailers and those living in houses. Further upriver, in Darlington, people (both Gypsies and non-Gypsies) remark upon the involvement of Gypsies in the making of the town, passing comments such as: 'Gypsies built this town.' 'Look at the names on half the firms around here – they are Gypsy names.' 'This town is half Gypsy.' This conversation with Davey reinforced a growing awareness that Teesside was a place that was imprinted with the memories and understandings of all those who lived there – that the Gypsies I worked with had made it as much their home as anyone else, that they weren't simply rootless, drifting nomads who happened by chance to end up on Teesside.

Whether or not it is the case that Gypsies 'built' Teesside, as Davey claimed, a casual passer-by (and even many local residents) would not recognise that it was a possibility, nor would they recognise the number of people living on Teesside who call themselves Gypsies. To all intents and purposes, and according to popular definitions, Gypsies are people who live in trailers – therefore their brothers, sisters, cousins and so on who live in houses are not viewed as Gypsy. This view of Gypsiness is even echoed in law, where people have had to prove that they travel in order to be legally classed as Gypsy (Hawes and Perez 1996: 7, 135ff.; Kenrick 1999). Or, in education policy at the time of writing, people who have lived in a house for more than two years do not qualify as Gypsies, according to the government department responsible for education, and therefore do not qualify for the services of the Travellers Education Service. These are illustrations of the way schematic understandings about what a Gypsy 'is' are reproduced in the public imagination (the law, policy documents, etc.) and in ensuing actions, including service provision, and thence also in space.[5] Through such processes, social relationships become concretised in space and those social relationships involving Gypsies are reflected in the physical environment. Sibley (1981, 1995) has effectively illustrated the ways in which schematic understandings about Gypsies are reproduced in terms of physical and social space. On Teesside, the marginalisation that Sibley describes is seen in the placing of official Gypsy sites on the edges of industrial estates, on the other side of wastelands and surrounded by barbed wire and brick walls. However, these are not the only places in which Gypsies are to be found on Teesside; in fact, the social relationships that are being concretised in space are complex and multivocal and incorporate an interplay of the differences between knowing about and knowing Gypsies to which I referred in the Introduction.

The Sites

There are three official Gypsy caravan sites on Teesside: one in Bankside, one in Middlesbrough and one in Stockton. These sites were established by Cleveland (formerly Teesside) County Council as a response to the 1968 Caravan Sites Act, which required local authorities to make provision for Gypsies and Travellers where there was shown to be a need (Kenrick and Clark 1999: 89ff.) – an act that was later repealed following the 1994 Criminal Justice and Public Order Act (ibid.: 108). The three sites were constructed in accordance with government guidelines (for more details, see Kenrick and Clark 1999: 84ff.) and have in common the fact that they are separated from the residential parts of the towns and they are built in semi-industrial areas that are difficult to get to. All three of the sites can only be reached by crossing a half-derelict ex-industrial wasteland transected by roads and railway lines. The sites also have in common the way they are made almost invisible to those who might be passing by – they are set off from the roads and surrounded by high banks of earth, thick hedges and barbed-wire-topped walls.

Bankside caravan site is the one I first visited back in February 1998. It is also the one that was most recently built. It has twenty-eight plots, each flat concrete with a gulley running down the centre for drainage (figure 3.4). Each plot is marked off from the one next to it by a low metal pole. In one corner of every plot is a brick built shed with kitchen, bathroom, toilet and storage area. These sheds also have service connection points so that the people resident on the site can hook up to running water and electricity. To get to Bankside site you have to walk past a couple of scrapyards and past a rarely used warehouse (figure 3.3). The road leads towards the docks, where huge cranes are visible but you turn off before you catch sight of the river and walk down a small side street. The street is called King George's Terrace and was once part of the residential area; the houses have long since been knocked down as the area was in the blast zone from the local industrial works and was therefore classed as unsafe for habitation. Although Bankside site is hidden from view by high earth banks, it is not walled in. The surrounding land was probably once part of the Tees flood plain, certainly part of the marshes – it has that flat and exposed feel. On the site itself, it is usually windy and dust blows across the concrete from the shifted earth piles of the landfill site adjoining.

Riverside Caravan Site in Middlesbrough is the oldest of the official sites on Teesside. It has eighteen plots, the sheds are older and more dilapidated than those on Bankside and there is nothing to divide one plot off from another. To reach the site, you need to cross the A66 and the railway, going from the centre of town towards the Riverside Industrial Estate (figure 3.1). The word riverside conjures up images of water in my mind, whether urban and edged by buildings and quays or field-bound in the countryside. On Riverside you cannot see the river. In fact, on Riverside you cannot see much other than the 10-foot-high breeze-block wall topped by barbed wire that surrounds the site on three sides – either that or the scrubby hedge that runs down the other side and is strewn with litter. Children ride their bikes down the short bank the hedge is planted on, through piles of litter and over broken bottles and discarded bits of toys. The roadside hedge is regularly cleared and trimmed by the Council and presents a neat face to passers-by, who would never know, unless it was pointed out, what lay on the other side. The site-side hedge, on the other hand, is never cleared as the council cannot agree which department has responsibility for it.

Stockton site is, like Bankside site, fairly new. Set back from a busy road leading to an industrial estate, the site has a couple of electricity substations at its gate (figure 1.2). A long driveway, with unusually high sleeping policemen, eventually opens on to a busy and colourful site; each plot has its own amenities shed, many with lace curtains. Many of the plots also have their own fences and gates; some even have brick walls, inside which are garden sheds and horseboxes. The site has twenty-seven plots and at its centre is a large house – a grade two listed building – where the warden lives. Part of this house is also used as a community centre for the residents of the site. Walking on to the site at any time of the day, you are usually surrounded by children, who come to check out who you are, what you want, who you are going to see and so on. If the children don't appear – perhaps because it's raining – you can guarantee a van will drive slowly past you and the driver will lean over and ask what your business is.

Apart from the official sites, there are also the unauthorised encampments. These are not permanent features of the landscape and appear and disappear with a speed that depends upon the speed of the legal system and the determination of the local authority to see them gone. Often this also depends upon the weight of public opinion. If the camps are in a barely visible place away from residential settlements and business premises, then they are often left for months at a time. If, however, the council begins to receive complaints – or the newspapers decide that the presence of Gypsies is a story that will stir people up and so help to sell newspapers – then evictions can take place over a matter of days. There are some places that are regularly used as unauthorised camps; they are usually fairly isolated patches of land where there is grazing nearby for horses, some hardstanding for the trailers and access to a good road. Roundabouts are very popular, as are the brownfield sites that have been cleared of the past industrial developments but have not yet been bought up for new use.

3.1 The road to the Middlesbrough site

3.2 The road to the Stockton site

3.3 The road to the Bankside site

3.4 Amenity
blocks on site

A Question of Culture

When I first visited a Gypsy site, I had a sense of travelling into another world or another land. This sense was bolstered by the ideas that I had about Gypsies being somehow different, belonging to a different culture, having particular ways of doing things and understanding the world, and that these things were what made them 'Gypsy'. This is, in many ways, the root of the anthropological and ethnographic project – roots which, certainly in the case of European anthropology, reach back into a colonialist past where 'other' cultures were not only behaviourally and conceptually different from 'us,' they were also geographically and physically distant, in terms of both place and appearance.

For Gypsies, a lasting legacy of the idea of a 'Gypsy culture' has been the fact that they are represented in terms of definable, identifiable and identifying cultural characteristics. Indeed, I had such ideas when I began working with Gypsies – and I have documented in chapter 1 how my ideas about the 'rules' of Gypsy culture had to change as I realised that people did not follow these practices rigidly and unconsciously; they were more creative and inventive with them than my early ideas about 'Gypsy culture' would allow.

In the end, I reached the conclusion that the culture of the Gypsies I was working with was not a set of defining, identifying and identifiable rules. True, some of the words they used could clearly be connected to a Sanskrit root, thus bolstering the frequent assertion of those who had worked with and written about Gypsies before that they (and therefore their culture) had originated in the Indian subcontinent (Kenrick and Clark 1999: 24). True, they lived in trailers, when they weren't living in houses, although sometimes they had both at once. True, they used different bowls for different activities, such as laundry, personal hygiene, washing up (but then so had my grandmother, who had been raised in rural Ireland but who was not from a Gypsy or Travelling background). True, there was a sense of Gypsies being generally more trustworthy and honourable than non-Gypsies in a way suggestive of the moral boundary separating Gitanos from Payos[6] described by Gay-y-Blasco (1997). There were times, however, when this idea of Gypsies' honour simply did not do justice to the subtle nuances of the ways the people I worked with spoke about themselves and others; there was an appreciation of there being 'good and bad in everyone', a phrase often repeated in many different contexts and again underlining the problems involved in using a boundary metaphor. True, many of them were self-employed or earned a living dealing (whether land, horses, scrap metal and so on), and so seemed to bear resemblance to the people who feature in Okely's (1983) and Sway's (1988) work. But, then, often men would take jobs at a local factory (reminding me of the people that Stewart worked with (1997b: 102)), whilst women would take cleaning jobs and many were dependent upon benefit. In fact, people would make a living any way they could, again reminiscent of Sway's Californian Gypsies (Sway 1988: 95ff.), and some were better at it than others and lived in large houses with land and stables whilst others were poor and lived in small trailers – often in unauthorised camps.

There was, however, a very important difference between the people I worked with and the people Sway described; Sway, drawing on the work of Simmel (1950), described the Gypsies she worked with as a 'middleman minority', part of the definition of which is that they are a minority 'not organically connected' to its customers, whether through kinship or locality or occupation (Sway 1988: 16). Conversely, the people I worked with were very much organically connected to the people around them – I never could draw a line around a group of people and say these are Gypsies and these aren't. As we shall see in the chapters that follow, the 'edges' of the 'family trees' that I drew were vague and uncertain and allowed Gypsies to be connected to the wider population around them. Similarly, I could not draw a line around them in space, for, whilst the sites and unauthorised camps were separate from the housed areas nearby, that did not stop people moving into and out of houses – sometimes having both a house and a pitch on a site at the same time. Nor was their a clear separation in terms of occupation: people made deals with friends and family, they worked for a variety of employers (as did many people when they got the chance), and at other times they claimed benefit alongside the very many unemployed people on Teesside.

This difficulty in separating the Gypsies I worked with from the wider world around them also made it difficult to apply Bancroft's (1999) ideas about Gypsies as 'strangers', who are, as a product of modernity, paradoxically defined as a 'fixed member of a spatially located group, but not of it' (ibid.: 4.6). Unlike the Czech Roma of Bancroft's studies, some of the Gypsies I worked with did own land, most of them did feel an attachment to place (as we shall see in chapter 10) and they were as likely to be viewed as local people who had grown up in the area as any of the people who had grown up on Teesside.

So what is it that distinguishes the people I worked with? What is it that allows me to write of them as 'Gypsies'? This is, in fact, a problem I struggled with for a long time. In the end I focused on a few individuals and their family networks; these individuals all recognised and accepted one another as Gypsies, thus fitting Okely's notion of self-ascription by the group (Okely 1983: 66), and they all had members of their families living on one or more of the sites for most of the time, although which particular member of the family it was might change. Finally, they all shared a love of going to fairs, such as Appleby and Yarm, where they would meet up with other members of their family.

I noted previously that one thing people would do when they were telling me what it meant to them to be Gypsy was tell me stories about their experiences. This constant use of storytelling encouraged the focus on stories that runs through this study. Like the Scottish Travellers that

Braid worked with, the Gypsies I worked with had a remarkable capacity for understanding the power and place of narrative thought in building a sense of being in the world (Braid 2002: 287). Whilst I couldn't point to a specific set of stories knowledge of which would help to identify Gypsies (such as Braid could point to as regards Scottish travelling culture), I could discern a recognisable style of telling stories – they were all particular and personal and certain themes cropped up time and time again. It was this that finally gave me the focus that enabled me to write an ethnography of Gypsies without relying on defining or determining cultural rules.

Putting Gypsies in Their Place

One aspect of a commonly held schematic understanding concerning Gypsies is the idea that they are dirty, that they 'mess up' the land (Sibley 1981, 1995) – they make it look untidy. As we have seen, social relationships are concretised in space and so it would be reasonable to expect that decisions concerning land use as it relates to Gypsies would take such an idea into account. This is indeed what happens and it is in this process of matching people and/or events to schematic understandings and so to actions that brings about changes in the physical and social worlds we inhabit. The following passage illustrates this process in operation; it is taken from a meeting in September 2001 of a local authority subcommittee dealing with Gypsy and Traveller issues. Greg is a public health officer for the local authority and he is discussing with Sarah, another local authority officer, and Len, a local councillor, the presence of a number of people in caravans on land near an industrial estate. Specifically, the passage illustrates the ways in which Gypsies are associated with dirty behaviour and non-dirty behaviour is associated with 'not-Gypsies' and how this 'knowledge' helps to form the basis of an understanding of a situation where a decision is expected to be made about what to do about it:

> Greg: … four vans, they come on Monday, four vans on the left hand side with three families and they're on British Steel – . British Steel come along and ask them to move and they moved straight away. But they don't look like Gypsies, they don't look like Travellers, they look like somebody that's just lookin' for somewhere to park up for a holiday y'know what I mean?

In this passage Greg makes explicit an association with Gypsies and the way things look. It also shows how, where visible behaviour somehow conflicts with what is 'known' about Gypsies, then there is a disassociation between the two. In this instance, the looks and behaviour of the people in question did not fit with the conceptualisation (schematic understanding) of Gypsies – the suggestion was that therefore the people were unlikely to actually be Gypsies.

Doubt is cast upon whether the people in question are actually Gypsies because they are behaving too well – they move when asked, there are no reports of threatening behaviour and there is no association with dirt or waste. Also, they 'don't look like Gypsies' as if 'Gypsy' is a visible attribute that can be used to identify a type of person. Sibley (1995) noted how the enactment of these ideas leads to Gypsies being forced into a physical and conceptual space where they can only be dirty and threatening – it is part of what defines a Gypsy. This point of view is returned to at the end of the meeting:

> Greg: There was quite a lot of Travellers actually on the P's land, seven caravans, so there was quite a lot. But they weren't particularly, I wouldn't say, Gypsies for want of a better word.
> Sarah: No – no.
> Greg: They come into the area for a week, looking for somewhere to stay, didn't want to pay the caravan park fees and just went and (inaudible) for a night. I mean they went – pulled all sorts out of their caravans and then, after a week, they left.
> Len: If people generally don't cause a nuisance …
> Greg: That's right.
> Sarah: Yeah.

In fact the people the above exchange refers to were Gypsies on their way back from Whitby Regatta, where I had been staying with them a couple of weeks earlier. They were slowly making their way back to their homes, some of which were houses where they would continue to be invisible as Gypsies – Gypsies, as we have seen, being schematically defined by mainstream imagining as people who travel around and live in caravans.

The extract above ends on a note of agreement, an agreement that does not contradict what Greg has said but that builds upon Greg's suggestion that the people in question might not be Gypsies. This agreement forms a common ground from which to make a decision about what to do about an unauthorised camp – the four vans that Greg refers to at the beginning of the extract. This decision is in fact a decision to do nothing – the people are defined as people by Len (in response to Greg's search for a 'better word' than Gypsies) and if people don't cause a nuisance then there is no harm in them staying for a little while. Gypsies, on the other hand, cause a nuisance by definition. And so the decision is made to do nothing, and so in one part of the place that is Teesside, for a short while in September 2001, an unauthorised camp of Gypsies was allowed to exist unharassed until they quietly went back to their houses on the north side of the river.

It goes without saying that this decision-making process is not the same all the time and in 'The Dark' section I explore more fully the complex and multivocal nature of the relationships that can become concretised in space. It is a story of conflict, contradiction and negotiation to which there is no final resolution, as there is no final resolution to the crucial February meeting described earlier. Before I do this, however, let us have a closer look at some of the people these decisions are made about.

3.5 Horses in Middlesbrough

3.6 Camp at a summer fair

Notes

1. http://clients.thisisthenortheast.co.uk/millennium/history/page76.htm
2. This development was not entirely without precedent – alum had been mined in east Cleveland since the Middle Ages, only stopping with industry's somewhat heavier demands. You can still see the weird lunar landscapes – scars of alum mining – on the cliffs at Boulby. In those days, the ports on the Tees imported urine (supposedly collected from convents and lunatic asylums) to process the alum.
3. http://www.teesvalley-jsu.gov.uk/tvstats1body.htm
4. For a useful review of the considerable literature, see Low (1996).
5. A process that will be explored in much greater detail in the final section of the book.
6. Spanish Gypsies' word for non-Gypsy, equivalent of gorgio.

PART II

THE FIRE

4.1 Yarm high street, looking towards the Show People's rides and trailers

Living to live in a world of time beyond me; let me
Resign my life for this life, my speech for that unspoken,

From T. S. Eliot, 'Marina'

4.2 Janey photographing Yarm high street, looking towards the Gypsy caravans

I love the fire as my own heart.
Winds fierce and small
rocked the Gypsy girl
and drove her far into the world.
The rains washed away her tears,
The sun – the golden Gypsy father –
warmed her tears
and wonderfully seared her heart …

From 'Untitled verse', by Papusza (Hancock et al. 1998: 43)

Chapter 4

STORIES AND TEACHING GYPSINESS

———— ⊂⊃⊃⊃⊂⊃ ————

An Introduction

Taking place in mid-October, Yarm Fair is usually the last in the season, but in 2001 it was both first and last. The foot-and-mouth outbreak had resulted in the cancellation of the usual summer horse fairs; Yarm Fair was still able to take place because nowadays there is little horse dealing – most of the economic activity is carried out by the Show People, who put their rides and stalls at one end of the high street. Gypsies fill up the other end of the high street with horse-drawn wagons and trailers and plenty of fortune-tellers or *dukkerers*.

This year, as usual, Yarm high street was lined with the living accommodation of Gypsies and Travellers. At one end of the high street were the traditional horse-drawn living wagons or *vardoes* that are becoming increasingly popular amongst the Gypsies I work with. Then there are the more usual motor-drawn trailers. Halfway down the high street, the fair starts and there can be found the enormous and flamboyant trailers of the Show People who travel around with the fairground rides. There is a history of rivalry between the Gypsies and the Show People, and many of the Gypsies feel that the fair is encroaching on their traditional horse fair, whilst the Show People blame the Gypsies for the negative reception they receive from the townspeople.

On the first evening I spent at the fair, Sarah said to me, 'Come on, get your camera, we're going to a christening.' I grabbed the video camera and we set off walking up towards the end of the high street where the living wagons were. Amongst all the wagons was one belonging to Tilly Wood – the oldest Gypsy in the fair – and outside it a group of people was gathering. On the street a little behind the wagon, a stick fire was burning, it was getting dark and the weather was cool and grey but it was not raining.

About ten minutes after we arrived, a man dressed in black made his way through the crowd, accompanied by a woman, also dressed in black and carrying a large wooden box. This was the Presbyterian minister, who had agreed to perform the christening (even though it wasn't to be held in a church), and his helper, who was carrying a kind of portable font with what I presumed to be some holy water in a bottle. These two set up the font at the steps leading up to Tilly Wood's caravan amidst a lot of wondering from the gathering assembly about whose christening it was. Tilly herself sat there looking on. Once the ministers had established themselves, a group of people came forward, one of the women holding a very small baby, the crowd settled itself and the christening began.

The baby was about six weeks old and its parents were keen that it should be christened and brought up as a Gypsy. To them this meant living most of the time in a caravan, at very close quarters with others who would share the same living space. Very probably, the baby would share its parents' bed until the next child came along, or until it was two or three years old. She (this particular baby was a girl, but all this could as easily apply to a baby boy) would not have the usual 'going to bed' routines of many mainstream[1] children – she would go to bed when the family went to bed and get up when everyone else got up. She would get used to a number of carers, all from the same family – close cousins, siblings, aunts and so on – all of whom would bring her up 'as a Gypsy.' Yet in all the time I spent with Gypsies I never witnessed anyone consciously teaching a very young child what 'being a Gypsy' involved. This baby would be brought up as a Gypsy simply because her world was a Gypsy world; she would be surrounded by people who were Gypsies and so she would grow with ways of teaching her how to be in the world that emerged from a particular tradition of practice – a Gypsy tradition.

The Intersubjective Process of Socialisation

Work by psychologists such as Vygotsky (1994) and Luria (1994) examined the ways in which culture becomes involved in the developmental process of the infant becoming an adult. Vygotsky noted how the social mediation of behaviour actually transforms the consciousness and conscious actions of the child (Wertsch 1991; Vygotsky and Luria 1994). In other words, a human being is not born complete but small, a huge amount of formative development continues following birth and this requires that the infant participate in a social world. The psychologist Premack (1984) refers to this distance between the cognitive abilities of the infant and the adult as a 'cognitive gap'. Premack also notes that in order to bridge the cognitive gap between the infant and the adult the social relationship is primary – the development of the human being depends more upon the social relationship than on the hard-wired systems of the biological organism existing at birth.

Building on these theories, more recent psychological studies have suggested that there is an innate capacity in human beings to recognise and imitate others – to fully enter into an 'intersubjective' relationship (Trevarthen and Aitken 2001). In the work of others (Schutz 1951; Berger and Luckman 1966; Jackson 1996, 1998), this notion of intersubjectivity forms the centre point of an understanding of intimate interactions between human beings who can experience one another as 'fully real' (Berger and Luckman 1966: 43). The implication is that the ability to engage in intersubjective relationships is an innate and necessary human capacity; moreover, it is a capacity that continues throughout our lives, thus enabling us to continually engage with and relate to one another. As we grow, the ways we learn to do this become ever more complex and intricate, building from the formative intersubjectivity of the infant to the very complex interactions of adult humans, who can convey a world of meaning in a glance, a gesture, an expletive – provided that the other participants in that interaction have learned how to interpret such glances or gestures or expletives and so on.

At this point, I shall focus upon the ways in which those social relationships are enacted – the ways in which our actions are mediated (Wertsch 1991: 12, 119ff.) and we come to cross and learn how to teach others to cross that 'cognitive gap'. This developmental process is carried out through the use of cultural 'signs' or artefacts (Luria 1994). Luria's experiments show how the artefacts or tools themselves are taught as well as their use – i.e. what is taught is not only how to use the tools but also what to use as tools; the uses of such artefacts or 'tools' are learned and taught by and to others in order to facilitate the development of the human being. Again, the emphasis is upon the social processes involved – and people from differing cultural and historical backgrounds have different traditions of what 'tools' to use and how to use them. What is more, they have different traditions or styles of practice – different ways in which to pass on the 'tools' and their uses.

Another Introduction

During my fieldwork, I had the good fortune to be involved in such processes myself; for instance, the day after the christening had taken place at Yarm Fair, I met up with William, whom I had been introduced to the previous day. William had agreed to teach me something about Gypsy culture for the book I was writing.[2] After spending some time showing me photographs of his family, William turned to me:

William asked me if I wanted to know some words. Of course I said 'Yes'! These are the ones he gave me:[3]

Gorgios	normal people/town dwellers
Gypsies	us (I asked if they called themselves Gypsies or Rom etc. – said no, Gypsies)
Danders	teeth
Yocks	eyes
Val	ear
Chockers	shoes
Eases	clothes
Tuvlers	cigarettes
Tattapani	any spirits, like whisky
Pani	water
Orben	food
Mora	bread
Luvva	money
Kitchima	public house
Hatching tan	stopping place
Dik akai	look here
Koorin mush	fighting man
Gavva mush	policeman (man you hide from)
Gavva	hide
Dindler	foolish person
Kosh pukker the drom	signpost (wood that tells the road to go)
Chavvie	child
Mandi juns	I know
Mandi	myself
Rokker	talk
Kerka rokker	don't talk
Kerka	don't
Jell on	come on
Grye	horse
Djuckel	dog
Cani	chicken (or other bird to eat)
Hingler	hare
Covvers	things

(Field notes)

The first word William chooses to teach me is 'gorgios', a word that immediately places what he is telling me in a world that is different from that of 'normal people' or 'town dwellers'. Importantly, William did not oppose 'Gypsies' to 'gorgios' – certainly there is a difference between Gypsies and gorgios but it is not necessarily an oppositional and excluding difference. That William chose certain words almost tells a story in itself; my own children sometimes come home from school with a list of words that they are to use to make up a story – if they were to be given (even in translation) the list of words that William gave me their story would have a distinctly 'Gypsy' feel to it. William chose to teach me words that convey a sense of 'Gypsiness' that is not contained solely in the meanings of the single words but that is built upon through the ways those words can fit together, the ways that they can give each other context.

Secondly, whilst this is the way that I wrote down the list of words and later copied them up more neatly, it is not the way William taught them to me; he also taught me contexts that gave them sense. For instance, when he spoke of the words for bread and food, he told me a story about how when he was at an Indian restaurant the waiters understood some of the things they were saying – how he could say 'What *orben*'s on the menu?' and it would be understood. Or, when he was telling me about the words *rokker* and *kerka rocker*, he would describe times when he was young when his parents would tell him '*Kerka rokker*' if a stranger approached and asked his name. Similarly he would expand on why a policeman was 'a man you hide from', telling me about the times when he had hidden to avoid being seen by a policeman and asked to move on. In teaching me words in this way, William was teaching me a whole world of Gypsiness – he was beginning with me a process of teaching 'how to do' intersubjectivity that I would need to have grown into to be a fully adult Gypsy.

Learning to Speak – Social Aesthetics and the Context of Socialisation

William provided a beautiful illustration of the connection between the world that we have grown up in, that we have learned to become part of, and the ways we use language:

> William said how he had grown up not speaking English – that he's had to learn that bit by bit since.
>
> He used to stop with his granny sometimes and with his uncles. He thought that they were the only Gypsies in the world. Then one day one of the uncles said to his dad that there was a big fair up north – Appleby. Some time later they sold their horse-drawn wagon and moved into a trailer with a van. 'The uncle said why don't you come with me – I was about 14 or 15. We did.
>
> 'When we pulled on to Appleby there were very many people there that I was nervous. I was that nervous I wouldn't come out of the trailer for two days, I could hardly speak.' (Field notes)

Here William makes explicit a connection between being able to speak and being in a world that you have learned to be a part of, an observation that runs through much of what he told me about his life and many of his conversations with others. For instance, on the last day of the fair Sarah and I were talking to William:

Then William and Sarah had a bit of a conversation about the different languages. Said how some people think that Cockney rhyming slang is Romany. Say that there are differences between the words people use in London and the words that he uses. For instance:[4]

	William	London
Woman	Rakli	Djuvel
Vonga	coal	money

They had a laugh about the way the London word for woman is very like their word for head lice (djuvvel and djuvvers) and also how they thought it was funny if a London Traveller went shopping they would take a pocket full of vonga (coal) and try to pay for things with coal. (Field notes)

Some of the things that William said also reflect upon the more poignant and difficult experiences of being a Gypsy that he had:

William noted that the English he speaks, and more especially that he spoke when he was growing up, wouldn't be understood because they pronounced it wrong. He said how he had grown up not speaking English – that he's had to learn that bit by bit since. (Field notes)

I made a note at the time that when William had told me this he had conveyed a real sense of frustration; he gave the impression that he had been ashamed of the way he spoke when he was younger (he spoke of being *'ladjed'*, a word used by Gypsies to denote shame or embarrassment) and that he had struggled to learn to speak in a way that was more easily understood by the non-Gypsy world and that conformed more to the social aesthetic standards of the non-Gypsy world that surrounded him.

In Vygotsky's work, there was a considerable emphasis upon the idea of language both as a system of cultural artefacts (tools) and as the means by which such artefacts and their uses are passed on from one generation to the next. The significance of language in this pedagogical process was also emphasised by Premack, who noted that in order to bridge the 'cognitive gap' language was needed – observation/demonstration alone was not sufficient to convey the complexity of the tasks concerned (Premack 1984). Further, language is not just how we are taught and how we teach – it is also what we are taught, what we learn and what we learn to teach to others. Moreover, we learn to do this in different ways, with different styles, depending upon the traditions of practice in which we are raised. Hence our language use, including the ways we are taught to use and tell stories forms a very significant part of that aspect of social life termed 'social aesthetics' (Carrithers 1992: 36ff.; MacDougall 1999; Highmore 2004).

The idea of social aesthetics has links to the notion of 'habitus', as developed by Bourdieu (e.g. 1977), in that it refers to socially accepted, taught and internalised standards of behaviour – what is judged to be fitting, appropriate or even tasteful. There are, however, significant differences between the two, which can be condensed to the point that the aesthetic standards of social aesthetics are conceived as socially distributed and, whilst individuals learn to use such standards, they are under-determining and so can be consciously rejected, manipulated and so on.[5] Habitus, on the other hand, is manifested and concretised in the individual, determining that individual's behaviour and expression. This point can be elaborated. A social aesthetic standard refers to something that the experienced instructor knows and understands and can transmit to the novice. Habitus is described as an embodied sense of 'fit' or the right/acceptable/appropriate way to behave, which is taught to us in ways that mould our bodies as well as language, and a part of which always remains in the unconscious of the individual and outside that individual's power to choose their actions. In other words, social aesthetics are intentionally taught to us and become part of our acceptable and expected behaviour but are open to change, adaptation and deliberate flouting, whereas habitus is an unconsciously internalised way of behaving over which we have little conscious control. As Bourdieu put it, 'The principles em-bodied [by habitus] are placed beyond the grasp of consciousness, and hence cannot be touched by voluntary, deliberate transformation, cannot even be made explicit' (Bourdieu 1977: 94).

We have seen that William was able to reflect upon and articulate the sense of being Gypsy that he had been taught as he was growing up, and which he taught to his children and grandchildren, and also (in a small way) to me. Nor was William alone in this, other Gypsies were also able to reflect upon their 'way of doing things' in a way that questions the unconscious and determining nature of habitus. Take, for instance, James and Rosaleen, a young Gypsy couple I first met in November 2001, when again I was introduced as someone who was writing a book about Gypsies. We talked about many things, including the 'way that Gypsies speak':

> At this point Rosaleen started talking about language and ways of talking, describing how although they spoke English they did it all wrong – 'backwards, opposite'. She illustrated this by saying things like – 'You say banana, we say panama.' I can't remember the other examples she gave, but it put me in mind of the way Gypsies often say revorced rather than divorced. (Field notes)

Here Rosaleen is aware of a style of doing things that is a 'Gypsy' style, but she is also aware of other styles and can use them as the basis of reflection and comparison. What is more, she can, if she so chooses, change the way that she does things to fit a different style.

This distinction between determining (e.g. habitus) and non-determining (e.g. social aesthetics) social contexts is developed in the work of Farnell (1995: 20, 2000), in which she rejects the determining (because unconscious) nature of the idea of habitus. Farnell concentrates upon the idea that areas of consciousness are 'out of focal awareness' – a notion developed from the insights of Polanyi (1958; 1969: 211–23) – which is not to say that they cannot become the object of focal awareness.[6] Farnell demonstrates the ways in which we learn to take for granted certain ways of being – certain practices that conform to the social aesthetic standards we have been taught. Such 'taken for granted' practices might involve the ways we walk, gesticulate and so on – here the links between this idea and that of habitus can be seen more clearly as we are reminded of the idea of habitus and bodily practices suggested by Mauss (1979 [1950]). What distinguishes Farnell's approach from Bourdieu's is the perceived ability of the individual to turn his or her attention upon the social contexts in which they operate and consciously and creatively examine and manipulate them. In the illustrations given above, we can see how 'taken for granted' practices are contained in the speech activities of Gypsies. It is, to a large extent, such 'out of focal awareness' ideas that make up an experience of what it is to be a Gypsy and that will be passed on to the baby whose christening I described at the beginning of the chapter.

In her work on gestural language, Farnell develops the links between language use and bodies. Through these links, we can see how it is the whole of the human that enters into the pedagogical relationship – the words they use to teach are enacted in the actions that accompany those words; the same point is also reflected in psychological investigations into mother-child interaction (see, for example, Brand et al. 2002). Hence, when we consider the nature of the relationships that form us into human beings we have to consider them in a holistic sense – words and actions together; it is in this way that we become socialised into a culture. But we do not become socialised into some determining prison of which we are unconscious, as suggested by habitus, but into a system of signs and meanings and understandings, by the use of which we can develop enormously subtle and complex relationships and which we can use, mould and manipulate to achieve our own personal projects.

Social Aesthetics and Socialisation – the Role of Stories

So far, we have seen how a sense of Gypsiness is taught and how it becomes part of an experience of the world that has a particular and recognisable style, but which is not constraining or determining. This sense of Gypsiness, the social aesthetics that inform the tone and style of being Gypsy, is shared by people such as William, Sarah, James and Rosaleen and other Gypsies. We have seen how a sense of Gypsiness is taught and conveyed through language: the words we are taught to use and whom we can use them with. Equally important is the way we are taught: as we saw when William was teaching me certain words; he did not simply use the words to label things, he put them in a context – a particularly Gypsy context – and he did this by using the words in stories.

In the relationship between the words William taught me and the stories he used to teach me, we can discern the social aesthetics that inform the whole process. It is this process as it can be seen in the lives of Gypsies and in their experience of a shared sense of Gypsiness that I shall now explore.

At this point I would like to introduce ideas about narrativity and the ability of human beings to think in a narrative mode, a mode that allows the comprehension of complex webs of meaning that stretch across time and between people (Bruner 1986, 1990; Carrithers 1992). My intention in what follows is to elaborate on some ways in which both narrative thought and socially distributed social aesthetic standards operate in everyday socialising processes.

There are many ideas and analytic approaches that draw on the word 'narrative', and one common way of understanding the capacity for narrative thought in human beings is in our ability to tell and understand stories. Stories are found in most cultures – and they can take many forms. Stories can be fairy tales, myths, legends, they can be religious and/or moral, they can be personal and relate to our own lives, people we know and so on. Anthropologists have used the stories that are peculiar to a people as a route into analysing the culture of that group (e.g. Bauman 1986; Riddington 1990), whilst other anthropologists use the stories that people tell about themselves and their lives as a route into understanding their particular position, for instance as regards an illness or a life event etc. (e.g. Mattingly 1994, 1998; Eschenbruch 2002). Here the word is equivalent to the phrase 'what people say' – i.e. what is analysed is what people say about their illness, their situation, their life, etc. Thus narrative is thought to provide a route into what people 'really' think and how they construct an image of themselves and their relationship to the world in which they are living.

What is common to all these approaches is the idea of a 'story' – a notion that encompasses an ability to think in terms of complex characters and plots and with an extended sense of events unfolding in time. The power of stories – or, to be more precise, the power of the narrative mode of thinking – lies in their ability to pull people in, to articulate and enact the sociality that we began discussing at the start of this chapter. It is this that Carrithers (1992) has referred to as 'confabulation', noting that the style in which (or social aesthetic standards by which) people confabulate society is related to the kind of stories that they tell about themselves and the way they conduct the telling.

Something more than this, though: the stories we tell are created within a particular socio-historical milieu – a particular tradition of practice. So stories can be seen as ways in which we are taught to process, to retain and recall information (e.g. Vygotsky and Luria 1994; McKeough and Sanderson 1996; Ramsey and Langlois 2002), and they help to form the total sense of being in the world (the embodied and enacted social aesthetic, including many things that become 'taken for granted') that allows them to interact in subtle and complex ways with other human beings. Right from the very beginning of our lives, both the stories we are told and the way we are told them have a significant impact upon the ways we learn to interact with others, and this is what William was both teaching and sharing with me when he taught me words and how to use them.

Stories and Teaching Gypsy Children

Contained in stories is a vast amount of information about the world that has generated the story in the first place, and we deliberately use stories in order to teach children about the world they are growing up in. In the mainstream, literate world of the West, children are not taught stories through simply having words read to them – in addition to the reading, pictures are pointed at and questions are asked (Heath 1986). Stories become part of the world in which the child learns to exercise his or her developing, and socially formed, cognitive abilities. It is evident that the stories we are told when we are growing up – and the way that we are told them – are a very significant part of the process of becoming a fully functioning and culturally situated adult human.

As we have seen when William was teaching me certain words, to Gypsies too stories are a very important part of the teaching of children – of bringing them up 'as a Gypsy', as it was put to me at the christening described earlier. William told me the following story at Yarm Fair, the day after the christening; and one of the reasons that I was introduced to him in the first place was because he is considered to be a good storyteller.

> Once when we were babies we were staying down a back lane with my mum, dad, brothers and sisters and an uncle who had never married.
>
> This uncle had a little wagon and one day someone shouted, 'Who's that sitting on your wagon?' There was a little man sitting at the front of the wagon. My dad chased him but he couldn't catch him so he turned round and went back to the wagons. When he got there the little man was sitting back where he had been before. So he chased him again, but couldn't catch him.
>
> Down the lane where the little man would run there was a stile that the little man would jump over but my dad wouldn't go any further. When the little man got there he would jump over the stile but that was as far as he would go.
>
> The next day we had to move on.

The first thing that William does with this story is place it in his own personal world, a world that will be familiar to Gypsies – they will understand what it is to stay down a back lane. The second thing that he does – and still in the first sentence – is place the action amongst people that he knows: members of his family. The overall theme of the story is one that is frequently repeated in Gypsy stories – the idea that strangers are dangerous. The image that is conveyed in William's story is that of a world of familiar people who behave in understandable and explainable ways, whilst unknown people – strangers – come into that world and behave in strange and unaccountable ways (for instance, sitting on wagons that aren't theirs) before disappearing back into their own world. Finally, the story ends on a note that will again be familiar to Gypsies – the need to move on.

These devices and themes are common to many Gypsy stories. The following was told to me by Deborah, whom I had met first at Whitby and then again later in York:

> I've lived in a trailer all my life and as winter was coming we decided to move into a house. We got a house in York and there was a spare bedroom in the house and this bedroom was so cold it made you shiver, but all the other rooms were hot.
>
> One night we were all sat in the living room watching telly and a gust of wind came out of nowhere and blew all the doors open and the pots down.
>
> The next day my dad was talking to our neighbour; my dad asked who used to live in the house and the neighbour said, 'Oh, it was a group of young ones but one of them died in the bedroom so they all moved out.'
>
> The next day we moved out of the house and back into a trailer. We've never been in another house since.

Here again the devices and themes illustrated in William's story are reflected – the teller begins with a scenario familiar to Gypsies – that of living in a trailer. She also places the events in an immediate and known circle of relationships – the 'we' refers to particular people who are known to her. In fact, the people of her 'we' are so well known that she does not even feel she needs to say who they are. The danger or threateningness in the story again comes from the anonymous outside – the world of strangers and people unknown – with the final result that the teller and her family need to move on.

Of course, the idea that danger and threats come from outside the immediate, known circle of friends and relations is not new, nor is it peculiar to Gypsy culture – but it is reacted to in the context of a Gypsy world (people who live in trailers at least some of the time) and in a recognisably Gypsy way (the Gypsies move on).

The strange and unaccountable nature of strangers is repeated in the following story, told by Ivy, Sarah's sister, who was telling a tale as it would be told to her around the campfire when she was a girl:

Listening to tales around the campfire at night was what everyone did for entertainment. Everyone flocked to the fire at a certain time just waiting for a tale to be told. This is one of the tales that I remember:

THE WHITE LADY
Me and a couple of others were walking down the lane without realising how dark it was getting. As we turned to go back, all of a sudden a lady in a white dress was standing next to us, she asked the time, and we gave her it. We walked a little way down the road and she disappeared.

The next night we did the same and the same thing happened. When we went into the village we asked an old man who was sat on a bench on the green and he began to tell us all about the lady in white.

At this time everyone was waiting for the very scary tale to continue, but the story would stop because it is too scary. Everyone would want it to continue but it never did. The same story would be told the next night and it would stop in the same place.

The story of the White Lady never gets ended.

This tale within a tale (Ivy telling me a story about a story that she was told) is quite consciously a tale for teaching and entertaining – it would be told to young people around the campfire. It repeats the image of a world where strangers do unaccountable things – appearing and disappearing – and so reinforces a sense of the world being a place where only those people that you know can be relied upon to behave in comprehensible ways.

Telling Stories and Enacting Stories

As we are told more and more stories, we gather a wealth of information about the world around us and, through the mediation of a more experienced person (e.g. a parent or a teacher or an older sister), we learn to put that knowledge into practice. The following passage is a transcript from a conversation I had with Robert, a well-known wagon painter – some familiar themes are repeated, but this time the story has been 'realised' (as opposed to real life being fictionalised) and this time things don't run exactly as one might expect in a story. Robert begins by talking about one of the wagons he has been painting:

Robert:	These, these type things – arts, that is like a work of art in its own right, innit?
Sarah:	Course it is.
Me:	Uh huh, that's beautiful.
Robert:	You know it (inaudible) I stopped by the roadside in them, I'm not telling no lies you know and the police come up to me, I thought ohh, I thought – one was in like plain clothes, was casual

kind of dress – uniform – you know I think it's the Council mush[7] coming to move – you know how you do. 'Are you all right?' – 'Yeh – can you do us a favour please?' 'What?' said, 'D'you mind moving?' I said, 'Look,' I said, 'I'm sick of moving.' He said 'No no no, don't get me wrong, we haven't come to shift you, we like what we're seeing and so does the villagers but it's going to cause an accident – people are driving past and gawping at it – on this bend – so do you mind moving a bit further down that lane so you just push back cos when people come round that bend ...' (Transcribed from video recording)

We can see in this excerpt the familiar themes and devices mentioned – situating the events in a familiar context (stopping on the roadside) and, of course, the action relates directly to Robert (although he was stopping on his own that time so he doesn't mention anyone else with him). The threatening nature of strangers and the associated need to move on – and this time with the unfamiliar twist of just having to move a little way down the road. This twist is even more unfamiliar as it is brought about by the fact that people in the village actually like to see Robert there – usually people are only too eager to move Gypsies on.

Deborah's story about the haunted house also includes another theme – the dangerous or frightening nature of houses. In a tape recorded by Sarah, this theme is repeated in the conversation of two women discussing what it was like for one of them to move into a house. Rose describes the way that being in a house on her own used to make her scared – she describes the feeling of the hairs on the back of your neck standing on end, as if someone's behind you. Then she describes how there would be noone there:

Sarah: What was it like, Rose, for you moving in?

Rose :   I, (inaudible) all the houses weren't I (inaudible) wouldn't move, wouldn't go upstairs, I wouldn't stop in by myself – no chance. We generally used to go out and I used to be in the house, see me washing up at the sink and I'm looking, y'know, like back of your neck in the sink, the stairs, you'd look at stairs – that was it, everything's done, lock the door, out and go, go down to Katherine's, sit round there all day, I would never stop in by myself, no. (Transcribed from tape recording)

These examples give a very brief outline of the ways in which Gypsies' stories teach about the world – how certain themes and possible responses are repeated, helping to create patterns of expectation about what the world is like and how to behave in that world. These stories introduce themes that influence the way the world is understood and reacted to, though not in a determining sense, as we saw with the unexpected developments in Robert's tale. For our current discussion the most significant points are that Gypsies' stories are set in a world that is familiar to Gypsies – a world of stopping in back lanes, by roadsides, of moving into and out of houses, of being moved on, etc. They are also set amongst familiar people, people who are directly known – usually members of the family. The world of unknown people – whether visiting strangers or previous occupants of a house – is represented as somehow dangerous or threatening.

The Real World of Stories vs. the Fictional World of Books

What I want to stress here is the stories' particularity: these are not general stories, fairy tales or such like that are common to a population and shared. These are stories that have been made particular, that cannot be shared. This leads to a very different understanding about how to use stories as a cultural, mediating, tool and in turn leads to very significant differences in understanding and using stories from those encouraged by the use of books.

In my work with Gypsies, the importance of this was underlined when observing the interactions of some of the young women who were entrusted with the care of small children. It is very common amongst Gypsies to expect young women of thirteen or fourteen to care for their younger brothers and sisters, and this has to be taken into account when working with them. It does, however, create considerable problems for mainstream education providers who are not able to accommodate young children in the classroom – this is just one of the many reasons why Gypsy girls are usually taken out of school at about age twelve. In response to this, I developed, alongside the Travellers Education Service, a project whereby some education would be provided on site. Some of this provision included the young women working with the Travellers Education Service to provide a 'pre-preschool' group for the very young brothers and sisters they were caring for. Activities that took place in these sessions included painting, modelling, playing with bricks and other such toys, and the sessions were always rounded off with a story. At some of these sessions I took a video recorder along, partly as a record of the project's activity, partly for my own fieldwork. The following excerpts have been transcribed from one of the recordings.

Sue is the schoolteacher who has been running the session. She and Lisa, a thirteen year-old Gypsy girl, have just tidied up all the paint and so on from the morning's activities, they have washed the children's hands and now Sue is trying to get the children (Beccy, five; Davy, four; and Chantelle, two) sitting at a small table to have a 'picnic'. Lisa, meanwhile, continues to tidy up, talking to me in a loud voice from across the other side of the room. Sue wants Lisa to read to the younger children as this will encourage her to read, something that she is generally reluctant to do, even denying that she can, and at times saying that it is 'gorgified'[8] and that she'd be 'ladjed'.[9] To Sue Lisa's reading to the children is an important way of teaching her how to read and how to use books and stories to teach younger children:

Sue gets the book – *Sean's Wellies*

Sue: (To Lisa) Do you want to do this story? (looks at the book and then speaks to Beccy) Lisa's going to do a story for you, all right? And I'll clear up. (*To Lisa*) I'll finish that and you can come and … (*doesn't finish the sentence. Sue starts humming and clears the little table that the children are sitting at.*)

The book is one that has been specifically designed to use in teaching Traveller children: it makes reference to things that these children will find familiar, such as pictures of trailers, horses and chickens. In fact, books are designed to encourage a referencing between things represented in the book itself and things experienced by the person reading the book or being read to and shown the pictures in the book (Heath 1986). This is a very simple 'lift the flap' book about a boy called Sean, who is trying to find his wellies. The reader lifts the flaps on each page to see if the wellies are under them (see figures 4.3 and 4.4). Lisa is a reasonably good (if reluctant) reader, but finds it difficult to put much expression into her reading. The following begins from towards the end of the book. Sue has now settled beside Chantelle and has her arm round her – she has been pointing to pictures in the book from time to time and asking questions about the pictures and the story.[10]

Lisa: **'Mrs Graham I can't find my wellies.' 'I know where they are. Look under Ben's coat.'** (*Lisa turns over the page*)
Sue: Hang on, turn round.
Lisa: Oh. (*Turns back a page*)
Sue: (*Laughing points at something and says something inaudible on tape but sounds like they've found the wellies*)
Lisa: **'Come on Sean we're ready to go. We we'** oossshh (*tongue-tied*)
Sue: (*Laughs*)
Lisa: **'Hurry up Sean.' 'I am coming, wait for me.'**
Sue: He'll be happy now, won't he? (*Looks at Beccy and nods*) Yeah. (Transcribed from video recording)

Sue's final comment has moved on from asking fairly simple questions such as 'What's that?' and 'Has he found his wellies?' to making a comment about something that isn't directly referred to in the story – the state of mind of the character Sean. This approach to the use of books as a way of 'taking meaning from' the world beyond the immediate context of the story in the book has been examined by Heath (1986) and it is important to note that it is the schoolteacher, Sue, who is doing this. At no point in the reading does Lisa – who is 'officially' telling the story –

4.3 Page from the book *Shaun's Wellies*

4.4 On this page the flap is one of the doors, which has been pictured open

attempt to relate what she is reading to anything more than what is actually in the book. A similar thing happens at the end of the reading:

Lisa: **'I did need my wellies today. Look, a fish!'**
Chantelle: (*almost shouting*) 'ishing! (*Sue smiles and nods*)
Sue: He needs his wellies so he doesn't get his feet wet, doesn't he?

Again, Sue draws more meaning from the book than is explicitly included in either the text or the pictures – she relates the book to a real world beyond the printed page where people's feet get wet. She is, in effect, teaching the children that books are about real things – real people and real emotional states – even if they are people and states that the children have not ever met or do not often experience (such as being excited about going fishing with the school). This moves the book from an object of entertainment to something that connects the reader and listener to a wider world, to a potentially imagined community.

This should be contrasted with the very particular stories told by Gypsies described above, which set the characters and the events of the story firmly in a world that is known, a world of an experienced rather than an imagined community. Whilst in both mainstream culture and Gypsy culture the use of stories as mediating tools is firmly situated within the intersubjective relationship, there is a significant, qualitative difference between the values attached to such relationships and what the stories are used to do between the two cultures. In the mainstream, the effect is to expand the sense of belonging to a community beyond the immediate environment of known people with whom one can enter into a direct relationship. In Gypsy culture, the effect is quite different: stories are used to root the sense of belonging to a community comprised of those relationships that can be directly experienced.

Stories – Real Life or Fiction?

The idea that fictional, printed stories about people you don't know can have much relevance to your real life is not an idea that is very familiar to Lisa and she does not extend the significance of the book in this way as Sue does. Stories, to Lisa and to other Gypsies that I have worked with, refer to actual events that happened to actual, known people. This was underlined in a conversation between Lisa and her friend Christine a little later on the same day. By this time, Sue, the schoolteacher, had left, as had Davy and Beccy. Lisa had been joined by Christine and Lisa was looking after Chantelle. The two older girls were there to do some work with me learning about IT: I had asked them to write a bit of a story, thinking that they could type it on the computer and I could help with spelling and so on. However, it turned out that they found the task I set them a particularly difficult one – not because of their ability to write and spell, but because the idea of writing a story was so strange to them.

Lisa: Tell you what, you've given us hard work this week.
Me: I know I have.
Christine: I've been going fourteen years and I can't say not one story.

What Lisa and Christine were finding so difficult was the idea of writing down something that happened to them as a story – fictionalising part of their life and removing it from the realm of direct experience, turning it into something that belonged to the more distant world of the imagination, or the imagined community. It wasn't that they had never been told any stories; it was that the idea of turning their story into something that could be made generally available, even to strangers, did not make a lot of sense to them. To Lisa and Christine, a story is something that is told about real, known people, to an audience of real, known people; it is, in other words, something that belongs more to the intersubjective world of direct communication than to the world of ideal types and indirect communication.

This association between stories and real-life events was again reflected some months later when I was supervising a class of young people on the Riverside site who were learning how to use the new laptop computers they had been provided with by the project. The tutor wanted to find a way of showing them how the publishing software worked and so he suggested making a poster. This was agreed, but what couldn't be decided upon was what to make a poster about. There was nothing of particular interest about to happen and the idea of just making something up didn't seem to make much sense to the participants at all – the reaction was one of being completely nonplussed. In the end, they agreed to make a poster about one of their relatives (this was a large family group of cousins and siblings), who was a good boxer – but then they needed to know when his next fight dates were and where. The point is that the activity had to make sense in the real, known and experienced world. The idea of imagining a fictional scenario didn't make sense at all.

In the examples above we can see in operation a contrast between different sets of taken-for-granted understandings that accompany ideas about what you do when you tell a child a story. Sue's ideas reflect a view that books can be used to reference things (both physical and social) in the world that exists beyond the book. Lisa does not share such 'taken-for-granted' understandings – hers are quite different from Sue's and have been learned through the telling of different stories (and different kinds of story). When Sue 'tells a story', what she is actually doing is sitting the children down and showing them how to read a book – pointing at the pictures and so on – and being physically close to them at the same time. Lisa was never taught like this when she was young: her parents do not (and largely cannot) read and there are no books in evidence in their trailers. The kind of storytelling she is used to is very different and consists of spoken tales about people that both she and the children being told the story know, with repeated themes that they can then see in operation in the lives of the people they are living with. Of course, this is not a clear and defining way of behaving that can be used to draw a line between 'what Gypsies do' as opposed to 'what we do' – most families have stories that they tell to themselves and about themselves (Langellier and Peterson 1993). What differentiates Gypsy storytelling is a combination of a preference for stories about known people, a lack of familiarity with using books and generally available stories as a teaching tool and the themes that are repeated in the stories that are told: it is a combination of practices that makes Gypsy storytelling distinctive rather than an absolute and definable difference.

As far as the discussion above regarding socialisation and social aesthetic standards is concerned this point is significant on at least two levels. First, we can see that there are different sets of expectation at work about what 'telling a story' entails. Secondly, these different expectations do not simply relate to the activity of telling a story, they also impact upon ideas about what a story is. Is it something that can be written down in a book and then told to anyone by anyone? Or is it something that draws upon and strengthens real and experienced relationships, something that 'belongs' to particular people and so cannot be told by just anyone? These two points relate to patterns of expectation and to the 'social aesthetic standards' that are operational in the cultures in question, influencing the pedagogical process in discernible ways. Implicit in this process is a set of judgements about what is the correct or 'right' thing to do in using a story to teach children, as well as a set of judgements about what makes for a 'good' story. In the process of making these judgements, we find the grounds for an assessment of not only the aesthetic aspects of the storytelling activity but also for making a moral judgement, as is illustrated by the very words we use when we speak of both social aesthetic and moral evaluations, words such as 'good,' 'right' and so on. It is this merging of the moral and the social aesthetic that I now wish to spend a little time exploring, drawing out some of the implications that different ideas about stories have for the moral 'grounding' of a culture.

Stories and Teaching Morality

We have seen how some Gypsies' stories repeat and reinforce an understanding of the world as a place where strangers behave in unaccountable or inexplicable ways. This theme is repeated in the following conversation where Sarah and her sister Ivy are talking to

Nancy; they had been discussing stories they might be able to put in their book.

Sarah	Tell us about when, when Uncle Isaac used to say that he, er, played cards with the mulla-mush.[11]
Nancy	Give us a clue.
Ivy	Oh, we were told that loads of times.
Sarah	Tell the story the way they said it.
	They were all round the campfire one night and then everybody had gone to bed and he was left by himself an, and, er, there was this man that come up and says do you want to play cards and …
Ivy	… and yess.
Sarah	And he started to play cards with him.
Ivy	And when they bent down he had the Devil's feet.

This cautionary tale that Sarah and Ivy were told 'loads of times' draws upon images of the unaccountable world of strangers, of unknown people, and adds to this image a moral aspect – a sense of evil that can come into the middle of the group if you aren't careful. Through telling such stories, a moral sense is combined with the aesthetic image, teaching a need to be wary of unknown people, not just because they act in odd ways, but because they are potentially evil or morally dangerous. Such stories then provide a basis of action in the 'real' world of direct experience.

As we saw with Robert's enacted stories about being moved on, a significant aspect of the role stories have in our learning how to operate within a cultural milieu is their openness. Whilst most books have 'a beginning, a middle and an end' (as we are taught at school), they also contain a wealth of other unstated possibilities. These possibilities are drawn out by interaction with a more experienced person who can talk to us about 'what might have happened if …'

Gypsies' stories also have an 'open' quality that allows for them to be 'realised' as we saw in the example from Robert above, where an unexpected ending was fitted into a familiar theme. Similarly, Rose's reaction to being in a house fitted a familiar theme that is repeated in Gypsies' stories. Through the telling of stories, and through fitting stories to our lives and our lives to stories, we are taught ways in which to make predictions and judgements about our own and others' behaviour; the patterns of expectation, the social aesthetic standards, also become moral standards by which we judge the actions of ourselves and others as 'good' or 'right'. To a great extent, it is through the telling of stories and the encouragement to apply stories to our own lives – to fit ourselves into the repeated themes, if you will – that we learn how to make such judgements.

'Fictional' vs. 'Real-Life' Moralities

In *Imagined Communities*, Benedict Anderson (1999) describes the impact that printed media have had upon the world, showing how they have enabled people to imagine a community to which they belong that extends beyond the people they know on a personal and direct basis. In these imagined communities – the communities we are taught to belong to through the use of books and other media – moral judgements are made according to some idealised standard about what is right or wrong.

In the face-to-face world of Gypsies, moral judgements are grounded in the actions and interactions of actual people, in a directly experienced world. Whether an action is considered 'good' will be based on the effect of those decisions in the experienced world, rather than their conformity to some kind of standard that can be taught through books. The real difference is that, in the abstract moral code of books and other print media, we are taught to consider the potential impact of our actions upon a number of possible people – 'types', as Schutz would put it. In the face-to-face world of direct observation, we are taught to consider the actual impact of our actions on particular, known people. This can lead to very different ideas about 'good' or 'right' actions and can also lead to considerable misunderstandings as the different ways of understanding the world and how to be in it come into conflict.

Through building patterns of expectations, we first build up aesthetic or sensed expectations – we learn the world, how it feels, how things happen in it – and we often do this with the help of stories and a mediating adult (or more experienced child). The particular stories that we learn with and the ways in which they are told/used form part of the total process: the interactions as we learn the stories teach us how to be in the world. So stories and their telling are a cultural product onto which our aesthetic attention can be turned; we can make aesthetic judgements about the quality of a story and its 'fit' to the patterns of expectation that we have learned.

Summary

I chose as my starting point for this chapter an occasion where a human infant was welcomed into the world. To be more specific, I chose an occasion when a human child was welcomed into a social world – I was present at her christening, not at her birth. In noting this, it emphasises the fact that we are not simply born into a physical world; we are also born into a social world and, just as we have to learn how to manage in the physical world, we also have to learn how to manage in the social world within which we are raised.

Whether made explicit and formalised through institutionalised educational processes, as with the reading of storybooks by schoolteachers, or part of the immediate social world, as with Gypsies' telling of stories, part of the educational or pedagogical process is concerned with teaching us how to choose what actions to make. We can learn to make these decisions according to whether they fit with our idea of a good story. What we learn to think of as a good story incorporates a great deal of information about the world that is taken for granted and remains 'out of focal awareness', whilst still forming part of our conscious understanding of the world. In other words, in stories we learn patterns of expectation that, like the stories themselves, are open and unpredictable by nature but from which we can internalise a sense of 'rightness' or 'fit'. These patterns of expectation are connected to the world that we live in – we are taught to connect the stories to our everyday lives. So we begin by telling stories about the physical and sensed world that we live in and gradually lead into the more complex social world of relationships and moral decisions and dilemmas. However, as the stories we learn become more complicated and as we learn to operate in a more complicated social world, the patterns of expectation begin to concern themselves less with sensed patterns – they become more concerned with moral or ethical issues and associated patterns of expectation. This is where the link between aesthetics and morality starts to become clearer.

If we move on, then, from the telling of stories and the building of patterns of expectation to the ways these become enacted in our social worlds, what we are looking at is the building of a 'community of speakers' – people who share a common practice in the telling of stories and the patterns of expectation, including taken-for-granted information, that are built up. This idea of a community of speakers is like that suggested by Machin and Carrithers (1996) as regards 'communities of improvisation' and also that of 'communities of practice' (see, for example, Erickson 2002). Such a community consists of people who understand, despite all the openness, all the possible actions and endings, etc., the kind of world we are living in and how to behave in that world. In doing this we are able to develop enormously subtle communicative abilities based on the assumption that we are all 'living in the same world'. This is of vital importance for human social life, as many of our social interactions depend upon being able to convey a wealth of information, including aesthetic and moral expectations and so on, without having to be explicit about them all the time. Indeed, if we did have to spell out all these assumptions all the time we would rarely get further than an introduction!

However, problems arise when the people engaged in the conversation have not been socialised into the same community of speakers; they have not been told the same stories in the same way and so have not built up the same patterns of expectation and understanding. An illustration of this was the situation we saw with the schoolteacher and Lisa earlier. Whilst very often these differences are clear because those involved actually speak different languages, this is not always the case and this can lead to some very profound difficulties and misunderstandings (Gumperz 1992; Watanabe 1993). What happens in cases like these is that the subtle nuances of speech are missed or not understood and often these subtleties are direct references back to the storytelling tradition, the learned patterns of expectation and taken-for-granted information of the community from which the speaker comes.

As noted at the beginning of this section, the intersubjective nature of human consciousness and human cognitive development is an essential factor in the socialising processes I have described above. The fact that we are able to use stories in this way depends upon our being able to interact with one another in an intersubjective way in the realm of direct observation and merging of streams of consciousness described by Schutz. I also noted the importance of very early social relationships in beginning these processes of socialisation and the fact that many of these early relationships are formed in the immediate social environment of the family. Family, however, is a word that means different things and that can vary from culture to culture, and the quality of those early relationships is coloured by the quality of that immediate social environment (the 'family') into which a child is born. In the next chapter I shall explore the relevance of this observation.

Notes

1. I shall use the term 'mainstream' throughout to refer to non-Gypsy culture as a counterpoint to Gypsy culture. However, recognising that non-Gypsy culture is not a homogeneous mass, I refer to a kind of 'average', a schematic understanding that is implicitly accepted by institutions and media (e.g. white, middle-class, literate ...).

2. When I was introduced to William, he had been told that I was writing a book. In fact, I was helping some other people compile a book of photographs and stories; this was not specifically connected to my research, but the two often seemed to become the same thing in the way they were spoken about.

3. William was very careful to tell me exactly what to write here: they were given to me in this order and the words/translations are his own rather than my interpretation or what I could remember after the event.

4. This was how I noted down what William said: he was making the point that, whilst his word for woman was 'rakli', a London Gypsy would say 'djuvel'. He also noted that when he said 'vonga' he meant coal, whereas when a London Gypsy said 'vonga' they meant money.

5. This is similar to the idea of aesthetics as used in music – as a standard by which we learn to expect (the next note of a phrase, continuation in a certain key, etc.), as a standard which can be deliberately manipulated for effect. In order for us to be able to do this, we must first learn (be taught) what the aesthetic standards are and then we must learn (again, be taught) how to manipulate them, and then we apply our own creative genius ...

6. In fact, it may well be that my presence encourages people to bring things into their focal awareness, things such as ways of talking that they don't usually consciously think about; the point is that they can do this.
7. Mush = man.
8. The sort of thing that gorgios do.
9. Ashamed or embarrassed.
10. Type in bold represents readings from the book, normal type is the speech of the people in the group and italics are my own comments and observations relating to what is going on.
11. Devil.

Chapter 5

STORIES AND THE TELLING OF FAMILY

In the previous chapter we saw how stories combine to form a cultural landscape that provides a sense-making context for one's own and others' actions. Such a landscape also affords possible future actions or projects, whilst not determining those actions or the associated patterns of expectation or aesthetic and moral judgements. We saw how Gypsies' stories have certain themes that can be drawn upon by individuals in order to create their own personal stock of stories. We saw, for instance, how ideas about 'strangers' described a world whereby what lay outside the immediate known circle was rendered strange and unaccountable. This unaccountability was told in different ways and with different stories – for instance, William's stories about 'little men' and Ivy's story about the 'White Lady', or Deborah's and Rose's different stories about the frightening nature of houses. Such themes are the landmarks around which a community of speakers is able to improvise its own stories relevant to the task in hand. The process is one of being taught how to tell oneself to and with others – of learning how to confabulate and confabricate (Carrithers 1992) one's place in a group of people and through this to create the shared cultural landscape of that group.

In the chapter that follows, I shall focus on the notion of 'family' itself in the creation of the cultural landscape of the Gypsies that I worked with. What I want to explore is the enabling capacity of storytelling, fitting it into an 'ethic of care' (Gilligan 1982; Borneman 2001; Larrabee 1993). In other words, I want to show how storytelling practices teach us how and who to be in the world and in so doing they describe the ethical and moral terrain of that world – how to be a 'good' person or a 'proper person' to use the words that Gypsies use. Faubion (2001: 18) has outlined this notion of an 'ethic of care' with regard to Foucault's analysis of ethics and techniques of subjectivation and with specific reference to performing kinship. The general theoretical argument here is that a person is the subject of his or her own creative capabilities and that through being taught techniques of subjectivation a person learns how to articulate him- or herself as the kind of subject s/he chooses to be. In terms of kinship we might speak of building up networks of people who both teach you how and who to be in the world and also allow you to be who you perceive yourself to be (i.e. they afford you the capacity to be the kind of person you are). Our kin, then, help to make us who we are, not simply by formalised or legalised or biological connections but because they and we emerge from a shared tradition of practice. As Foucault puts it:

> it is not enough to say that the subject is constituted in a symbolic system. It is not just in the play of symbols that the subject is constituted. It is constituted in real practices – historically analyzable practices. There is a technology of the constitution of the self which cuts across symbolic systems while using them. (Rabinow 1984: 369)

So, tying together ways of telling stories (a tradition of practice) with kinship (those who practise the tradition) will demonstrate not only the cultural landscape of a tradition; it will also show how that landscape affects and is affected by the understandings and associated actions of the people who live it. William's way of introducing himself to me demonstrates this process:

> William began – 'My name is William Wood, Charles Wood was my father, my mother was Rowan after the tree that she was born under – a rowan.' He is a Welsh Gypsy.

> William was born just after the war when there was hardly any food – there was still rationing and they didn't give much to Gypsies. He had an older brother called James who had a half-mongrel lurcher, a ferret and net and a catapult and with these he could catch pheasants and hares and the like and keep his family well fed.

> They used to collect elder sticks to make the flowers with, William's mother used to sell the flowers. When William and his father used to go cutting the sticks his father would have to sit down because he couldn't breathe properly, his chest was bad. (Field notes)

William begins his story by placing himself in relation to a past that he has shared with particular people doing particular things. A crucial point about this analysis is that it relies upon an understanding of the human being as socially and cognitively situated in a network of face-to-face relationships. These relationships entail an element of caring about one another in that we matter to one another – in other words our sense of who we are is tied into our relationships with one another. It is this mattering or caring that forms the basis of an 'ethic of care' – an ethics of practice rooted in a network of lived relationships. An ethic of care is an ethics of acting in ways that strengthen our networks of relationships and so preserve both our own and others' sense of what kind of people we are. This notion of an 'ethic of care' has been very influential in feminist studies, particularly through the work of Gilligan (1982), who contrasted what she saw as a feminine (and therefore largely ignored) 'ethic of care' with a masculine (and therefore representative of the mainstream) 'ethic of right'. Challenging the dichotomising of women's and men's experiences, both Borneman (2001: 43) and Faubion (2001: 11) link such a notion of care to Heidegger's thematic concept of *Sorge* – to care is an essential aspect of human beingness and as such is neither a feminine nor a masculine quality.

My work with Gypsies also persuades me to question the opposition of 'feminine' and 'masculine' ethics. For the Gypsies I worked with an 'ethic of care' emerges in a focus on face-to-face relationships, relationships with people to whom one owes some sort of moral responsibility. Such an ethic is, however, opposed in what Borneman might term the 'master narratives' (Borneman 1992: 19 and *passim*) of the mainstream world, with its notions of abstractable moral codes. Seen in this light, the 'ethic of care' is that which belongs to the world of known others – those whom we have grown up with, whom Gypsies tell their stories of and to and with whom the stories are made. The 'ethic of right' is that which belongs to the world of contemporaries or ideal types, the imagined world of people taught through the use of books, people with whom Gypsies have not lived or acted or interacted. These two ethics are not necessarily in opposition, nor are they necessarily harmonious, but for the Gypsies I worked with I would argue that an ethic of care more accurately reflects the ways that people are taught to make moral decisions. Just as the mainstream 'ideal type' that is applied to 'Gypsy' sets up conflicts and contradictions for those who identify themselves as such (see chapter 1), so also does Gypsies' understanding of ethical behaviour conflict with mainstream ideals about ethical behaviour.

Borneman (1992: 43), developing the insight of Todorov, focuses upon the way the caring relationship is implied in the symmetry and reversibility of relationships between individual 'I's and 'you's. Amongst the Gypsies I worked with, the caring relationship is primarily a manifestation of a 'we' relationship, a relationship in which individual 'I's and 'you's gain their sense from being part of the 'we'. In this chapter, I explore an ethic of storytelling as a voluntary expression of a caring 'we' relationship, carried out within those relationships lived by Gypsies in the realm of intersubjectivity, of face-to-face interaction, of the self with other selves rather than the self contrasted with Others – in other words, as an expression and construction of relatedness. For the Gypsies that I worked with, these relationships are made manifest in family networks – close networks of known people who carry out the projects of their lives within a shared cultural landscape, though each in their own particular way. I should note here that the terms 'kin' and 'family' are somewhat problematic as they carry many associations about their meaning and significance, both in everyday understandings and in their specific usage by anthropologists. For the most part, I shall use the term 'family' to refer to groups of real people (for instance, William's 'family', rather than his 'kin network'), as that is how those people would term themselves. I shall use the term 'kin' when discussing more theoretical ideas.

One mediating, or connecting, factor that keeps people linked together is found in the stories they tell and the ways they teach one another to tell stories. The potential for kinship networks to provide a clue to the links between the individual and the cultures they live in and through was noted by Barth (1973: 5), and it is useful to contrast his work then with his more recent work, which underlines the need for a cognitive theory of culture (Barth 2000: 20). The suggestion is that our understanding and enacting of kinship are the way in which we create and continue culture and they are also the way we fulfil our cognitive development as human beings. This is done (at least in part) through the telling and teaching of stories, creating ourselves as subjects of the stories of our lives, and hence in the ways in which we learn to be kin.

As pointed out in the previous chapter, the way we are taught to be in the world encourages us to develop a sense of 'fit', a sense of a certain way of doing things being right. In terms of our personal interactions, this sense of 'fit' is taught in the context of close and intimate relationships, relationships where we learn to feel at home, where we feel we belong, relationships with people for whom we care and in which we are cared for. One of the most noticeable ways in which any such study of belonging differs from more traditional studies of kinship is in the focus on the ways in which our experience of kinship ties us into webs of meaning through which we come to understand ourselves as particular people. It is through the struggles of particular people to achieve the kinds of relationships they imagine and desire that kinship terms become actively contested and redefined (e.g. Bargach 2001; Borneman 2001; George 2001; Karim 2001). It is also through such struggles as lived by particular people that prescriptive ideas about culture – for instance, in sets of ideas about determining rules and accepted ways of behaving – are challenged (see, for example, Carrithers 2000). All these studies make it clear that ideas about relatedness as they are lived are about direct and mutual relationships – relationships that are not determined by the cultural landscape in which they take place, although the existence of a shared cultural landscape facilitates the mutual expression of the caring nature of the relationship.

A further and very significant aspect of kinship as a site of contested meanings is that we frequently see it played out in places where there is a considerable degree of social change and cross-cultural interaction going on (see especially studies in Faubion 2001). It is at such times and in such places – places that I have metaphorically referred to as wastelands and shown to be an important feature of the cultural landscape of both Gypsies and non-Gypsies – that individuals are challenged to re-imagine themselves and their relationships in ways that maintain a sense of belonging without denying the possibility of and the necessity for change.

Parenting and Teaching How to Be

Particularity is a necessary part of belonging; it is not, however, enough to be able to juxtapose that sense of belonging with a notion of kinship, to say that if I feel I belong with you then you and I are kin. To link kinship and belonging it is necessary to make the particularity span generations, to form some sense of shared origin. That this is an important factor of kinship is noted by Hayden (1995), who studied issues surrounding gay couples' parenting. Returning to William's story above, we can see that he places himself in a web of relationships in which he has learned how to be in the world. The first set of relationships he refers to are those with his father and mother, so illustrating the importance of parental relationships in introducing us into and nurturing our inclusion in a social world: 'William began – "My name is William Wood, Charles Wood was my father, my mother was Rowan after the tree that she was born under – a rowan." He is a Welsh Gypsy.'

The parent–child relationship is of profound importance; it is the realisation, the 'familiarisation' of the pedagogical relationship, it is how belonging is transmitted (or where it breaks down). However, the parent–child relationship is not a simple construct and here we need to spend some time examining what is going on in this relationship.

The simplest understanding of the parent–child relationship is that of a biological relationship, although, of course, it is more complex than that. This complexity becomes apparent in any discussion centring upon issues concerned with adoption, new reproductive technologies and so on (e.g. Strathern 1992). In her study of fostering in western Africa, E. Goody (1982) pointed out that parenting incorporates a number of responsibilities that may or may not be carried out by the biological parents of the child and that parenthood is about establishing 'social replacements' (ibid.: 8). Goody presents five different types of activity that can all be associated with parenting: (i) bearing and begetting; (ii) endowment with civil and kinship status; (iii) nurturance; (iv) training; and (v) sponsorship into adulthood (Goody 1982: 8).

Whilst I would prefer to use the phrase 'social continuation' rather than 'social replacement', Goody's analysis of the tasks of parenthood makes clear the range of duties involved and the extent to which they can be carried out by people other than the biological 'parents' of the child (see, for exmple, the role of school and college in George 2001). In this analysis, the various roles of parenting can be seen as relating to those in which responsibility for transmitting cultural values is vested,that is, for reproducing not (just) human organisms but human beings who are fully integrated members of a culture. This focus on the role of parents emphasises ongoing, intimate relationships and has clear links to the notion of pedagogy. It is in the parent-child relationship (i.e. as we understand it in its broader definition, not simply as a biological relationship) that a pedagogical relationship is formed – a relationship that can include members of the extended kin network, teachers, friends and so on. In fact this point is commented on and understood by Gypsies – for instance, in the following conversation between two women on the Bankside site where they comment specifically on how children learn to speak, thus reminding us of the importance of speech, an embodied articulation of a tradition of cultural practice:

> They talked about who else was in London, and more about how there's a good living to be made. Most of this part of the conversation revolved around money. Then got onto when Janey and Pat were in London and how they liked the sites but they didn't like the 'Cockney Travellers'. Pat talked about how she had cried to come home and how she had eventually been 'taken bad' and so she had to. Janey said she didn't know why she had stuck it so long – nearly 7 years living all over London. Some talk about which of the London sites was the best and then quite a bit about the different accents the children picked up. Pat said how at one time she had three children living with her – the eldest spoke like a Geordie, the middle one like the Irish and the youngest like a Cockney. Janey said that Annie picked up more of the Irish as that was who she spent almost all her time with. (Field notes)

It is through such parental/pedagogical relationships that the cognitive gap is bridged through the use of cultural artefacts, including stories. Through these processes we learn the technologies of the self that enable us to author our interactions with others, which enable us to be subjects within a network of caring relationships (i.e. relationships that we care about one way or another) and enable us to tell our stories and be told in the stories of others. These networks can be, and frequently are, referred to as families – the networks of belonging in which we have developed as human beings and through which we have learned and developed the stories of our lives and the ways to tell those stories to others. It is through the telling and the realising of stories that an understanding of one's place in a 'family' is built upon and becomes a resource for negotiating tensions and moral decision making. Hence for each person their family is experienced as a system of stories that can be drawn upon in order to understand and explain both one's place in the world and the decisions that one makes in that world.

In order to clarify this point further, I shall look at the various ways in which these processes work in the lives of the people I have worked with. I shall focus primarily on the family of one of the women I have worked with over the past few years and draw upon other examples where appropriate. Thus I show further how 'family' is understood and experienced as a collection of stories, stories that are taught in pedagogical, parental relationships and provide a basis for making moral decisions. In doing this I show how, in their bridging of the 'cognitive gap' discussed in the previous chapter, they also bridge the individual and social divide, thus providing a 'cognitive theory of culture', such as was sought by Barth.

Family as a Collection of Stories

On the outskirts of Middlesbrough, just off the road that takes you into North Yorkshire, there is a piece of land with stables and a couple of trailers. This is where Naomi lives with her husband Billy and whoever happens to be visiting them at the time. One beautiful day in March 2001 I went to visit them, the late snow was melting and everything was beginning to smell like spring. Naomi had phoned me to ask about a project we were working on together – making a video about Gypsy life – to find out if I had managed to get any funding. I had, but there were some things I needed to sort out, and it was a great excuse to go and see them: I really enjoy Naomi's company but don't get to see her very often.

When I arrived, Naomi had gone out to the shops but Billy greeted me with a shout from the tractor he was driving. He turned off the motor and climbed down, looking very stiff and not very well; he had been ill at the end of the previous year and he still hadn't properly recovered. He explained where Naomi was and showed me into their main living trailer. Billy had fitted a wood-burning stove into the trailer. I asked, 'Do you cook on it?' to which he immediately replied, 'She does.' I asked for it – there's no way Billy would cook or clean or do any work in the house; in fact many people had commented on how hard Naomi had to work because Billy was 'even worse than most Gypsy men'[1] – she has a hard life, Naomi.

Naomi arrived back from the shops laden with biscuits and straight away put the kettle on and made herself and me a cup of tea. She remembered how I liked mine, which surprised me as I hadn't seen her for a while. She didn't make Billy a cup but gave him a pack of cigarettes, after which he got up and said, 'Well, you don't need me anymore then, eh?' and headed back to his tractor to finish off levelling a bit of ground in the corner of the field. This left me alone to have a chat with Naomi and I asked how she was coping after Billy's illness; things hadn't been easy, and they were not made any easier by Billy's stubbornness – he just kept on smoking and working all the time. After a short while, the conversation drifted away from Billy and Naomi told me that she was going to become a granny again. This time it was her youngest son's wife who was pregnant with her first child. Naomi said she hoped it would be a girl – 'They're easier and they can help with the cleaning' – but then she laughed and said she was joking, that 'you get what you're given'. Talking about children and grandchildren soon led on to a discussion of Naomi's family, and I asked if she minded me noting it down. She said 'No,' but she didn't want to be recorded on tape.

I asked Naomi if she had a bigger sheet of paper and she went into the back room of the trailer and got a sheet of ruled A4. Then we began, and Naomi proved to be an absolute mine of information – she could remember back to her great-great-grandparents. Figure 5.1 is what we ended up with. This drawing of Naomi's family can be read as a reflection of the conversation I had with Naomi through which it was produced. Although I have since 'tidied it up',[2] the version here is more faithful to the conversation we had which was somewhat 'messy', weaving in and out of

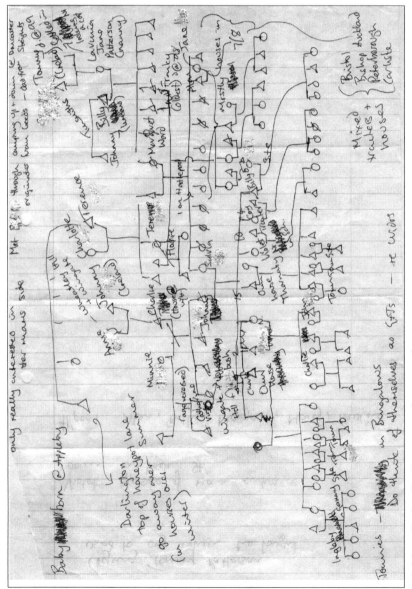

5.1 Naomi's family diagram as drawn at the time

different events and characters in Naomi's life, linking one to another and knitting Naomi into a strong system of relationships through which her life made sense.

What I would like to focus on here is the nature of the relationships, relationships that are represented as lines both in more conventional (tidied-up) anthropological kinship diagrams and also in this one. Perhaps partly because of the static nature of lines once drawn, these relationships are often seen as fixed (although contestable, or able to be interpreted in various ways). I suggest that the relationships represented in Naomi's diagram are routes through which stories are taught and told, emphasising their changeable and fluid nature: more than one story can be told for any of the lines that could link Naomi to her kin. Further, the nature of the story will depend upon the context of its telling, without calling into question the fact of a strong relationship that need not be defined as specifically biological, institutional, etc. However, the nature of the diagram is somewhat misleading here, because it looks as if each relationship (each possible route through which a story might be made and told) is mediated through people who are 'between' the two parties involved (see figure 5.2). What actually happens is that the genealogical distance between relatives is 'collapsed' in the face-to-face nature of the parental relationship, and here specifically in the storytelling act, thus creating and keeping as close kin those with whom most such experiences were lived. In other words, a 'line' could be drawn between Naomi and any one of the other symbols in her chart, thus representing an experienced, face-to-face relationship. We shall discuss this in more detail later on, but let us start with the characters and relationships themselves, as they were told by Naomi.

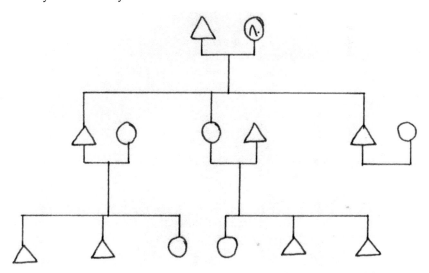

5.2 Here it seems that Naomi's (n) relationship with her grandchildren is mediated by her children – her grandchildren's parents

A Sense of One's Beginnings

Naomi always confined her talk to people that she knew or had known personally. People that she had never known she said she 'knew nothing about' and this can be seen in the diagram by the way that it peters out around the edges. The importance of knowing the people in the family was also underlined in another way, and repeated in every single one of the conversations that I had with people about their families, although it cannot be seen in the diagrams themselves: babies who had died young were usually not spoken about unless they had actually been met – occasionally someone would speak about someone who 'had had a hard time' with children and say that they had had some who had died young, but this was told as part of the mother's story rather than referring to the story of another person, that of the child who had died. Frequently I would be told that such a person 'had had others, but they died' and people were unable to be more forthcoming. Neither of these features, in themselves, define a particularly 'Gypsy' way of thinking about family and kin; nevertheless, what is reinforced is a sense of the world whereby family is understood as denoting a network of relationships between people who know one another on a direct and face-to-face level.

The characters that Naomi spoke about were always introduced with something of a story; there was nothing like enough room to put all the stories down on the one piece of paper, so the letters represent the stories that I was told, and which I wrote separately. For instance, (a) represents the oldest ancestor that Naomi could remember and that she had some personal, i.e. face-to-face, knowledge of – Laughing Billy Lee, her great-great-grandfather:

> (a) LAUGHING BILLY LEE
> Originated in Ireland, but Naomi doesn't know which part he came from.
>   A well-known historical figure (apparently) Naomi told me to 'ask Sarah about him – everybody knows about Laughing Billy'. He was called Laughing Billy because he used to get himself so excited when he got into a fight that he used to laugh as he fought.
>   It's something people say to their children, according to Naomi – 'You're a real Laughing Billy'.

What this story underlines is that Naomi's sense of where she comes from is rooted in her interactions with real, known people. She can state a direct link, through the story that she tells, to a specific character who was real and present when she was a young girl. Laughing Billy Lee was actually beginning to slip out of known memory and it is for this reason that Naomi mentions him as 'a historical figure'. But this is not historical in some 'lost in the mists of time' way. Laughing Billy is not the stuff of mythic heroes or totemic ancestors; he was a real, known and experienced person. This is what Naomi pointed towards when she said to 'ask Sarah about him' – Sarah is of the same generation as Naomi and had also known Laughing Billy when she was a very young child. However, he is beginning to crystallise as something other than a dynamic personality and as he does this he ceases to figure in people's family networks; he was very rarely mentioned by any of the people that I worked with – just once by a lady who was older than Naomi. So, when Naomi says 'everybody knows about Laughing Billy', this isn't really true – many younger Gypsies have no direct experience of him. At this point in the research, I had been interested to see if there were any shared stories people used to tell their children, and so I had asked young women with small children about Laughing Billy to see if he was referred to in any way as some kind of 'folk character'. My enquiries were met with blank looks and shrugs, and when I explained who he was people said something to the effect of 'Oh, yes, big Naomi's grandad – I never knew him.'

The fact that Naomi talks about Billy is also an important reminder that Naomi is a specific individual: she is interested in her family history and has made an effort to find out about it and to remember it. Not all Gypsies are so interested and so they don't know anything of 'Laughing Billy' and, contrary to Naomi's suggestion, the phrase is rarely used these days.

Repeated Story Themes

Someone who was a little closer in Naomi's memory, and whom she had more to say about, was Margaret Lee (d), her great-grandmother, and this is what Naomi told me about her:

MARGARET LEE (called Nanny by Naomi)
Eventually settled in a house in Darlington, where she kept herself to herself and kept a cat. Naomi told me a story about how her next door neighbour used to keep an eye on her and once, when she didn't seem to be very well, she called the ambulance and had her admitted to hospital. According to Naomi, Margaret was furious about this – she'd never even been into a hospital in her life, but she forgave her when she came out.

Margaret eventually died at the ripe old age of 99 – Naomi said how they were a bit disappointed because they were sure she was going to get a telegram from the queen. The story was that Margaret died because she had gone out to look for her cat on a frosty night and had slipped. She was found in her yard the next morning, dead.

Again, this is a story about someone who was known to Naomi and, as with the stories discussed in the previous chapter, the action takes place in a world where there are known people and strangers – strangers being people who act in odd and unaccountable and frequently threatening ways. Given that Naomi's story about Margaret takes place within a recognisable cultural landscape, and given what we have seen about the themes of Gypsy storytelling, we might well expect to see some of the themes repeated here – as indeed we do. For instance, Naomi describes how Margaret kept 'herself to herself' after she moved into a house. As we have seen, from a Gypsy point of view, the idea of living in a house has quite negative connotations: they are dangerous and unwelcoming places. What is more, the world of non-Gypsies (most of whom live in houses) is strange and unaccountable, and here again Margaret's neighbour did something that would not happen if she had been living with Gypsies – she called an ambulance and had her admitted to hospital. The suggestion is not only of doing something that Gypsies wouldn't do, but of forcing Margaret to do something against her will. The way the story ends, with Margaret being discovered dead in her yard, underlines something else that would strike a chord with most Gypsies; to lie dead and undiscovered for a whole night would be unthinkable to people living in trailers, where it is rare for someone to live alone; it is something that could only happen in the strange and lonely world of houses – places full of empty spaces rather than the crowded fullness of life in a trailer.

Here Naomi is demonstrating an awareness of the different qualities of different spaces as they are experienced in the world of people. But it is not only that the spaces of houses and the spaces of trailers feel physically different; there is the suggestion of their being somehow morally different as well, in that the actions of people who live in one kind of space are 'wrong' and cause anger (for instance, sending someone to hospital against their will). It also illustrates a sense of the uncaring nature of the non-Gypsy world: how else could an old woman lie dead in her yard for a whole night? Again, we can see the close link between the idea of an articulated social aesthetic and a sense of moral judgement – what feels right.

The theme of the dangerous and frightening nature of houses was revisited by Naomi a little later:

> Naomi related a story about when her mother was ill and they all moved into a house in Darlington. Naomi told how it frightened her and her brothers – they were afraid to go upstairs and when they were sent to bed their mother would come up with them. When she got downstairs again, she would turn around and all her children would be there behind her, frightened of staying upstairs by themselves.[3]

In the first story above we find Naomi making a link between Margaret's death and the point that she had settled in a house. This was combined with the idea that neighbours, whilst perhaps being well-meaning, were 'uncaring'[4] and would do things wrong – sending her to hospital, not noticing that she had fallen down until the next morning and so on. Through the making and telling of such stories with characters whom Naomi knows (or has known) on a face-to-face basis, Naomi grounds and makes real an understanding of houses as 'bad' and strangers as somehow associated with danger or unpleasantness.

So far, it might seem as if I am suggesting that there are certain stories that Gypsies learn to tell and thereby learn how to be Gypsy. To an extent this is what I mean; however, Gypsies' stories are not in any way defined or determined by this. Naomi, for instance, has lived her own particular life and many of the stories that she tells do not necessarily repeat common themes. So Gypsies' story-making practices are not confined to the realising of common themes and Naomi's stories also include very personal events, but these too are tied into her understanding of herself in a group of related people with a shared cultural landscape, as the following story illustrates:

> Naomi can only remember a long way back on her mother's side – she said she'd never taken much interest in her father's family. She related a story to me about how when she was about 6 her paternal grandmother gave her a cheap plastic basket, rather than the doll that she'd given her daughter's children. Naomi told how that has stuck with her and how she never really took to her father's side of the family after that. She also says how it was always them (her father's daughters) who had to go and clean for her paternal grandmother – not her dad's nieces (daughters of her dad's sister).

Although this story is peculiar to Naomi, it does have certain things about it that mark it as a Gypsy's story – for instance, the mention of cleaning, which Naomi did not feel needed any more explanation. I understood the context of Naomi's story because I knew how ordinary it was for young Gypsy women to go to their relatives and clean for them; though for many in the more mainstream culture that fact would probably attract a lot of attention, for Naomi it is part of the background, 'taken-for-granted' cultural landscape. This little story also shows how very important kin networks are to Naomi; she was very clear about how it was her paternal grandmother, her 'Dad's Mum,' whom she used to clean for and who didn't give her a doll for a present. Naomi also pointed out that the girls who did get a doll were her Dad's sister's daughters not her Dad's brother's daughters. In many ways, this would seem to lend itself to a fairly traditional interpretation of kin networks, emphasising the ways that affection or indulgence is expressed through the female line (grandmother, mother, daughter), whilst services (such as cleaning) are taken from the male line (grandmother, father, daughter).

Whilst this may well be a plausible interpretation (and indeed I do know of cases where such a pattern could be discerned, although I know of others where it couldn't), it misses the point as far as Naomi's telling of the meaning of the relationship is concerned. For Naomi, the point is that it was a particular, personal relationship that she did not enjoy and that she has since chosen to minimise, thus making her father's side of the family more distant than her mother's. Naomi has, however, chosen to minimise her relationships with her father's side of the family from within a cultural

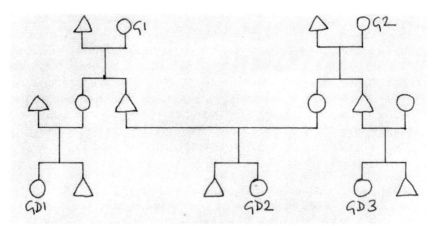

5.3 Showing a possible (and more traditional or structuralist interpretation) of the kin relations expressed by Naomi in the story about the plastic basket and the dolls

landscape that accepts, for instance, doing the cleaning for your grandmother as unremarkable. Also implied in Naomi's story is the suggestion that her grandmother could have behaved differently – that she chose to give Naomi a cheap plastic basket rather than a doll because she didn't like Naomi. Naomi interpreted her grandmother's behaviour as issuing from personal choice, not from some social structure that determines that all paternal grandmothers treat their son's daughters in this way. So we see that Naomi's stories are told (and describe) a cultural landscape that is at once 'taken for granted' and inscribed in the fact of people's relationships. On the other hand, it in no way determines how people express the fact that they matter to one another, nor does it determine people's allowed actions or affections, etc. Such a cultural landscape is also apparent in the following passage, where Naomi talks about different kinds of living accommodation, yards and names of familiar people:

> Naomi spoke a bit about her childhood; she spent much of it in York (on the Compound yard …?), where she used to spend a lot of time with the Lees who were like brothers and sisters to her (actually they were cousins – … x[5] …). I asked if she had grown up in a trailer and she said, 'Yes, well … I think it was more a selection of vehicles including wagons, trailers – possibly tents …' She mentioned how she used to spend a lot of time in Old Charlie's trailer, how they all used to play in there and get sent out for misbehaving.

The importance of closeness and of sharing stories in making people part of the family is reinforced here when Naomi describes her cousins as being 'like brothers and sisters' to her. These are people who shared much of the same spaces when they were younger, they shared many of the events that took place in those spaces, and so they share the same cultural landscape.

Another notable point draws upon more mainstream ideas about parents and the way that siblings share parents. In the passage above, Naomi refers to a character – 'Old Charlie' – who can be seen as fulfilling for all the children (Naomi and her cousins the Lees) some of the parental tasks above, thus making them all in some way siblings – they shared the parental attention of Old Charlie, so in some ways they were more than simply 'like' brothers and sisters to Naomi. Sharing parents made them closer members of the family than if they had simply had the same biological mother and father. At the time, I also made the following observation:

> (*x*) Note how Naomi gives more information about her 2nd cousins – from Franky and Violet's marriage, than she does about her 1st cousins from her mother's brothers and sisters. Naomi explains this by saying that she was always closer to them because they were closer to her own age. But, also, these 2nd cousins have settled around the Riverside site – in fact, most of them are on the Riverside site, whereas her 1st cousins are settled in houses in Darlington.

This point is important when considering Naomi's understanding of her family relationships in that it underlines the way it is time spent with people and having stories to tell of them that makes them a more integral part of the family group. Such varying degrees of closeness and relatedness are not reflected in traditional kinship charts, as they would show first cousins as being closer (i.e. more closely related) than second cousins. To Gypsies who travel around and live in trailers such closeness is achieved through being together in camps. To Naomi the closeness of kin has more to do with the extent of shared space and time, or, to put it another way, the extent to which people move through the same landscape, the same landscape of consciousness and action. For Naomi, those she feels are close kin (like brothers and sisters) are gradually made through the build-up of shared stories. Naomi is aware of other possible understandings of kin and relatedness – hence she says they are 'like brothers and sisters' – but these ideas are not part of what she feels is important in telling the stories that place her within her family.

What's in a Name?

Naomi does not, however, suggest that just anybody might become 'like brother and sister' to her. This is a process that is only open to a few people, people whose families already share a cultural landscape and some degree of physical space (and who therefore could be potentially considered as candidates for shared parenting). Family names are important here, as names are one way of signifying (or indexing) the shared experiences – the shared stories and associated cultural landscape not only of oneself but also of those that taught you. Family names have long been recognised as important in studies of kinship; they are, however, generally used in such a way that suggests they refer to something fixed – be that a particular individual, a particular relationship between individuals, a particular family group and so on. In other words there is assumed to be some sort of definitive relationship that the names refer to. In my conversation with Naomi, however, it became apparent that the family names were actually doing something else, they weren't so much a fixed pointer to something definite as a changeable suggestion of association. We are not talking here of fixed categories of kin (father's mother, daughter's daughter, etc.) – such categories or classifications tell us little or nothing of a sense of belonging – rather, we are talking about whom we identify with, whom we feel we share a relationship of relatedness with.

Knowing the names of people is really quite an important aspect of belonging in the face-to-face culture of the Gypsies I worked with and this is reflected in Naomi's telling of her family:

> It also turns out that Naomi's name is Lee and that Billy's name is Roberts – even though most people refer to Billy as Mr Lee. I asked Naomi how she had come to meet Billy and she explained how it was through 'camping up and down at Lancaster way', how Billy had originated in Lancaster and how his father came from there too. Naomi says how it's no good asking Billy about these things as he's not interested and most of his family are dead.

The fact that Billy has taken Naomi's name is significant; certainly it is important enough for it to be mentioned. What is more, the mention is done with reference to a story – how Naomi met Billy – that is recognisably Gypsy in that it refers to 'camping up and down'. That Billy has taken Naomi's family name is even more significant when you combine it with the fact that Billy has also moved to a part of the country where Naomi grew up and where her family have largely stayed. Billy, on the other hand, has left behind the places and the people that he grew up amongst and he has also left behind their name. Through using the name of a group of people who are much in evidence around where he is currently living, Billy ties himself into a stock of stories that are shared.

In fact, if Billy had kept his original name, he would not have been able to claim a share in the stories of the people around him and so would have had no clearly recognisable place there; he does not come from a family that is well known in the north-east. We can see how words, names, places and events combine to give a person a place in the physical and social world, connecting them to others in time and space. This was brought home to me when I was first in Whitby at the regatta that many of the Gypsies on Teesside and around the north look forward to in the summer. Whitby regatta, like the horse fairs, is an important chance for families to meet up with one another and so to reinforce their ties. There is one pub in Whitby where most of the Travelling women go in the evening – and as I was there with a group of Gypsies I went along too. As the evening drew on, people who didn't know one another began to introduce themselves and the young woman sitting next to me turned to me and asked:

'Where've you come from?'
'Durham,' I replied.
'What's your name?'
'Sal.'
'Your second name?'
'Oh, Buckler.'
'You're not a Gypsy then?'

If I had been able to say that my parents had had a recognised name, connected to a place – one of the Smiths from Lancaster, for instance, or a Lee from Hull – then I could have claimed to be a Gypsy. From this we might have been able to establish someone that we both knew, so establishing some kind of common ground. This is in fact what one of the women I was with did when she was asked about her name. She was a Smith from York who married a Harker from Darlington; people then listed some names until they found some people they both knew – her claim to be a Gypsy was based upon her ability to link herself with particular people through names and places.

This focus on the importance of knowing names, of having a known name and the way that names connect people to places in the world, was also reflected in the conversation I had with William – you will remember how he introduced himself: 'my name is William Wood, Charles Wood was my father, my mother was Rowan after the tree that she was born under – a rowan.' William then continued, saying that he is a Welsh Gypsy, from South Wales. The link to names and places is reinforced. These links are told and retold through stories, stories that are shared between groups of people who understand themselves as kin, as related to and belonging with one another through the telling of shared events and places.

Writing about the family of one person such as Naomi, gives the impression that her idea of family and the stories that form it belong to her as an individual, as do also her connections to the places told. What are not shown are the ways in which the family is dynamic, the ways in which the characters of a family weave in and out of one another's stories, the ways in which they together create a shared sense of belonging. This sense of belonging is not so much situated inside the mind or body of an individual, it is created and maintained through the interactions of members of a family. In the following chapter, I shall explore the 'jointness' of creating a sense of belonging, focusing on ideas about 'home' in the talk of Gypsies.

Notes

1. Although this seems like some kind of judgement about whether Billy is a good husband, it isn't really meant like that because the nature of the gender roles in Gypsy society (see, for example, Okely 1983) mean that Gypsy women often tell me that they wouldn't want their man to do the cleaning or any work in the house because, as Sarah once put it, 'we're not used to men being soft like that'.
2. See appendix I.
3. This story also reinforces what has been noted as a general preference amongst Gypsies for bungalows – if they are to be housed, then they would prefer there not to be a second level.
4. 'Uncaring' in the sense that they did not express their care in a way that either Naomi or Margaret would understand or accept, not in the sense that they didn't care.
5. Marked by the x and the horizontal } on the diagram (figure 5.1).

Chapter 6

HOME IS WHERE THE HEART IS

———— ⨾⨾⨾ ————

In the previous chapter I examined how stories about family and about family members create and maintain a sense of belonging within a network of relationships. So far, we have examined these stories as they were told to me by individual Gypsies talking about their lives and their families. In the chapter that follows, I shall examine the ways in which these relationships are continually recreated and so maintained through the everyday talk of Gypsies. We shall move from a discussion of how a sense of being Gypsy is articulated in the exchange of a single person talking to another person (an 'I : you' relationship) to the ways in which Gypsies share the creation and articulation of their Gypsiness (a 'we' relationship, where 'we' is a term I use to refer to a shared sense of togetherness, rather than an explicit use of the word 'we' evident in Gypsies' talk). Many of the examples I draw on here refer either explicitly or implicitly to ideas about land and place. This is deliberate, as the issues discussed will then provide a link to some of the issues surrounding attitudes towards land, as discussed in council meetings, which will be examined later in the book.

Let us begin with a reminder of the place where I was working because, after all, this is about real people in a real place, not abstract and disembodied words and theories:

> It was a beautiful day – the air was crisp, the sky was blue and the frost was having a hard time being melted off the street. On the bus on the way down from Durham I had seen the cooling towers belching out their steam for many miles. There is a peculiar poignancy about a day like today when visiting the Gypsy sites on Teesside. The apparent beauty of the day can never quite get rid of the dirt, the litter, the general sense of squalor that permeates the whole of these desolate settlements that line the Tees Valley. The sites, while sharing in this general run-down air of dereliction, have somehow managed to distance themselves – they are not part of the same world. Walking on to the Bankside site I pass a couple of scrapyards and orient myself by the huge cranes that mark the docks ahead. I never actually get to see their bodies – only the huge necks that continually peer out from the unseen river and towards the scrubby fields of the industrial wastelands.

I walk on broken glass and ice; an oily black mud somehow prevents the road from ever having that crispness I associate with frosty mornings elsewhere. Birds in trees are replaced by torn plastic bags and the road that leads to the entrance of the site is lined with scrap cars and taxis waiting for their next job.

A car speeds past and honks its horn – it's either at me or at the men stood looking out of the scrap yard entrance across the road. It's at me, I think – I see the back of Carla's head and think I recognise the car – I never was very good with cars. Anyway, I'm almost at the site so I'll soon find out – sure enough, the car slows and indicates to turn left on to the site. It was Carla.

Arriving on site I am struck by how much fuller it now is compared to some time ago. In fact it is now the fullest I have ever seen it. Carla is out of the car and talking to Bernie – she smiles and waves, I do the same back. I don't go over to talk, I carry on to where Maudy has her trailer as I have arranged to see her about 10 minutes ago; Jim's car is there so Maudy must be in. Sure enough she has just boiled the kettle and makes me a cup of coffee. Last time she served me in a cup with a chip in. I mentioned it and she threw the tea away and made me another in another cup. This time the cup is fine and we get down to the serious business of catching up with what's going on. (Fieldnotes 29/01/01)

It was very warm in the trailer, the fire was on, the TV was on, but Maudy switched it off when I arrived. It was homely, comfortable and (to my more chaotic and less house-proud eye) sparklingly clean. As we talked, there was a continuous stream of visitors: people coming in, people calling across the site, people banging on the window asking for things, asking for people, offering to run errands. This was Maudy's home, a home that only partly consisted of the place where we were sitting talking, a home that was characterised just as much by the toing and froing of particular people. Whilst home is usually associated with a place in space – i.e. the place of residence – to Maudy, and to other Gypsies, home is about place among people. However, in all the tapes I have of Gypsies talking, I looked for mentions of home – and reached pretty much a blank. The two mentions I did find equated home with house or *ken*,[1] a place to be sure, but without any of the other connotations that are generally associated with the idea of home – in fact, as we have seen, 'houses' are frequently talked of as alien, negative and unwelcoming places.

Whilst 'home' does not figure as a significant marker in Gypsies' talk, there are other things that describe a relationship to the material world, that suggest a sense of belonging. Through an exploration of these aspects of talk, we can begin to see articulated a sense of being in the world that might be translated as a notion of home. However, this is not a located sense of home and in the translation would lose some of its subtlety; perhaps a better description would be 'sense of place' rather than home. Gypsies do have a sense of place in the world, so let us stick with that and tease out from there any sense of belonging there might be.

Homing In

One dismally grey and rainy day in August 2001, I went to visit Sarah and Nancy, two women, both grandmothers in their fifties who were living on the Riverside site. It was unseasonably cold and very dark – the sky was the same colour as the concrete ground and the wall around the site. As usual, when I walked on to the site, a couple of dogs started barking and some of the net curtains in the trailers twitched. Sarah came out to meet me and we went and knocked on Nancy's door – we didn't wait for it to be answered as it was raining so hard. Inside the trailer was warm, the windows were steamed up and the rain made a continuous pattering noise that was very soothing. Nancy made a cup of tea while Sarah chatted about the book she was making with her sister. This book was the reason why I was there – Sarah and her sister Ivy were collecting old photographs, stories and recipes to make a record of Gypsy life on Teesside. The small talk turned to memories; the recording on the tape begins:

Me:	No, you didn't tell me about sleeping outside.
Nancy:	Well, we did, underneath me granny's wagon, with a cover round it.
Me:	Well, they …
Nancy:	I used to sleep under the bed piece.
Me:	They must have because you had such big families.
Sarah:	Aye, they did.
Nancy:	No I'd sleep with me Granny.
Me:	Mm?
Nancy:	I'd sleep with me Granny, see me Granny bought me up.
Me:	Yeh.
Nancy:	An' she brought Frankie Boy up, didn't she – me dad's sister's lad.

This exchange begins with something that marks it as different from many people's ideas of home and that immediately distinguishes Nancy's ideas about something that could be called 'home' from a non-Gypsy one that would equate home with house – it is about sleeping outside. Nancy describes sleeping arrangements that were common to those Gypsies fortunate enough to have a horse-drawn wagon. The wheels on the wagons are huge and this means the wagon stands a long way off the ground, leaving lots of space underneath (see figure 6.2). Inside the wagons there was room for the equivalent of two double beds, not nearly enough for everyone at a time when the average number of children in a family was seven or eight.[2] What people would do was fix a tarpaulin (a 'cover') around the base of the wagon and make a sleeping place on the ground. Generally it was the boys and the men who would sleep outside like this, and this is backed up by Nancy when she says she used to sleep with her Granny under the bed piece. The bed piece is the seat in the horse-drawn wagons that opens out to a double bed and which has what looks like a couple of cupboards underneath. These cupboards store bedding and a feather mattress that rolls out to make the second bed inside the wagon.

Nancy then goes on to explain how it was her Granny who brought her up and that it was her Granny she used to sleep with. This is the first indication of the significance of people in creating a sense of belonging; this is not just a memory of where but of who. Included in that 'who' is Frankie Boy, Nancy's dad's sister's son, who was also brought up by Nancy's Granny (who is also his own Granny). Here we are reminded of the way that Gypsies' stories concern events between a group of known people – the family – and that one of the things that make people family is the way they share stories. Nancy is remembering relationships with particular people, rather than specific events, and in her remembering she is recreating her place in the family network that includes those people.

So far, Nancy's remembered sense of belonging sits with a way of making a space to sleep in and the people who shared that space. There is nothing to connect this sense of belonging to anywhere particular in the world, to any geographical location or to any place in a landscape that is even theoretically separable from the people included in the memory. Finding a place in relationships with people is a theme that is reiterated in the following passage, which follows shortly after the one above:

Me: Why were you bought up by your Granny?
Nancy: I don't know, cos me mam an' me dad, as far as I know, were
           stopped together – with Sarah's Granny and me aunt Annie,
           which was the other sister. They always pulled around together,
           and me Granny had just 'ad like Frankie or Frank and I just used
           to stop over at first.
Me: Right.
Nancy: Right, sleep over an, that.
Me: Yeh.
Nancy: An' then when my dad went his way an' me mam when she went
           her way I went with her. She asked my dad could she take me
           with 'er and I was with her all ever after that until I got married.

Here Nancy is quite specific about who stopped with who, who 'pulled' with who,[3] again emphasising the importance of having a place amongst people. This sense that it is people who give a feeling of being rooted is emphasised by the changing relationship between her biological parents that Nancy describes; Nancy's relationship with her grandmother and her cousin provided stability in a way that her parents did not or could not, her grandmother fulfilling many of the parental tasks outlined by Goody (1982) and her cousin becoming as close as a brother to her.

Note also that Nancy doesn't say that she 'stayed' with her Granny, but that her Granny took her with her – a phrase that suggests movement rather than being settled in one place. It is often the case that grandparents provide Gypsy children with a deeper root in a family network than their biological parents alone could provide, enabling children to form strong bonds with relatives beyond the parental, nuclear unit. This is underlined by the following exchange, which follows almost immediately after the one above:

Sarah: Lot of the Grannies did, Grannies.

Nancy: Yes.

Me: Is it …

Nancy: It's like our Cheryl she does with you, she stops with you don't she, our Cheryl.

Me: Yeh – well, it's like when I was talking to, well a couple of the women I've spoken to really said that they were y'know closer to their Grannies.

Nancy: Yeh.

Me: It's just that it's a bit different, isn't it, it's a bit … it's more common with Gypsies and Travelling people than it is with …

Sarah: Gorgios.

Me: Yeah, wi' gorgios, yeah.

Nancy: I mean Cheryl, she'd live permanently with Sarah, wouldn't she Sarah?

Me: Yeah.

Nancy: Aye, she likes stopping with her Granny, doesn't she, Cheryl … It's like our Lizzy – out Iris's always wanting to come back here with me y'know …

Sarah's initial statement emphasises the importance of Grannies. Although it is stated in the past tense, Nancy joins in to assert the same way of doing things today. Cheryl is Sarah's granddaughter, and is linked into the wider family network through Nancy and Sarah's relationship – they are second cousins, but, more importantly, they are close in that they share experiences both in the past and in the present. If Cheryl didn't stay with Sarah very often, she would lose that sense of being connected to the wider family network that includes Nancy – Cheryl would no longer be 'our Cheryl' to Nancy because they wouldn't be sharing experiences, they wouldn't share a 'we' relationship. In fact, staying with her Granny keeps Cheryl in contact with many of her aunts and cousins, who regularly visit one another, with Sarah, Cheryl's Granny, being the focal point. Doing this also enables the 'collapsing' of distance in the family network discussed in the previous chapter – i.e. relationships are not mediated by those who are deemed to be genealogically closer. So again we see that close kin relationships are dependent upon shared experiences and the stories that you can tell of them, rather than a place in a fixed structure.

The extent of Cheryl's network is illustrated in figure 6.1, where, as with Naomi's kinship diagram in figure 5.1, a line denoting a face-to-face relationship could be drawn between any of the people symbolically represented.

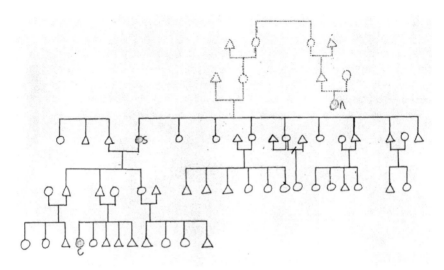

6.1 Cheryl's and Sarah's family, as told by Cheryl

The importance of people and kin relations in forming a Gypsy sense of place and identity has been commented on by anthropologists working amongst Gypsy communities in other countries. For instance, both Stewart (1997b: 28) and Gay-y-Blasco (2001: 641) have noted how people are not considered properly Gypsy unless they are linked into a network of relations in this way. The importance of these networks in forming Gypsy identity also sheds light on how children born into marriages of a Gypsy with a non-Gypsy are only considered part Gypsy, but their children are acceptable as full Gypsies (Okely 1983: 69) – those children who only have one biological parent who is a Gypsy only have access to half a network of Gypsy relations with all the possible people who can fulfil the (non-biological) tasks of parenting that go along with teaching 'how to be' a Gypsy.

In the above exchange I comment on (what I think of as) the particularly Gypsy way that children come to be linked into such a wide network of relationships, my contribution is intended as an encouragement:

Me: It's just that it's a bit different, isn't it, it's a bit … it's more common with Gypsies and Travelling people than it is with …
Sarah: Gorgios.
Me: Yeah, wi' gorgios, yeah.
Nancy: I mean Cheryl, she'd live permanently with Sarah, wouldn't she, Sarah?

I meant my comment to be an affirmation that what they were saying was true on a wider basis, but it also underlined a difference between the way Gypsies and non-Gypsies do things that probably wouldn't have been commented on if I hadn't been there. The irrelevance of my statement is emphasised by the way Nancy pays little heed to it – she continues to talk about Cheryl and is unconcerned about how gorgios do or don't do things. This in itself underlines the importance of placing oneself in a web of relationships, a web that orientates around a group of known people and not around theoretical others (in this case either gorgios or other Gypsies not known personally to either Sarah or Ivy).

This lack of emphasis on unknown others and the associated emphasis on known people is quite different from a picture of Gypsy identity that is frequently found in ethnographies of Gypsies, especially those that stress boundaries and binary oppositions (e.g. Gropper 1975; Sutherland 1975; Okely 1983; Fonseca 1995). In these studies Gypsy identity is described as if it were one half of a Gypsy/gorgio divide, as if being Gypsy depends upon people being not-Gypsy. However, what seems to be more important for all of the Gypsies I have worked with is that being Gypsy depends on being included in a network of relationships with other people who are Gypsies. Whilst many anthropological accounts of identity stress the relationship between self and other in enabling the formation of a stable and coherent sense of self, the emphasis for the Gypsies I worked with was not on this opposition. Instead the stress was laid on a network of relations between people who were known personally to one another – the 'we' relationship explored in the previous chapter. In such a relationship people focus on known others, and, in order to make sure that significant others are known, children are raised by people other than their biological parents, thus weaving together the relationship networks. Similar ways of 'doing kinship', recognising both the part played by relatives other than the biological parents in raising children into a social network and the role of children in performing kinship, has been noted by Goody (1982) and Carsten (1991). In other words, it is not enough to know who your relatives are; it is necessary to know them as individual people, and this is done through performance and participation, including making and telling stories.

A further aspect of the importance of interaction within the realm of face-to-face interaction is also highlighted in the above passage when I say, 'Yeh – well, it's like when I was talking to, well a couple of the women I've spoken to really said that they were y'know closer to their Grannies.' Here I was going to mention Naomi, the person who featured in the last chapter, but I stopped myself because, whilst Naomi is known to both Sarah and Nancy, she is not a member of their 'family' – i.e. she 'belongs with' a different family and in a different set of stories. Naomi had also been largely brought up by her Granny and had had a lot to say to me about how she was closer to her Granny than she was to her own mother. However, just before I was about to say her name I remembered that it was 'not done' to talk about people in any sort of intimate or personal way if they weren't part of your own group. If you are talking about something that doesn't have any direct impact upon yourself (for instance, me talking

6.2 The author's children sitting on a vardo

about Naomi's relationship with her grandmother), then it isn't considered polite to mention other people's names. In the subtle insistence of only naming people who are part of your family, or who are actually present and taking part in the conversation, a sense of a close-knit family group surrounded by an unaccountable world populated by strangers is reinforced. There is also a repeat of a general social emphasis on face-to-face interactions, thus adding to a general feel about how to behave – the enactment of a social aesthetic, part of the Gypsy style of telling stories and maintaining relationships. It was never actually put to me in those terms; it was more of a gradual realisation that there are some things and some people that you can talk about and some things and some people that you don't – which stresses again the way I had to learn to be in their world and operate according to their social aesthetic standards.

Telling Family Together

The intimacy and intricacy of people's family networks – those webs of relationships in which they find a sense of belonging – is emphasised in the following excerpts. They come after Sarah has been asking about old stories for the book and where she is likely to get them (I have cut them down a bit for the sake of space, which is why there are two excerpts, rather than just one long one):

Nancy:	I tell you who'd tell you an all cos y'know Eileen, Charlie's Eileen, she were bought up wi' me mam. They were pals, best o' pals, me mam married me dad an' – Eileen married Charlie. She said they were down here Monday.
Nancy:	Charlie …
Me:	Yeah.
Nancy:	… is me mam's cousin. Charlie's dad and my granddad – were two brothers.
Me:	Right – what was Charlie's dad called?
Nancy:	Me Uncle Billy.
Me:	Billy.
Nancy:	Yeah.
Me:	Right.
Nancy:	'E's Charlie's – Charlie is his son.
Me:	Did he have any others?
Nancy:	Yeah.
Me:	How many, d'you know?
Nancy:	fffuuuu (intake of breath).
Sarah:	Hee hee hee hee.
Nancy:	Err, hang on a minute – Charlie, Jane, Lizzy, Maria, Dougie, Iris, err, he had seven – two boys, five girls.
Me:	Right … and, so, Charlie is your mother's cousin.
Nancy:	Yeah.
Me:	And they were brought up together and then …

Nancy	No, his wife was.
Me:	His, his wife were …
Nancy:	Yeah, Eileen.
Me:	Eileen
Nancy:	… were brought up – with me mam. They were pals – y'know, when they were kids and that.
Me:	Yeh.
Nancy:	Teenagers.
Me:	Yeah.
Nancy:	Pulled around together.

Here we can see familiar and intricate knowledge of family relationships connected to the way people 'pulled around' together, connected, in fact, to the context of sleeping arrangements (for instance), with which I began this chapter. It is important that these relationships are experienced, that they don't remain theoretical, as they can quickly become so complicated that they become almost meaningless unless particular known people are involved. Such complex relationships are difficult to imagine and understand if they remain as words alone: hence my confusion in the excerpt. Nancy and Sarah don't get confused by this complexity because they have grown up among these relationships, they are part of what makes them (and for this reason it is OK for them to talk about them – this is their own personal knowledge).

For those of us who don't have such an intimate understanding of these relationships, a diagrammatic representation can help us to visualise how the people in question are related to one another: hence the (much truncated) version of Nancy's kinship chart in figure 6.3. Again the sense

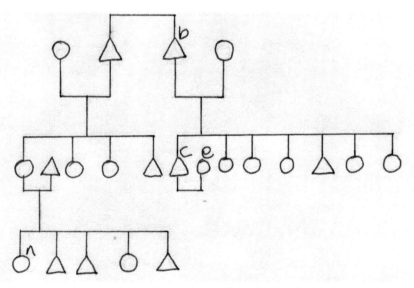

6.3 Diagram showing Nancy's relations referred to in the text

of belonging is connected to having a place amongst people, and specifically to having a place amongst particular people – people with names and histories, people with whom you share experiences and memories and with whom you remember and relate stories, people who are known 'vividly' and as 'fully real' (Berger and Luckman 1966: 43; Bird-David 1995: 69).

The way that Nancy and Sarah are sharing something through the telling of these relationships is emphasised when I ask about the number of children that Billy had. Nancy's intake of breath and Sarah's answering laugh affirm the fact that both Nancy and Sarah know the answer to the question (hence they both know the relationships being talked about). They also share a sense of amusement because they both know that the answer to my question further complicates something that I already find confusing. Such shared stories enable Nancy and Sarah to reaffirm their relationships to one another and their respective places in a network of relationships. The stories that do this are not necessarily event-rich stories; they are more repetitive and evocative, they are rememberings of the mundane, told in a way such that Nancy and Sarah share their telling and the remembering.[4] For instance, in the following example Nancy and Sarah remember one of the meals they used to cook around a campfire, a typically domestic tale but framed in the context of a lifestyle of travelling around and living outdoors. Nancy and Sarah are not describing a time when they cooked a meal together; they are using the notion of a meal in order to emphasise a sense of connectedness, of understanding, of shared (if separate) experiences:[5]

Sarah:	Panakilty.
Me:	Panakilty – what's that?
Nancy:	Bacon.
Sarah:	It's er – go on.
Nancy:	Bacon, onions, sliced tatie – all put in together – yeah.
Sarah:	Corned beef.
Nancy:	Corned beef.
Me:	Yeh.
Nancy:	Used to put anything in it, didn't you.
Sarah:	Sausage.
Nancy:	Sausages wi' mainly bacon, innit – and one piece of bacon cut up.
Me:	What all fried up together?
Nancy:	Yeah – no, boiled.
Sarah:	No, boiled.
Me:	Right.
Sarah:	All boiled – yeh, like a stew.
Nancy:	Yeah.
Sarah:	And that was all done on all on a fire.
Nancy:	Yeah.
Sarah:	Campfire was'n' it – panakilty – hare.
Nancy:	Yeh – 'ares – old boiler – chickens.
Sarah:	Mm.

The sense of sharing in telling such stories reaffirms the relationship between Nancy and Sarah, who have spent a lot of their life together; indeed, they still spend much of their time on the same official site as each other. This sharedness is made evident in the way that they talk with one another, which displays evidence of mutual understandings of the world and their closeness in that world, very suggestive of Bernstein's 'restricted code' (Bernstein 1964). Nancy and Sarah also use many linguistic devices that are common in conversational remembering (Middleton and Edwards 1990: 26) such as repetition, agreement and appeals for confirmation – 'put anything in it, didn't you' and 'Campfire, was'n' it'. In using these devices their talk emphasises the shared nature of the memory and also a shared understanding in the present of what such a story is for. Nancy and Sarah are both well practised at telling such stories, but they have chosen to tell this one, now, for me, because they are using it not only to affirm their sense of relatedness but also to teach me something about what it is to be Gypsy.

Learning when is the right time to tell which story to which person and in which way is an important part of becoming 'fully practised' cultural participants (Middleton and Edwards 1990: 9). Nancy and Sarah are well practised in telling the right kind of story, at the right time, to the right person and now, together, they are teaching me. So we are reminded of the ways that stories are used to teach 'how to be' in the world, and I am shown here how Gypsies use stories to ensure a continuing sense of sharedness, one that can be passed on to others.

Individual and Family – the Interplay of 'I' and 'We'

It is, however, important not to overstress the extent to which being a part of a group and sharing memories gives a sense of being 'Gypsy'. Being part of a 'we' relationship comprised of people who are known intimately and on a face-to-face basis is important and, as we saw in the previous chapter, it is from such a relationship that people develop their particular sense of 'I'. Nancy and Sarah happen to be second cousins, but the closeness of their relationship means that their sense of relatedness, their sense of sharing a family and hence a 'we' relationship, makes them closer than is suggested by the term 'second cousin'. Both Nancy and Sarah are in their fifties and are grandmothers – they have a lot in common, both now and in the past. They have also led quite different lives; they haven't been together all the time and sometimes Nancy's and Sarah's talk works on the times when they haven't been together. When this happens the stories and the memories they relate to are not shared, but in their telling they emphasise the knowledge between the two that is shared – the relationships and understandings that are at work in creating a sense of belonging in a family. This sense of sharedness provides a backdrop, the cultural landscape, against which the particular events of an individual's life are played out:

Nancy: You know, the best laugh I ever 'ad with a chicken [was at] Topley Fair.

Sarah: Have we got the tape rollin'?

Me Yeh.

Nancy: Right – wait a minute – I were, I weren't so old. Me Granny's wagon that way, me Aunt Sylvia and Uncle Jim's in the middle – right – an' me mum an' dad's in the corner. In the field at Topley Fair. Aunt Sylvia: 'Jim, Jim – croak me that chicken, I'm sick of it. Croak me that chicken and I'll – boil it up for tomorrow.' Right, and, cos she had him under the thumb, didn't she – she were the boss where he jumped at. Anyway, he gets this chicken. Croaks it, passes her it. She sat on – on the edge of little field like that – bowl – chicken in it – plucking it. Well, I'm stood there watching her and when – plucking it, all of a sudden chicken jumped up – he hadn't croaked it properly.

Me: (gasp)

Sarah: Heh heh heh heh!

Nancy: Hee hee hee, well I, right, well I set off running, me mam come out – I'm screaming, me. And you know Aunt Sylvia she didn't know what to do – legs cocked up in the air. He'd only stunned it – and you know with her pulling the feathers out – she'd wokened it up. Well, this chicken running off up and down, half feathers and half non-feathers. Well, you know me, don't you, nobody could stop this chicken. She's screaming 'I'm gonna kill you, Jim. Jim, when you come near me I'm gonna croak you.'
'Why Sylvia, whatever's the matter?'
'You killed chicken, did you? Yeh, well what's it runnin' up an' down for then?'
Honest to God. Mother run out at me, picked me up, thought what's ever the matter and I'm screaming, thinking of chicken – you know, a babby seen a chicken jumping out of a, a bowl.

The setting of this tale is laid out from the start, and assumes a level of shared knowledge and understanding that includes a vivid knowledge of the people involved. It is also a knowledge of place – Nancy knows that Sarah knows where Topley Fair was, what it was like, what it looked like. From this she can describe the relative positioning of her relatives' wagons and so describe a domestic, even homely, scene that will be familiar to them both. Again, specific people are important: Nancy is quite particular about whose wagons were where, about the placing of people in a familiar landscape. This familiar landscape is also a temporary landscape, as it is tied into the event of a fair; this brings with it even more information about the time of year, other people who were likely to be around, the kinds of activities that were taking place and so on. The closeness of the relationship between Sarah and Nancy is also played upon by Nancy when she appeals to Sarah: 'Well, you know me, don't you.' Through this appeal Nancy draws Sarah into the story, she includes her in her telling of it, so acknowledging her place in a shared world. All this reaffirms and draws upon something shared between Nancy and Sarah from which Nancy can then tell her tale of the chicken that Sarah had not heard until that day.

This linking of place to people is emphasised in the following excerpts of talk, taken at a different time when Sarah is talking to her sister Ivy. They had begun the tape talking about old recipes that they used to cook around the campfire, but had gradually got on to talking about other things that they remembered from their childhood:

Sarah:	When we were on t' tip ...
Ivy:	Yeh but you ...
Sarah:	... what what I call the tip.
Ivy:	Yeh, yeh, but at the same time (inaudible) you only come t' visit us.
Sarah:	No, I was stopping with Aunt Christa.
Ivy:	But not as long as I did.
Sarah:	No, not as long as you did, no.

Almost immediately the place, the tip, is defined in terms of who was stopping with who and for how long. In fact, it might not even be a tip; that is just what Sarah calls it. What the place is doesn't really matter for the telling of the story, but who was there matters enormously. In this exchange, however, there is a subtle interplay between sharing and resisting a sense of sharing; Ivy doesn't want to share too much and so she also stresses what was different – the fact that she's been with Aunt Christa for longer than Sarah (with the implication that she was closer to her than Sarah was). This shows again the ways that stories are deliberately used to both reinforce a sense of being Gypsy (Sarah and Ivy share the cultural landscape that provides the setting for their talk) and a sense of being individual people.

Sarah's and Ivy's talk shows a very careful balancing of sharedness with individuality, and their talk continually plays on one and then the other in order to achieve a balance between the two. The following excerpt comes a little further on in the tape recording:

Ivy:	(Sigh) An' I'll tell you another thing. Can you remember when I was on a' at Appleby? With me Granny?
Sarah:	Yeh.
Ivy:	An' them?
Sarah:	Yeh ... with Granny Smith.
Ivy:	Y'know? Yeh, she was there.
Sarah:	Yeh.
Ivy:	Lee an' that, Granny Cooper.
Sarah:	Ohhh yes, that's right.
Ivy:	And family Cooper.

In this exchange it is the shared knowledge between Sarah and Ivy that is being stressed, although Ivy begins talking about what seems to be a story that is particular to her – 'when I was on at Appleby' – she deliberately draws Sarah in, asking her if she can remember. What is being remembered is a place – Appleby – which needs also to be understood as an event – Appleby Horse Fair – and it is remembered in terms of the people who were stopping there together with Ivy and Sarah. This emphasises and reminds both Sarah and Ivy of their place in a wide network of people. We are also reminded of the importance of Grannies in providing the connections into such a wide network of relations and associated stories, networks that are recognised through the family names 'Smith' or 'Cooper'. We might expect that these bits of talk are the preliminary scene setting to other, more eventful tales, as in the story of the chicken, but this is not the case. These shared rememberings are about the day-to-day details of a life lived together in a shared cultural landscape as part of a 'we' relationship.

A Variety of Possible Stories

As we have seen, particular events happen to individual people and can be thought of as the property of those people. Stories about these events might be told when the differences between people are being worked on, whether to explain a feeling of distance and unrelatedness (as with Naomi and her paternal grandmother in the previous chapter) or to bring someone closer (as with Nancy's telling of the chicken story above), thus emphasising the joint nature of the storytelling performance. This echoes the way in which people are only spoken about if they have a direct relevance to yourself – events are only related if they are yours. This is very different from the way the mundane details of everyday life are used to affirm a sense of belonging. In fact, there are different sorts of stories used to do different things. Some of them (those concerned with the details of everyday life – cooking a meal together, describing a scene at a fair) emphasise a sense of belonging to a family group. Others (getting upset because your grandmother didn't give you a doll, seeing a dead chicken come back to life) portray a sense of individuality within that family setting. Still others (stories about strangers and haunted houses) combine the two through repeating certain themes, which can also be metaphorically described as landmarks within a cultural landscape, in a particular and personalised way. Yet others (references to particular family names, talk about Grannies) are almost not stories at all, although they could be spun out into a whole variety of stories about the people, places and events that form the basis of the family. All these possible stories are implicit in the exchange between Sarah and Ivy above.

The conversation continues on its theme of shared ordinariness: having remembered the time, the place and the people that provided the

important reference point, the talk moves on to more talk about the place
– what and who were there:

Sarah:	Horses and vardoes, wasn't it? Wasn't no trailers.
Ivy:	No, it was wagons. Living wagons.
Sarah:	Was wagons, wasn't it.
Ivy:	You go (inaudible) on living wagons.
Sarah:	Vardoes.
Ivy:	Living wagons, oppenlots.
Sarah:	Well, whatever.
Ivy:	Once called them oppenlots.
Sarah:	Oppenlots, yes. And square tents.
Ivy:	Yes … yes.
Sarah:	The square tents, wasn't it?
Ivy:	Yes – mm.
Sarah:	Yeh.
Ivy:	Mm.
Sarah:	Yeh, you went with Aunt Lizzy Lee, didn't you?
Ivy:	An' me dad [and] them landed up.
Sarah:	Yeh, yeh.
Ivy:	When it was finished I went with Aunt Christa. I told her that me mam an' me dad says it were all right. I, uh, went with them (ha). An' we travelled down the road (heh). Me dad come racing after us in the car an' took me back. Stopped us.

Here Sarah and Ivy reminisce about the way a place used to look, firmly
tying the landscape to the actions and movements of Gypsies, tying the
geographical landscape and the cultural landscape together. It also ties
Sarah and Ivy into a shared past that is recognisably Gypsy – with the talk
of living wagons, vardoes, oppenlots and square tents. All these are the
dwellings that Gypsies used to have before the motor-drawn trailers
became popular, and mention of them underlines a sense of shared origin,
of coming from the same place, thus underlining their relatedness and
suggestive of an idea of home, such as I was looking for at the beginning
of this chapter.

Very soon the talk returns to particular people and the excerpt ends
with an event that describes Ivy moving from stopping with one lot of
people (Aunt Lizzy Lee) through trying to stop with others (Aunt Christa)
and ending with her father. The fact that Ivy refers to her dad – 'me dad
[and] them landed up' – reinforces an understanding of kinship that is less
tied to rules and roles than that of the mainstream society that surrounds
the Gypsies. Ivy is talking to her sister, Sarah – Ivy's father is also Sarah's
father – however, they do not talk of their father as if they shared the same
sort of relationship with him, that of daughter to father. The suggestion is
rather that they each have an individual and particular relationship with
the man who is their father. In other words, it is a relationship defined by
people's personalities rather than their roles – a relationship defined by a
directly conscious awareness of one another. This particularising of

relationships, rather than a typifying based on generalised roles and relationships, is frequently done in the talk of the Gypsies I worked with – they would talk of 'my mother' when talking to a brother or sister, 'my brother' when talking to another sibling, 'my aunt Christa' when talking to another Gypsy who was also Christa's niece or nephew, and so on. This means that the importance of face-to-face interaction is again emphasised and is in contrast to the more role-based expectations of the mainstream society. Bird-David (1995) explored this phenomenon amongst hunter-gatherer societies, noting how the particularising of individuals led to a strong sense of a known group where one's sense of self and place in a group hinged upon performed relationships rather than ascribed kinship (or other) roles. I would contend that a similar group building activity is going on amongst the Gypsies I worked with, and that much of this activity is performed through storytelling and affirming the place of the individual in a 'we' relationship.

Where in the World?

From the passages above and the references to places and events (Topley Fair, the tip, Appleby, etc.) it is clear that, for Gypsies, finding a place amongst people also involves knowing where in the world you are. That personal relationships and where people are in the landscape are vital to establishing a sense of home was underlined whenever the Gypsies I worked with came together. This finally became absolutely clear to me in the summer of 2001, when I went with a group of Gypsies to stay at Whitby Regatta.

We were all excited about going to Whitby; because of the foot-and-mouth outbreak, almost all the horse fairs had been cancelled and this was going to be one of the few big gatherings that summer. The people I was with would talk all the time about who was going, who would be there, who they might meet and so on. When we arrived, almost the first thing we did was go out into the town and walk along the quayside, where people were putting out stalls for the main regatta days on the Sunday and Monday (we arrived on Saturday). We spent the best part of three hours walking up and down, looking to see who was there. When we did meet up with someone the conversation would follow a well defined course:

> 'Hello, –, haven't seen you in ages, who are you with?'
> This would be replied to with a list of names and then would follow a series of questions:
> 'Where are you staying?'
> 'When did you land?'
> 'How long are you stopping for?'
> 'Have you seen anyone else?'
> 'Where are they stopping?'

This was not a one way process: each of the questions was asked and responded to by each party. At first I thought these were the preliminaries before asking people how they were and what had been going on in their lives recently – the sort of conversation I was more used to. But this never happened; the conversation followed the same course every time without fail and, having established who was where and for how long, might close with a 'See you in the pub later?' It was never even necessary to say the name of the pub, as all the women went to a particular one and all the men went to another, as they did every year. I soon began to realise what was happening, because as we walked and talked to people I was beginning to build in my mind a picture of who was where, for how long they might be expected to be there and who was with them. This picture was especially clear when it involved people I knew personally.

So it was that for four days we established a place in Whitby that consisted of the relationships between people played out in time and space, built and continually reinforced through the walking and talking that was going on (and that continued to go on for the four days that I was there). That place would then dissolve in order for another place to be established in another time and space and involving some of the same people and others who weren't there earlier.

Conclusion

Gypsies' ideas about home are not tied to notions about fixity and property (and associated notions of ownership and power), as is the case in the popular understandings of home mentioned at the beginning of the chapter. This is not to say that Gypsies don't have a notion of property, as has sometimes been claimed and counterclaimed (see Hancock 1997: 183). Nor is it to say that Gypsies don't have a conception of power, though it can be claimed that their conception of the world is based on a less hierarchical and status-driven sense of power than the non-Gypsy world (Stewart 1997b: 91). Instead, 'home' – and with it land, space and place – is about the ability to maintain and reproduce relationships. Such relationships are maintained and reproduced through the use of different sorts of story, which are told in a recognisably Gypsy way and which repeat and reinforce recognisably Gypsy themes. Gypsies are taught how to do this through their interactions with others who are more practised in the skills and styles involved in Gypsy storytelling – i.e. they are taught through a pedagogical relationship with reference to a recognisably Gypsy set of social aesthetic standards.

Carrithers (1992) has pointed out how people use stories, including the mundane stories of everyday talk, to formulate a sense of community that extends through time (past and future). Ochs and Capps (2001) have noted the way joining in telling stories together reaffirms a sense of belonging and builds a shared social world. We can see that both everyday talk and stories are used by Sarah, Nancy and Ivy in order to maintain relationships, to give a sense of continuity and connectedness, despite differences and distances. All this helps to strengthen a sense of belonging amongst people, which gives them their sense of home. This isn't just a remembered sense of home – it is recreated in the telling and so provides the ground from which to project into the future and imagine a sense of continuity. The future is imagined as a place where networks of people and relationships continue, which entails that the networks and relationships of the past be continually remade in the present; placing people in the world and teaching people how to use stories is an important part of this.

Notes

1. Ken = house or other static dwelling.
2. An average based on the genealogies I have collected.
3. 'Pulling' is a reference to the way the wagons were pulled and, whilst the horses did the pulling, groups of people pulled together.
4. The close and intimate nature of the talk is also suggestive of Bernstein's 'restricted code' (Bernstein 1964), in that there is an awful lot of 'taken-for-granted' information that does not need to be made explicit.
5. The lines down the side indicate when two people spoke at the same time.

Chapter 7

THE NEGOTIATION OF MORAL AMBIVALENCE

As part of the process of teaching 'how to be', stories need to teach ways of dealing with tensions, such as those between ideas about 'real' Gypsies and tinkers, etc., which were outlined in chapter 1. In this chapter I explore how learning these strategies through stories allows for cultural scenarios to be realised in the narratives and social action of everyday life. So far, I have shown how a practice of storytelling articulates with the construction and experience of the world, and I have focused on the idea of 'family' in order to do this. In the chapter that follows I shall use this understanding in order to examine interactions both between Gypsies and between Gypsies and non-Gypsies. The intention is to explore how understandings about the world that have been taught through the use of stories operate in the less obviously story-based interactions of everyday life. I begin once again with ideas about belonging, but I move away from the notion of 'family' in order to see how relationships are both formed and informed by a rhetorical use of language. I look at how understandings about what it is to be Gypsy are grounded in an understanding of relationships between people as those relationships are articulated through talk. The focus then returns to the idea of 'family' and builds upon the associated ideas about moral values looked at in chapters 4 and 5.

What's In and What's Out – or Who Belongs and Who Doesn't?

In chapter 5 I described a conversation I had with Naomi; she spoke about her family and I made notes and drew a diagram of her family as she was talking (figure 5.1). Throughout our conversation a process of moral evaluation was discernible, which shows how Naomi deals with ideas about Gypsiness. Take, for instance, the following excerpt from my field notes:

> I ask her if they all think of themselves as Gypsy Travellers and she says, 'Oh yes.' Most of them still move out into trailers in the summer, some travelling

as far away as Germany on a regular basis. Naomi explains how there's a group of people they refer to as 'wide-ohs', who have moved out of houses and into trailers but who aren't really Gypsies, even though they try to pass themselves off as Gypsies. I ask if there are any of these people on the sites on Teesside at the moment and she says no, they were moved off a few years ago. Some of them still camp on the Macro's roundabout – these are the people who leave the rubbish, says Naomi. She tells me about a time when she was happily camped on a forecourt car park, with the owner's consent. But when a group of 'not real Gypsies' moved on she insisted on being pulled a few hundred yards away – she didn't want to be associated with the mess they left behind. (Field notes)

Here Naomi adopts a position that I have noticed is used frequently amongst Gypsies and Travellers – that is, to associate known members of the family with an idea of being a 'real' Gypsy and other people as 'not real Gypsies'. This stance is implied rather than made explicit in Naomi's tale – for a start, Naomi had begun by talking about her family, a family that includes all those people who do still think of themselves as Gypsy Travellers and who were referred to at the beginning of the excerpt.1 Naomi then juxtaposes these known people, many of whom live in houses at least over the winter, with unknown people, an anonymous group of people called wide-ohs, who might look like Gypsies but who aren't really. Naomi's suggestion is that the wide-ohs don't have the history of being Gypsy that 'real' Gypsies do. As we have seen, Gypsies know their history through family stories – tales of known people doing recognisably Gypsy things. What Naomi is doing here is using her knowledge of what a Gypsy is (a known person with whom she shares some history) to place unknown people in a comprehensible position relative to those she does know. Naomi is describing a sense of the world where her consociates are those who have shared some time with her in an intersubjective relationship and so have helped to make her who she is. Naomi's contemporaries are those whom she has not known in this way and who exist only as representatives of the type 'not Gypsy'.

Such a stance does not mean drawing a clear-cut, albeit symbolic, line between Gypsies and gorgios; Schutz (1972: 177) described the extent to which these worlds of contemporaries and consociates fade into and out of one another and how people can move from one realm to another. In fact, it is a stance that cannot accurately be reflected by any kind of metaphor involving boundaries, divisions and separations. The feeling is more accurately captured in a favourite image of the Gypsies – that of a campfire in the dark. The idea is that a fire casts light and heat that cannot be neatly separated from the darkness; metaphorically Gypsies are known people who share the same fire – and fire is like family, it is that which gives life. Of course, there is always the danger that strangers might enter the circle of known people, along with their doubtful morality (remember the stories about the devil and unaccountable people recounted earlier). It is also possible that there are people who are not currently present who are properly part of the circle of known people. So an important aspect of the stance that Naomi adopts is the possibility that unknown people can become recognised as kin – but only once they are known, as we saw in chapters 5 and 6.

Because of the close association between a group of people (e.g. members of a Gypsy family, including those who could become kin) and ideas about morality, the boundary between the morally desirable and undesirable realms is not clearly defined. This reflects the somewhat vague and mutable nature of the distinction between the known characters in a story and the mysterious strangers from the unaccountable world of non-Gypsies, as well as the impossibility of drawing a line around the light and heat from a fire. As noted previously, the negotiation of potentially conflicting representations of what it is to be a Gypsy is something that Gypsies have to learn to cope with. Stories teach how to do this through creating 'cultural scenarios' (Schieffelin 1976) or themes of interaction, which have a certain 'open' quality and which take place in a shared cultural landscape that displays a fluid and vaguely defined separation between the known world of Gypsies and the unaccountable rest of the world. However, this strategy also has to be realised in everyday interactions – interactions that do not fall into an easily recognisable 'storytelling' mode. This strategy was well used in a conversation I had with Rosaleen and James:

> James described how 'Years ago people in council estates would throw stones at us – dirty Gypsies, they would say, that's what we had to put up with.' Said how now those same people couldn't cope with all their debts and they're buying trailers and moving on to the road and calling themselves Gypsies. Said how they weren't Gypsies – 'if it ain't travelling blood …' But then he said that he doesn't mind people doing it – it makes things easier for them, 'makes it better for us'. (Field notes)

Here James places himself within a known group – an 'us' – that is positioned in opposition to those outside the group – 'they'. Those outside the group are said to be taking actions that are recognisably wrong but that those in the group 'put up with'. What James then does is place those outside the group in an apparently contradictory and unsustainable position – they are both attacking the Gypsies and trying to be Gypsies at the same time. These 'wannabe'[2] Gypsies are both those who attack and those who actually make life easier for the 'real' Gypsies – those in the known group. So what we have here is a description of a group of people whose current behaviour (whatever it happens to be – good or bad, attacking or helpful) can be explained by referencing it both to their past behaviour and to their position relative to Gypsies – i.e. 'not-Gypsies.'

James achieves this by creating a history for the 'wannabes' that links people who lived on council estates in the past with people who claim to be

Gypsies today – making them 'those same people'. James also depicts them as carrying out offensive behaviour (throwing stones) whilst at the same time saying that they make life better for Gypsies; this collapses any moral distinction between the ways various groups behave and places the 'wannabe' Gypsies, alongside people on council estates, in a morally ambivalent place. The result is that this group of people is placed in a position relative to Gypsies whereby whatever they do, however they behave, can be explained in such a way as to maintain the relationship, i.e. in this instance the distance between Gypsies and non-Gypsies. This means that, despite being people who might look like Gypsies, if they are not known, then their behaviour can easily be used to show the fact that they are not real Gypsies, that they belong to that group of people called 'wannabes'.

Naomi also uses such a strategy in the passage above when she talks of 'not real Gypsies' or 'wide-ohs' being the ones who leave the rubbish behind; what makes them not real Gypsies is not the fact that they leave rubbish but that Naomi doesn't know them. What this strategy does is create a kind of 'moral wasteland', an area of moral ambivalence and ambiguity through which people can be moved either to bring them closer to the known group of Gypsies or to send them further away into the unaccountable world of non-Gypsies.

Making a Place in the World – Rhetoric and Meaning

There must, however, be some means of distinguishing between those who belong and those who don't, some way of marking the difference. Naomi makes it clear in her tale above that, in belonging to the known group of real Gypsies, people inhabit a place in the world that is recognised as clean and honest. Those people who are not known but who are known about (for instance, people who 'pass themselves off' as Gypsies) occupy a place in the world that is associated with rubbish and dishonesty. This, of course, leaves all those people who are neither known nor known about, who can come into the world of the Gypsies and prove themselves to be either acceptable or unacceptable, desirable or undesirable, honest or dishonest and so on. As noted previously, such a construction of the world is reflected in the writings of many ethnographers of Gypsy culture and would seem to support the division of the world into, if not neatly Gypsy and non-Gypsy, at least reflecting an idea of pure and impure, desirable and undesirable. However, the more I spoke to Gypsies, the more I had to question this view; again it seemed as though the distinction did not fit. In fact, the idea of dirtiness and cleanliness appears to have very little meaning other than as a device for showing, at any one time, who is in and who is out. In other words, ideas about dirt, cleanliness, etc. do not carry any associated moral significance; ideas about 'dirt' are not indicative of some overarching, structuring cosmology that links Gypsies to purity and non-Gypsies to pollution. On the contrary, ideas about dirt are simply a theme around which Gypsies improvise in order to maintain some sense of a difference between Gypsies and non-Gypsies, without that difference ever becoming fixed. I must stress that I am referring specifically to what people say, not to what they do – because I have always found that Gypsy women work extremely hard to keep their homes clean and that in practice dirt is never thought of as desirable. I would, however, question the profound symbolic significance a desire for a clean home has been given by more structuralist-oriented ethnographers, such as Okely and Sutherland.

In my conversation with James and Rosaleen, themes concerning dirt and cleanliness are elaborated on, as are the differences between different sorts of Travellers, their behaviour and what this means for the moral judgements gorgios make about Gypsies:

> Said how they weren't Gypsies – 'if it ain't travelling blood ...' But then he said that he doesn't mind people doing it – it makes things easier for them, 'makes it better for us'.

> I asked if that was really true – and James and Rosaleen both agreed that it was as far as the people in 'accommodations' at Yarm were concerned – but no – not the New Age Travellers. Then described how the New Age Travellers left dirt behind them and got the Gypsies a bad name as being dirty. (Field notes)

In this statement the now familiar themes of dirtiness and Gypsiness are used in such a way as to stress their contested and contestable nature. In this passage, dirt is something that is left by non-Gypsies but that is attributed to Gypsies because it is left by people who look like Gypsies. As noted above, the significance of ideas about dirt, pollution, impurity and so on in a Gypsy world view has been well documented, but the suggestion is always that there is a definite idea about what is dirty, who is dirty, some kind of absolute distinction between the pure and the impure realms of Gypsy and non-Gypsy. This again reflects a largely non-Gypsy view of the world, a view perhaps built upon binary oppositions (e.g. Okely and Sutherland's structuralist accounts) or upon Freudian and other psychoanalytic notions of self and other, desirable and abject (Sibley 1995). It is not a view that is reflected in the ways that the Gypsies I worked with spoke. In Gypsies' talk, the idea of 'dirt' was a rhetorical device used to position people within a cultural landscape; it had in itself no absolute definable value or any definite referent in the 'real' world. This point can be illustrated in the following note I made about a comment by James a little later in the same conversation: 'James began talking about how it was the gorgios made the Gypsies clean. Said how when they lived in tents they weren't clean but they were made so much fun of that it forced them to become clean. Here the suggestion is that, far from Gypsies having always had a sense of cleanliness that they have jealously guarded, they were once dirty themselves. This is not really the point of the comment, though; the point is that the idea of cleanness or dirtiness is again used to draw a distinction between Gypsies and non-Gypsies that is not dependent upon having a different cultural landscape so much as being in different places relative to one another in the same landscape. It serves to maintain a certain kind of relationship between the known world of Gypsies and the strange and unaccountable world of gorgios.

James does make a statement that appears to assert some kind of definite idea about what it is that makes a Gypsy when he says 'if it ain't travelling blood …' On the face of it this seems to imply that there is a definite idea that Gypsies are descended from particular bloodlines, and if you don't belong to one of them then you cannot be a Gypsy. Such talk could be used to bolster a 'purity'-based conception of Gypsiness, linking cultural traits to race, such as is suggested in some folklore studies (e.g. Jarman and Jarman 1991: 12), however, references to blood are more appropriately viewed as figures of speech – a metaphor for a sense of belonging. Also, just as 'dirt' did not have any definite values ascribed to it – it was more a tool used to maintain a sense of stability in relationships between Gypsy and non-Gypsy – so the same thing applies to ideas about 'blood'. 'Blood' is a figure of speech used to denote and maintain a sense of Gypsiness without referring to absolute and fixed qualities. This kind of talk is evident in the way James spoke about living patterns or lifestyles, etc. Take, for instance, the following comment made as the conversation continued:

> This led somehow to James explaining how if they ever were to move into a house then they would have trouble with the neighbours and that would make things difficult for them. I asked if any of his family were in houses and he said that his mum and dad took to houses. Explained this by saying that there is hardly any stopping.

So the people that James is descended from – his mum and dad – live in houses and they have pretty much the lifestyle that James described of the people living in 'accommodations'[3] at Yarm. He gives a reason for his parents being in a house, saying that there's no 'stopping' – i.e. there aren't so many places these days where Gypsies can camp without being harassed by the police and other officials. In other words, although his parents live in a house, this fact becomes evidence of their bad treatment by the non-Gypsy world and so does not challenge their Gypsiness – it confirms it. However, houses, as we know, are not considered desirable places to be and James affirms this at the beginning of the statement by saying that they would have trouble from the neighbours – the threatening world of the housed non-Gypsies looms once again. However, the possible positions and ensuing moral stances of the central characters (James, Rosaleen and the Gypsies that form the 'us' referred to at the beginning of the passage) have not yet been fully explored, and Rosaleen continues the conversation:

Rosaleen then returned to the topic of conversation we were having before and said that they wouldn't be Gypsies if they were in a house. Interestingly the reason she gave was not that they wouldn't be travelling around but that they would become isolated from other Gypsies – 'When you live in a house people don't come and see you so much.'

So here we have another statement about what it is to be a Gypsy, and the idea revolves around how much you interact with other Gypsies, thus stressing, once again, the focus on relationships. This reminds us of how important it is to be part of a network of shared experiences – shared stories – and it is these that make you kin, that give you the 'travelling blood' that James referred to at the beginning. But, again, this would be too simple: to fix on one single definition of what it is to be a Gypsy would not allow for the negotiation of ambivalent representations by the mainstream. In the statements that follow both James and Rosaleen play on this, agreeing upon a direct contradiction about the nature of the Gypsy experience:

Then the discussion turns to what makes a Gypsy a Gypsy. James says how you could take anybody and put them in a trailer on the side of the road and whether they were a Gypsy or not the police would come and move them on. The point seems to be that you can't tell by looking at them whether someone is a Gypsy or not.

Rosaleen seems to agree with this but then says that there must be something – there must be a funny look about her or something because people can always tell that she's a Gypsy.

So it is agreed that there is both something that looks Gypsy and no way of telling by looking whether someone is a Gypsy or not.[4] To agree on a contradiction is significant in itself, but what adds to the impact is that in the context of the telling, in the narrative confabrication of a shared cultural landscape, the whole passage made sense. This is not something that comes easily or naturally; it is something learned through the teaching and telling of stories and the realising of stories through the project of lives lived together.

Rhetoric, Symbols and Values – Introducing the Inchoate

In *Persuasions and Performances*, Fernandez (1986) develops the idea of a 'quality space' through which people can be persuaded to move in their thoughts and in their actions by the use of metaphorical associations between one set of qualities and another. Features of different domains of experience are placed relative to one another such that everything is imbued with some kind of aesthetic/moral value. Fernandez uses this idea to go on to analyse the rhetorical effect of various speakers' metaphors, noting how the metaphors are used to persuade people of an aesthetic/moral point and so also to persuade them of the appropriate action to be taken.

In the conversation with James and Rosaleen, as in many other conversations I had with Gypsies, what became apparent was that the qualities and associated values could easily change – that a metaphorical association of Gypsies with cleanliness or non-Gypsies with houses could shift from one sentence to the next and become their opposite. What was important was the maintenance of a distinction between Gypsies (known people) and non-Gypsies (a type), a distinction grounded in the relationship of one to the other rather than in any difference of attributes or qualities or values.

Carrithers (2003) has since developed Fernandez's idea and extended it to cover more than the use of metaphor, showing how stories provide an effective ground for the use of rhetoric, outlining both the aesthetic/moral stance to be taken and the range of possible actions implied. Certainly with James and Rosaleen it was the stories and the style of telling stories that were the most important thing; qualities, values and so on changed in order to maintain a set of social aesthetic standards, which was based on an understanding of the relationships people have with one another. These social aesthetic standards are taught and used in telling stories and it is through the stories that possible moral/aesthetic stances and associated actions gain their coherence. What James and Rosaleen do is string together numbers of possible stories – for instance, stories about their bad treatment by non-Gypsies, about the undesirable nature of houses, about the dirty ways of 'wannabe' Gypsies, about the potentially helpful nature of non-Gypsies and so on; in this way a vast array of potential values are played with and made available to draw upon for whichever rhetoric end is wanted at any one time. The metaphorical association of one thing with another in and of itself has no fixed meaning; it only has meaning when set within a story or at least within a potential story.

Both Fernandez and Carrithers draw upon the notion of 'the inchoate' to develop their ideas. 'The inchoate' is used to recognise that area of human experience that is 'an uncharted and imperfectly chartable hinterland to thought and feeling which nevertheless exerts its plenipotentiary attractions and repulsions upon us' (Fernandez 1986: 215). Carrithers relates this idea to rhetorical acts of story making and telling, noting how we use a 'story consciousness' (Carrithers 1992: 116) to try and gain some purchase over what is inchoate in our experience of the world, in order to try to form that inchoate into some understandable, perceivable, graspable sense from which we can persuade ourselves and others of the most appropriate course of action. What we see above in James's and Rosaleen's conversation is something of the way this is done. We also see something of the way in which the inchoate remains and can thereby be continually formed and re-formed, depending on need, desired effect and context. Both Fernandez and Carrithers use an analysis of pronouns to focus upon attempts to grasp the inchoate in human interaction, pronouns being slippery words (shifters), and so do not simply refer to the inchoate but allow for its articulation in language as well. In what follows I shall adopt the same approach in order to see how, in an interaction of Gypsies and the non-Gypsy world, the inchoate is formed into one kind of story or another, depending upon the learned social aesthetic standards of those involved.

Families Real and Imagined – the Idea of a Moral Community

I shall here look at this process of making sense from the inchoate as regards ideas about family, the area of Gypsy experience with which we have been most concerned so far, and in doing so we shall be reminded of the importance of ideas about whom stories are told to and whom and what they are told of. What we saw Naomi, Sarah, Nancy and Ivy doing in telling their stories of family is recreating for themselves a cultural landscape – a cultural landscape that has been taught through the ways that they have learned to tell their stories and the events that form the basis of the stories they tell. It is a cultural landscape that is populated by real characters and it has recognisable landmarks or themes. It is a 'unified landscape of consciousness and action' (Carrithers 1992) that has real people in it, who form Naomi's family, that group of known people with whom she lives out her life as a participant in a 'we' relationship. This 'we' relationship is not only very important in Gypsies' interactions with one another, as we saw in the previous chapters; it is also of great importance in interactions with the mainstream, as I shall go on to explain.

At the beginning of chapter 5, I described a christening that took place at Yarm Fair in October 2001. This description served as an introduction to an exploration of some of the ways in which we are taught about the worlds we are born into and brought up in, with a particular focus on stories. By the end of the chapter, I had shown how it is real, concretely known people who are the basis for moral decision making, rather than a possible or imagined community of people and an idealised moral code, and this is reflected in the style of Gypsies' storytelling. The notion that this process hinges upon is that of 'family', a notion that amongst Gypsies points to face-to-face relationships with people who have shared at least some of the parental attentions or tasks[5] of other members of that face-to-face community. This emphasis on the concretely known rather than the imagined marks a significant difference from more mainstream ideas about the basis of moral decision making, in other words, it is an emphasis on an ethic of care, rather than an ethic of right. Such a difference in ethical emphasis also leads to differences in values, which are reflected in differences in attitudes towards the 'family'. On the one hand, the notion of 'family' refers to a network of relationships rooted in the shared experiences of people who know one another as individuals rather than as types. On the other hand, 'family' refers to a bounded group of people with fixed and determined, structured relationships to one another.

I shall now return to the christening at Yarm to examine in more detail just what these differences mean in terms of relatedness and moral responsibility, notions that follow on from the ideas about 'fit' and a sense of belonging that were introduced in the last chapter.

A crowd had gathered outside Tilly Wood's caravan and through them passed the Presbyterian minister who was to perform the service. Behind him followed his helper, carrying a kind of portable font, and they set themselves up at the foot of the steps leading up to where Tilly Wood was sitting looking on. Once the crowd had settled (as well as it could do, being in the middle of a main road with buses and so on trying to get past), the minister began. What follows is a transcript from the video I took of the event where the minister is beginning the service:[6]

'Good afternoon, ladies and gentlemen. This is a very special occasion for Lizzy-Beth. It's good to have so many of God's people drawn together to share in this service of baptism. It's an absolutely wonderful experience for me, I've never done this before and I'm really looking forward to being part of your community for a short while.

'Lizzy-Beth is going to join the family of Christ, of whom we are all members, and we look forward to you supporting her with your prayers and good wishes through a long and happy life. Baptism is, as I said, an introduction into the church of God in whatever denomination. Audrey and I, as it happens, are Presbyterians, if you like, Church of Scotland. So I'm a Church of Scotland minister. Umm. We welcome to the Christian faith for the many denominations so the fact that I'm a Presbyterian makes no difference – she's going to be christened into the family of Christ and so, let us worship God as we come together for this very special service.'

(*Silence – and noise of traffic, coughing, etc.*)

'In this service we desire to acknowledge God as the source of life, as the giver of all good. To thank him for the tender and solemn hopes which gather around the newborn – the newborn, the young and the slightly older. And to pray that this child may be abundantly blessed by God and may learn to love God and to serve his kingdom.

'Inasmuch as we believe that all who are born into this world are children of God we reverently acknowledge the fatherhood, the divine fatherhood of God.'

(*others talking, heckling quietly, inaudible on tape, laughter*)

Father calls out: 'This child is all ours.'

'Seeing that new responsibilities have come to the parents Robert, Katherine, of this child …'

(*More heckling – someone calls,* 'Which parent?')

(*Child is crying and mother says something to the minister*)

'Caitlin, through the gift of this new child we solemnly rededicate our service to the presence of God and ask for his help worthily to fulfil these new and sacred duties.

'It is written that thou shalt love the lord thy God with all thy heart, with all thy soul, with all thy mind and with all thy strength, and thou shalt love thy neighbour as thyself. These words should be in your hearts and you should teach them to your children.

'Hear the words then of the Gospel of Luke of our lord Jesus Christ (*reads from the Bible the story of 'Suffer the little children …'*)

'Robert and Caitlin, you have brought this child for Christian baptism and dedication. Do you promise that she shall be brought up as a Christian child in the nature of that ministry?'

(*nods*)

Caitlin passes the baby over to the minister who says:

'Lizzy-Beth, I baptise you' (*rest is inaudible as he leans over towards the little font and dips his fingers in the water, then draws a cross on her forehead with the water*)

The crowd shuffle about a bit with more talking, then someone calls out: 'Take your child back mate.'

The father says: 'Give her back, chief.'

The minister hands the baby back to Caitlin.

Having now an idea of the fuller context of the christening and the exchanges that took place, let us go back and examine in more detail some of the implications, intentions and expectations that were contained in this brief service.

Rhetoric and the Creation of Social Space

That this christening is taking place in a different kind of space from more mainstream versions is clear from the outset as it is taking place on the high street of a market town in north-east England. What is more, the high street itself is not as might be envisaged in everyday popular imagination.

Instead, Yarm high street has become the embodiment of that linking of people, places and times that we saw happening at Whitby. The christening is taking place set against a backdrop of Gypsy caravans, stick fires, fortune-telling advertisements and so on. It is also taking place in the context of a community of people who are known to one another and whose limits are set – in a very clear and evocative way – by the presence of Tilly Wood (the oldest Gypsy at the fair) and young Lizzy-Beth, the baby about to be christened and the youngest Gypsy at the fair, a point that was commented on by a number of people standing in the crowd waiting for the christening to begin.

We saw in chapter 3 that the arrangement and placing of things and people in space carries meanings and symbolic messages that reinforce the underlying ideas behind the space (see Lawrence and Low 1990: 466ff.). In fact, the placing of people and things in space can be seen to reinforce power relationships, and this is clearly so in the case of churches, where the whole design of the building is to deliberately reinforce a sense of hierarchy and one's associated place within that hierarchy (Halbwachs 1980: 140). In the usual course of carrying out his job, the minister will be able to draw upon the space of the church he preaches within to reinforce his message and, what is more, he will be able to fairly safely assume that the people who come to his church accept the power relationships that are articulated in the physical space they have chosen to enter. In this case, however, the minister has stepped out of his familiar surroundings into the world of the Gypsies and it is in this space – a space that is temporarily turned into a Gypsy space and reflects Gypsy relationships and values – that he is carrying out the service.

What the minister needs to do is recreate the social space (Bourdieu 1990), including the moral values, that is reflected in the physical space of a church. He needs to do this in order to guide more fully the understandings and ensuing actions of his congregation on the High Street. In other words, the minister needs to establish his position and authority to carry out the service without reference to either the supportive framework of a familiar church building or the associated understanding that a certain authority has already been accepted. The minister has nothing but his words (and a portable font) with which to establish his position; he is almost entirely dependent upon the effectiveness of his rhetoric. Were the space a little different, were people not so crowded together and all on a level, it might be that his attire (a black clerical gown) would have helped the minister convey a sense of his status; however, in the event, most of us could not even see him properly (I had to hold the video camera at arm's length above my head to get him on tape). What the minister needs to do is use language in order to persuade people to agree with him about the nature of the social space they are in – and the associated arrangement of moral and aesthetic qualities – in order to confirm his social position and thereby his authority to perform the christening as he understands it. He is here entirely reliant on language because all the usual social props are not available: he is in Gypsy space, not in his church. The minister began:

> 'Good afternoon, ladies and gentlemen. This is a very special occasion for Lizzy-Beth. It's good to have so many of God's people drawn together to share in this service of baptism. It's an absolutely wonderful experience for me, I've never done this before and I'm really looking forward to being part of your community for a short while.

> 'Lizzy-Beth is going to join the family of Christ of whom we are all members ...'

I pause at this point to consider the scene as it is being set by the minister. He begins by placing himself in some sort of 'we' relationship to the gathered congregation of Gypsies – a group that he characterises as a 'community' in which he is temporarily included. It is, however, a community of which he has no personal knowledge – he doesn't know their names, their likes, their dislikes, etc. What allows the minister to include himself in this way is the notion that they are all alike in that they all share the same relationship to God. In order to do this, the minister draws upon the notion of family – a notion, as we have seen, that can have quite a different connotation amongst Gypsies than it does in the mainstream.

Carrithers (2003), following Fernandez (1986: 8), has noted how a 'strategic predication' upon an inchoate 'we' allows a speaker to include himself amongst a group of people. This is what the minister does in his speech: the 'we' is the group of Gypsies present at the christening together with the minister, the 'strategic predication' is the placing of the notion of 'family' upon that 'we'. In the move from talking about 'your community' to 'the family of Christ', the minister moves from a position of being excluded and so uninfluential to being included and able to assume a position of moral authority. This is underlined in the second section of the speech, when he draws attention to the point that 'we' are all members of the family of Christ. From what we have already seen about Gypsies' understanding of family, we can surmise that this notion of 'family' is pertinent because it immediately brings us to a point of disagreement between the minister and the Gypsies – a point where the differences between the concretely known and the imagined worlds become apparent. For the minister a family could consist of any group of people that share a common ancestor or point of origin – in this case 'God'. In this conception of family it is not necessary that the relationship can be clearly traced back and defined, nor is it necessary that people be known; it is sufficient that the connection be recognised. In fact the minister seems to assume that it will be recognised. This assumption illustrates some of the 'taken-for-granted' understandings that the minister brings with him to the service and that he simply imagines the Gypsies share; thus he imagines that they act according to the same understandings and associated expectations as he does.

The minister proceeds to build upon this point. His intention is to place himself in a position of some authority and at the centre of a group of people who share a common purpose (a position that would be evident were this christening taking place in the space of a church building where the minister would be at the centre of everyone's attention and set a little higher than the congregation):

> 'and we look forward to you supporting her with your prayers and good wishes through a long and happy life.'

Now it would seem that the minister falters here, making a rapid shift from a 'we' to a 'you'. Who is looking forward to who supporting Lizzy-Beth with their prayers, and why is it no longer all of them together? It appears as though the minister has given voice to a recognition that his inclusive 'we' is not durable and that the grounds of his moral authority are flimsy and changeable. Indeed, he continues with an attempt to shore up his moral authority:

> 'Baptism is, as I said, an introduction into the church of God in whatever denomination. Audrey and I, as it happens, are Presbyterians; if you like, Church of Scotland. So I'm a Church of Scotland minister. Umm, We welcome to the Christian faith for the many denominations so the fact that I'm a Presbyterian makes no difference – she's going to be christened into the family of Christ and so let us worship God as we come together for this very special service.'

In this passage the minister does something else when he refers to 'we'. Here he opposes it to 'you' – in fact, it is not entirely clear just who the minister is referring to when he says 'we', which emphasises the shifting nature of the pronoun and hence its role in trying to articulate and make sense of a shifting, inchoate situation – a situation where he is not sure what is going to happen next, how the Gypsies are going to respond to him, whether he is going to achieve what he had set out to achieve. Perhaps the minister's 'we' refers to the Christian church – and after all he does go on to explain why he is there as the representative of the church and what gives him that authority. However, if this is the case, then in opposing the 'we' of the church to the 'you' of those he is addressing he implies that the Gypsies are somehow outside that church. On the other hand, the minister could be referring to the 'we' that is him and his assistant minister, Audrey – and after all he does go on to introduce his assistant into his speech, calling her by her name – in which case he apparently recognises that there are differences between the 'we' that refers to his own known associates, the 'you' that refers to the Gypsies, and the 'we' that he uses as a means to establish some kind of common purpose and his place in guiding that purpose – i.e. the imagined 'we' of the church and the family of Christ. Whichever it is, in opposing a 'we' to a 'you', the minister distances himself from his Gypsy congregation on the high street and so separates himself from them, contradicting the attempt to include himself with them, which is how he began his speech.

Now it would appear that the minister is aware that there might be some who could question the authority that he is taking for himself – and he explicitly addresses himself to this potential conflict, stating why he can assume authority amongst people who might not be of the same church as himself. Once again, he draws upon the notion of family in order to do this – family becomes the means by which he can include himself:

> 'the fact that I'm a Presbyterian makes no difference – she's going to be christened into the family of Christ and so, let us worship God as we come together for this very special service.'

There is more to it than this, though, because what the minister is doing is using the notion of 'family' to make a moral point and to persuade the Gypsies at the christening about how they should behave in the future. In the cultural landscape of the minister, the notion of 'family' is such that it allows for the transfer of ideas about moral responsibility etc. from the world of the immediately known, face-to-face community to the world of ideal types, or an imagined community – the movement from an ethic of care to an ethic of right. It is significant that, although the notion of 'the family' has been shown to be vague and contestable (e.g. Harris 1969: 62), such a vague notion is used to outline the grounds for moral responsibility and decision making. There is a suggestion in the speech of the minister that the idea of family that he is using, and even the possibility of using 'family' in order to move from the world of the immediately known to the world of ideal types, can be 'taken-for-granted' – that it forms part of the common ground, the cultural landscape that links him and the group of Gypsies for whom he is performing the service. But, as we can see from the previous chapters, the idea of 'family' that the minister is using is at odds with the idea of 'family' as Gypsies use it. To Gypsies 'family' is one of the means by which a sense of Gypsiness is maintained in the face of the inchoate (it is the fire that burns in the dark) and so it cannot be used to incorporate the strangeness and dangerousness of the non-Gypsy world. In fact, by trying to include himself in the group, the minister takes on a character reminiscent of that of the Devil in the card-playing story told earlier – an irony to which the Gypsies are very responsive, as we shall see.

In his speech the minister's use of the notion of 'family' is what Fernandez would term a 'strategic predication', in that it places a term with its associated moral/aesthetic qualities (the family) upon an inchoate pronoun (the 'we' that includes both the Gypsies and the minister) and through this aims to achieve a sense of moral coherence and agreement. The minister's intention and expectation are that he and the Gypsies inhabit the same 'quality space' (Fernandez 1986: 12–13) and that referring to 'the family' will move the Gypsies' thoughts and actions in an expected direction – a direction that holds implications for the grounds on which moral responsibility is felt and moral decisions are made.

Now, whilst it is very likely that the Gypsies present are sensitive to the minister's intentions – they are, after all, not the naive inhabitants of some distant, different culture, but sophisticated participants in the heterogeneous culture of north east England at the turn of the second millennium CE – they have also been equipped with the whys and wherefores to resist the minister's intended move. The Gypsies are able to refer to stories and a storytelling style that refuses the minister's move from the world of known others (the fire) to the world of imagined others (the dark) and so can refuse to grant the minister the moral authority he desires. The minister is attempting to place the Gypsies, and specifically Lizzy-Beth, in a story that extends beyond the face-to-face group and in doing this the minister's projected story goes against the grain of the Gypsies' social aesthetic standards. In other words, the minister's taken-for-granted understandings are not shared by the Gypsies he is addressing. This is further illustrated in the following passage, where the assumptions of the minister are challenged. Having introduced the service, himself and the context of the christening, the minister then goes into more detail about the particular beliefs that shape the world he expects the child has been born into, and again a degree of conflict between different notions of family and responsibility makes itself felt:

'Inasmuch as we believe that all who are born into this world are children of God we reverently acknowledge the fatherhood, the divine fatherhood of God.'

Here again the minister's use of 'we' is intended to be inclusive, to draw the Gypsies into some shared sense of community and common moral values. However, the 'we' is also, once again, vague or inchoate – it is not clear exactly who 'we' is. The minister's 'we' could refer both to the 'we' of the Christian church and the moral values defined by that group – abstract values made absolute. It could also refer to all those actually present at the christening, thus referring to an idea of community and morality that might be more familiar and acceptable to Gypsies – a face-to-face community similar to their sense of family. It is this articulated inchoateness that affords potential to move people through social space as it can form a strategic predication linking one group and its associated values (e.g. Gypsies) with another (e.g. the Christian church). However, this inchoateness also allows for contest as it highlights some of the different possibilities and so allows the Gypsies to move against the minister's rhetoric, which is what happens next.

In the above statement, the minister builds upon the idea that all those present at the service are members of the same family. He makes this explicit by placing 'God' as the father of all there – a claim that finds resistance amongst the Gypsies, who also find it amusing that Robert's claim to be the father of the child might be challenged. In fact it is the ambiguous nature of the 'we' that allows for Lizzy-Beth's father to interject and claim some control over how the inchoateness of the situation becomes formed:

> (*others talking, heckling quietly, inaudible on tape, laughter*)
> Father calls out: 'This child is all ours.'

In this interruption the ironic nature of the situation is remarked upon by Lizzy-Beth's father. The irony plays upon the discrepancy between the taken-for-granted assumptions of the minister that allow for the association of 'father' with something/somebody who is not directly known (God) and the Gypsies' experience of the world in which family relationships such as 'father' are limited to relationships between people who are directly known to one another. Specifically the minister's inclusive 'we', with its associated move towards acceptance of a set of moral values, is replaced by an exclusive 'ours', which resists the expected or intended move and so removes the moral expectations and values of the minister from those of the Gypsies.

The minister, however, ignores this interruption, choosing instead to build upon his preferred scenario – one that places all there within the same story (the projected story of Lizzy-Beth's life), a story based upon a set of social aesthetic standards that accepts 'reverently' the authority of God as a father figure. This set of social aesthetic standards incorporates ideas about moral responsibility and the grounds for moral decision making. Building on this, in his attempt to move the Gypsies in the direction of his thinking, the minister explicitly introduces the notion of parental responsibilities:

> 'Seeing that new responsibilities have come to the parents Robert, Katherine, of this child …'

The Gypsies, however, do not accept this move which is perhaps not surprising given the different ideas and attitudes that Gypsies have towards the carrying out of parental tasks, as discussed in chapter 5. Whilst the minister attempts to link the parental responsibilities of the people that the Gypsies accept as parents of the child to the acceptance of the authority of God and the associated inclusion in the same community as the minister, members of the Gypsy congregation continue to voice their challenge to this point of view:

> (*More heckling – someone calls*; 'Which parent?')

Despite the interruptions, the minister continues – and it is not clear whether he is choosing to ignore them because they challenge his views, or whether he is unaware that there might be a challenge to his views, his taken-for-granted assumptions about the world he imagines both he and the Gypsies share.

In his next statement the minister makes explicit his intention to place those present at the christening in a moral context, a context that acknowledges the authority of God, the figurehead of a moral community that extends beyond the known and experienced relationships that form the face-to-face community that the Gypsies know and prefer to move within. In order to do this, the minister does not rely only upon the metaphorical move that links the people present, through the idea of family, to a wider, 'imagined moral community' (Gullestad 2002: 59). In addition to this move, in the following statement the minister becomes quite explicit about the kind of mood that ought to be adopted – i.e. solemn, worthy and sacred – which is in sharp contrast to the laughing irreverence that has been displayed by the Gypsies so far:

(*Child is crying and mother says something to the minister*)

'Caitlin,[7] through the gift of this new child we solemnly rededicate our service to the presence of God and ask for his help worthily to fulfil these new and sacred duties.'

To the Gypsies present it is important that people can name and know their relatives; the idea of a family being something beyond that, in the unaccountable world, is somewhat absurd. What is more, the idea that the child is being welcomed into a 'family' that is wider than the known family and that includes strangers is seen as something of a threat – and something that they are only prepared to go along with for a short while. This is reinforced a little later in the service when the minister takes the baby in order to perform the baptism.

Caitlin passes the baby over to the minister who says:

'Lizzy-Beth, I baptise you' (*rest is inaudible as he leans over towards the little font and dips his fingers in the water, then draws a cross on her forehead with the water*)

The crowd shuffle about a bit with more talking, then someone calls out: 'Take your child back mate.'

The father says: 'Give her back, chief.'

The minister hands the baby back to Caitlin.

The exchanges above describe contested perspectives between sets of understanding about what the world is and what the values are in that world, as well as what projected storylines are being played out. Once the christening was over, Sarah took me to meet Caitlin, Lizzy-Beth's mother. In my brief conversation with her, the contrast between her own set of expectations and those of the minister was expressed. Caitlin's expectations relate not to some notion of community based upon an idea of a father in common; they are grounded in the importance of known people and bringing Lizzy-Beth into an experienced or 'unimagined' community (Lemon 2000), a community that was made up of people that

Lizzy-Beth would come to know. As Caitlin put it: 'We wanted her christened at the fair because we hadn't seen most of our friends all year because all the other fairs have been cancelled.'

Between the two sets of expectations expressed by the minister and by Caitlin concerning what the christening was about there is a degree of tension – there are different taken-for-granted understandings about what the christening is to achieve – and this is articulated in the different moods and behaviour of the crowd and the minister. There are also different understandings about what kind of cultural context it is taking place within. This is a tension between a notion of an 'imagined moral community' and a face-to-face community, where moral decisions are grounded in a knowledge of particular people. There is a difference in moral attitudes: the assumption from the church that one covers all – they can all become part of the family of God and thus subscribe to a moral code that stands good for all people at all times – as opposed to a more specific face-to-face morality governed by relationships of those you care for and who care for you.

Notes

1. It was because Naomi had commented that these people live in houses in County Durham that I asked the question referred to at the beginning of the passage.
2. 'Wannabes' is a term commonly used by Gypsies to describe people whom they consider not to be Gypsies but who want to become accepted as Gypsies.
3. In the second statement above, James and Rosaleen refer to people who live in 'accommodations'. This was their term for people who were in 'traditional' horse-drawn wagons, but ones that they had made themselves. This is itself something of an unclear distinction, as many of the Gypsies had made (or their relatives had made) their wagons. James and Rosaleen had earlier described the way that many of the people in the 'accommodations' at Yarm spend most of their time in houses and only come out to go to the fairs as if to show how they differ from 'real' Gypsies. In fact this pattern is common amongst many people recognised as Gypsies, including people from James's own family.
4. This is a significant strategy when set against discussions regarding what 'real' Gypsies look like, which we saw with Greg in chapter 3
5. I.e. they either share parents or have shared parenting.
6. I include the full transcript before examining it in more detail, because it gives a clearer sense of the context of the things that I shall be talking about.
7. It is evident from watching the video that the minister has got the name of the mother wrong, something that stresses the fact that he doesn't actually know the 'community' for which he is performing the service and in which he is including himself.

PART II
Summary

As we have seen in chapters 4 and 5, the importance of an intersubjective relationship is fundamental to the socialisation process through which we cross the 'cognitive gap'. Such a relationship, to work effectively, must incorporate more than a style of speech (for instance, the 'motherese' referred to in the work of various psychologists (see Trevarthen and Aitken 2000)); it must also incorporate certain emotive and affective actions. In these first intersubjective relationships, we are cared for and begin to learn how to care for others – a process that continues throughout the developing complexities of becoming an adult. In its connection to the parent-child relationship (parent being defined in the broad terms we have used above, rather than as a biological relationship), caring is first enacted and embodied in kinship relations – i.e. intimate relations of passing on ways of being-in-the-world that span generations.

Tension between continuing traditions of practice (those ways of being-in-the-world that we have been taught from our earliest pedagogical or parental relationships) and dealing with the changing world around us is often enacted in the arena that we call our family. This tension at least partly concerns how we are to express our caring for others and how we are to appreciate and acknowledge being cared for by others. As the world changes, so do the ways that we learn to live in that world, and so this tension also concerns how we live out the changes in 'technologies of the self', which Foucault so effectively documented for past times and cultures (Foucault 1979). It also concerns how we are to understand ourselves and those we are closest to amidst all those changes. These changes have been very effectively documented as regards changing family patterns in the West (Strathern 1992; Simpson 1994, 1997, 1998) and as regards the difficulties faced by those from emigrant or immigrant backgrounds (Bargach 2001; Karim 2001).

Amidst all these changes, Gypsies could be seen as a group who have deliberately isolated or excluded themselves, choosing to maintain traditional practices within a closed kinship group. This is not, however, the experience of the Gypsies that I have worked with on Teesside, and conversations with Gypsies from further afield suggest that such a view is not entirely reflective of their experience either. It is true, however, that, whilst the nuclear family appeared to become the norm and the focus of nurturing and caring relationships with the onset of the industrial revolution (Collier et al. 1982), Gypsies resisted this movement, choosing not to become involved in the wage labour of the growing industrial economies (Okely 1983: 36) and at the same time choosing to maintain an emphasis on the wider kin group as the focus of socialising relationships.

In the growing capitalist economies, responsibility for socialising children beyond the earliest years began to fall more to schools, and certainly older children were expected to participate in the corporate culture and find fulfilment through that (Rose 1999: 123ff.). Much of this was tied up with processes of formal education, which relied on the printed word and the ability to duplicate teaching materials so that people were all taught to 'sing from the same hymn book'. This process led to the emergence of 'imagined communities' (Anderson 1999) and the cultivation of a sense of belonging that reached beyond the interactions of the realm of direct experience and became thoroughly rooted in the 'realm of contemporaries'. Gypsies, however, resisted this and did not participate in the educational practices of the mainstream choosing to stay semi-literate – or, rather, choosing not to focus their teaching upon printed words and pictures. Perhaps this was choice, perhaps it was the result of the ways Gypsies had of making a living – moving around to carry out seasonal work on farms, to go to horse fairs to deal their horses, overwintering in the growing industrial centres, where they could sell their wares and deal in scrap metal and rags. But, whether by choice or default, the resulting lack of inclusion in the educational system was the same.

I have described one of the ways in which kinship is a site of the socialisation of children: it is where we are taught how to be and, as such, it is where we are taught various techniques of subjectivation. These techniques of subjectivation Foucault also called 'technologies of the self', and they relate to the ways in which we are taught and the ways we come to learn how to experience ourselves as subjects amongst other subjects. Faubion points out the implications such a notion has for the study of kinship, making the point that by learning how to place our selves relative to one another, thus defining and delimiting some of the qualities that comprise a self, we make it easier for us to articulate ourselves to one another and also to ourselves. As he puts it, the terms and categories of kinship and the parameters these place upon our relationships, whilst not ultimately determining or completely defining our 'self', enable us to live in a social world in a way that falls 'at least somewhat short of a constant and full-blown identity crisis' (Faubion 2001: 15).

I have described something of the social world that Lizzy-Beth was welcomed into, the kind of social world that other Gypsy children are also welcomed into – a world of face-to-face and particular relationships, a community that is directly experienced rather than imagined. However, Gypsies do not live in a world apart, and the tensions between different sets of understandings and associated moral values that are illustrated in the passages above have to be dealt with. In the behaviour of the Gypsies and the expressions of the minister, we can get a sense of how the 'quality space' of the Gypsies differs from that of the mainstream[1] without being explicitly opposed to it – for instance, there is an agreement that the family can provide a basis for a moral community and moral responsibility. Part of the learning process of becoming an adult Gypsy must incorporate strategies that allow the negotiation of such tensions. This is a very important part of Gypsiness, as was pointed out in the introduction, especially as regards the tension between 'real' Gypsies – or, in other words, Gypsies as an 'ideal type'– and those perceived as interlopers. The experience and negotiation of such tensions is an inevitable part of Gypsy life, as their understanding of morality rooted in face-to-face, experienced relationships challenges the assumptions of a hegemonic mainstream view that stresses 'imagined' or idealised relationships and fixed and abstractable moral codes.

Whilst their history might not be the same as that of the mainstream West, Gypsies' history is inevitably linked with it, and, just as all cultures continuously change and transform themselves, so too does Gypsy culture. The Gypsies that I work with struggle to imagine and make their relationships with one another and with non-Gypsies in ways that allow for change and also for the continuation of practices that create and maintain a sense of belonging. Their family structures are as complex and diverse as any documented in the 'unclear' (Simpson 1994, 1997, 1998) mainstream, and yet they are still Gypsy families, and what makes them Gypsy is the tradition of practice from which they have emerged and which includes a tradition of stories and storytelling that has provided a route for the socialising process through generations. This tradition of storytelling is grounded in a set of social aesthetic standards that focuses on the face-to-face group conceptualised as 'family'. This set of social aesthetic standards incorporates ideas and attitudes towards those not in that known group in such a way as to reinforce the relationship between the two, whereby, no matter what the behaviour or attitudes concerned, Gypsy and non-Gypsy always and necessarily inflect one another.

Notes

1. Although the minister is quite clearly a representative of a particular religious faith, I would argue that his views more accurately reflect those of the mainstream – i.e. those taught in schools and which form a reference point for the media, etc. – than they reflect the views or attitudes of Gypsies. Just what the mainstream, hegemonic view of Gypsies is will be further discussed in chapter 8, 'The Mediated Moral Imagination'.

PART III

THE DARK

If the lost word is lost, if the spent word is spent
If the unheard, unspoken
Word is unspoken, unheard;
Still is the unspoken word, the Word unheard,
The Word without a word, the Word within
The world and for the world;
And the light shone in darkness and
Against the Word the unstilled world still whirled

From T. S. Eliot, *Ash Wednesday*

We were silent for thousands of years
But our hearts are full
Of unuttered sentences,
Like a sea receiving
Blue river waters
All its life long

From 'The People With the Face of the Sun', Dezider Banga (Hancock et al. 1998: 11)

Part III
Introduction

In the previous section I explored the ways in which telling stories and the stories that are told constitute a social world that is distinctly Gypsy and which, at the same time, articulates with and inflects the non-Gypsy world. This is carried out in ways that are fluid and underdetermining, whilst still being recognisable as belonging to a tradition of practice. In the following section, I shall look at a similar process but from a rather different perspective. I shall concentrate on the ways that Gypsiness is told in the non-Gypsy world, again looking at the telling of and content of stories and how such stories are then implied in the everyday interactions of people who, for one reason or another and in one way or another, come into contact with Gypsies.

My intention is to put into operation the understandings we have gained so far, to see how the ways that we learn to 'do' intersubjectivity and our understandings of the wider context in which we learn to do this affect the ways in which we interact with one another. In the chapters that follow we see people struggling with the implications of what it means to care about one another – that is, what it means to matter to one another. We see people pulled in different directions whilst all the time attempting to achieve some consensus that will allow them to agree on a plan of action, to agree upon a way of building the world together. These are not the governed and governing subjects of systems of rules or regularities (Bourdieu and Wacquant 1992: 98), subjects created by the workings of systems of power (Rose 1996: 152). These are people who reflect upon their relations with one another, aware of the potential irony inherent in their relative positions (Rapport 2003: 42) and the creative challenge that such awareness imparts. However, just as these are not the determined subjects of structuralist (or post-structuralist) accounts of the social world, nor are they the autonomous, free-floating and projectile-like individuals of Rapport (ibid.). In the chapters that follow we see people acting consciously and self-consciously as agents who are acutely aware of, and take into account, the possible impact of their actions on others and of others' actions on them. Further, we see people who have learned to do this in particular ways and who draw upon this learning in order to achieve a joint project. Such a project might succeed or might fail, and is, furthermore, beyond the capacity of any one individual to achieve.

There is a desire in the history of anthropological investigations to provide generalised descriptions and understandings of cultures in accordance with the desire to show anthropological knowledge to be on a par with that obtained by the natural sciences. Thus far the understandings I have proposed are of two kinds. On the one hand, there are the general theories about the nature of human consciousness, the realms of consociates and contemporaries, the need for narrative structures and so on. On the other hand, there are the ethnographic descriptions of the lives and stories of people that I have worked with, most of whom are Gypsies. My intention in the section that follows is to explore the ways these two kinds of knowledge can work together in order to allow me to make sense of a situation and also to describe and explain that situation and the sense I have made of it to you. It is tempting to describe the tradition of practice of the Gypsies I have worked with and written about as indicative of the 'culture' of Gypsies in general. I must emphasise, however, that I do not want to generalise about Gypsiness in this way; instead, what I want to do is see how far the very specific knowledge gained through anthropological fieldwork can be used to illuminate more wide-ranging and generalised theories about human experience and especially those theories that I have drawn upon thus far.

Chapter 8

THE MEDIATED MORAL IMAGINATION

I noted in chapter 4 that stories are used to teach people how to be in the mainstream world (the dark), though not in the same way as they are used in the Gypsies' world. In this chapter I shall explore some of the ways that people from the mainstream are taught to know about Gypsies and the impact this has upon the actions of people from the world of the non-Gypsies when they enter those wastelands that are meeting points of different perspectives, understandings and interpretations and that are the ground for different motivations, intentions and actions.

In order to tell the stories of this section, I need to move away from the close, familiar world of Gypsies' storytelling into the world of the non-Gypsies – the unaccountable world that surrounds the light and heat of the fire. In so doing, I shall also move away from exploring ideas about family, though staying with an exploration of how people struggle to make or maintain for themselves a sense of belonging in a world that stretches out beyond the reach of everyday, interpersonal experience, into the realms of the imagined, the impersonal and the unknown. I show how a schematic understanding of what a Gypsy is becomes socially distributed through an imagined community – i.e. a community of people whose members need not necessarily be personally known to one another. I then demonstrate how such a schematic understanding is used to try to make sense of a particular situation – the situation that lay behind that inconclusive February meeting I referred to in the Introduction.

The Character of the Gypsy

Heath (1986) has shown how using books to tell children stories can encourage them to link those stories to a world that reaches beyond that of their immediate face-to-face environment and experience. In chapter 4 we saw how schoolteachers attempted to put this process into effect in a teaching situation with a group of Gypsy children. Heath demonstrated how in the mainstream world this process was more or less taken for granted; in this kind of environment, children soon learn to use books and the characters in the stories that they read to map on to the world around them. In this way, the types demonstrated by characters in books become attached to ideas about people in the world; in other words, if Gypsies are portrayed as romantic, mysterious and devious, then when we come across Gypsies in 'real life' we will interpret their behaviour accordingly.[1]

Edward Said noted that, when certain typical characteristics are repeated time after time, in a variety of genres and in a number of contexts, a 'strategic formation' comes into being that has 'density' (Said 1978: 20) and thereby seems to carry a self-evident truthfulness. This 'truthfulness' then allows for more such representations to be added to this body of knowledge, thus maintaining it and keeping it relevant in the contemporary world and available as a reference point when examining events in that world. Such a process has thoroughly embedded a schematic understanding about what a Gypsy is in the public culture of the UK today, which is available through and represented in museums, books, films, TV programmes and other media. In the section that follows, I shall demonstrate how a schematic understanding about what a Gypsy 'is' is contained and conveyed beyond the immediate face-to-face contexts we have looked at so far. Specifically, I shall draw attention to particular ideas about Gypsiness that are referred to later in the chapter when I look at these same themes as they are picked up and used in newspaper articles concerning the presence of Gypsies on Teesside. My intention is to be illustrative rather than exhaustive, to show how schematic understandings are carried through printed stories and so are made available to an imagined community. There are many examples of schematic understandings of Gypsiness in the printed word (see, for example, Kenrick and Clark 1999: 71–78); however, as my intention is to illustrate schematic understandings in print rather than to make a detailed study of them, those that follow provide sufficient background before going on to look at their use in the particular situation described through the newspapers.

Typifying representations of Gypsies reach back a considerable distance in time and so have grown deep roots in our cultural history. When looking at historical representations of Gypsies, we can see how the folk truths of the past are carried into the present. For instance, the following passage introduces Arnold's poem 'The Scholar Gipsy[2] in Palgrave's 'Golden Treasury' (Palgrave 1926 [1861]: 427) and is cited as coming from 'Glanvil's *Vanity of Dogmatizing* 1661':

> There was very lately a lad in the University of Oxford, who was by his poverty forced to leave his studies there; and at last to join himself to a company of vagabond gipsies. Among these extravagant people, by the insinuating subtilty of his carriage, he quickly got so much of their love and esteem as that they discovered to him their mystery. After he had been a pretty while well exercised in the trade, there chanced to ride by a couple of scholars, who had formerly been of his acquaintance. They quickly spied out

their old friend among the gipsies; and he gave them an account of the necessity which drove him to that kind of life, and told them that the people he went with were not such imposters as they were taken for, but that they had a traditional kind of learning among them, and could do wonders by the power of imagination, their fancy binding that of others: that himself had learned much of their art, and when he had compassed the whole secret, he intended, he said, to leave their company, and give the world an account of what he had learned.

Depictions of Gypsies go even further back than this to the court of Henry VIII, who passed a law expelling 'Egyptians' from the country and introducing the death penalty for anyone who was found guilty of being a Gypsy (Hancock et al. 1998: 36). For my purposes, however, it is sufficient to go back to 1661, when even then it would appear that Gypsies were associated with ideas about mystery, secrets and vagabonds. What is more they were also seen as objects of curiosity – something that could be studied and then related to the non-Gypsy, educated world – and a people who were accused (possibly unfairly) of being impostors. Some 200 years later, Arnold uses such associations in the poem itself:

And near me on the grass lies Glanvil's book –
    Come, let me read the oft-read tale again!
      The story of that Oxford scholar poor,
    Of shining parts and quick inventive brain,
      Who, tired of knocking at preferment's door,
        One summer morn forsook
His friends, and went to learn the gipsy lore,
    And roam'd the world with that wild brotherhood,
    And came, as most men deem'd, to little good,
But came to Oxford and his friends no more.

But once, years after, in the country-lanes,
    Two scholars whom at college erst he knew
      Met him, and of his way of life inquir'd.
    Whereat he answer'd, that the gipsy crew,
      His mates, had arts to rule as they desired
        The workings of men's brains;
And they can bind them to what thoughts they will.
    'And I,' he said, 'the secret of their art,
    When fully learn'd, will to the world impart;
But it needs heaven-sent moments for this skill!'

But what – I dream! Two hundred years are flown
    Since first thy story ran through Oxford halls,
      And the grave Glanvil did the tale inscribe
    That thou wert wander'd from the studious walls
      To learn strange arts, and join a gipsy tribe.

Arnold's romantic imagining of Gypsies ties the mysteriousness of Glanvil's account to ideas linking Gypsies to nature and the divine realms of Heaven – they are the epitome of the 'wild Other', both dangerous and desirable, that is still so often repeated in our present-day imaginings of 'real' Gypsies (for a fuller description of this 'othering' of Gypsies, see Okely 1983: 201ff.; Greenfields 2003). If Arnold's poem shows us what Gypsies have that the mainstream doesn't have, the following excerpt shows us what they have that the mainstream doesn't want:

> Miss Smith, and Miss Bickerton … had walked out together, and taken a road – the Richmond road, which, though apparently public enough for safety, had led them into alarm. About half a mile beyond Highbury, making a sudden turn, and deeply shaded by Elms on each side, it became for a considerable stretch very retired; and when the young ladies had advanced some way into it, they had suddenly perceived, at a small distance before them, on a broader patch of greensward by the side, a party of gipsies. A child on the watch came towards them to beg; and Miss Bickerton, excessively frightened, gave a great scream, and calling on Harriet to follow her, ran up a steep bank, cleared a slight hedge at the top, and made the best of her way by a short cut back to Highbury. (From *Emma*, Jane Austen 1996 [1816]: 299)

Of course, children are not generally taught about the world by reading to them extracts from Glanvil, or Arnold's poetry, or Jane Austen's novels – though television period dramas have made these last more accessible. Instead, children are taught about Gypsies through products aimed specifically at children that reflect the knowledge and understandings of the adult society into which they are becoming socialised. The following excerpt is taken from an award-winning children's book set in the late twentieth century:

> Mind you, my great-great-grandad, Snowy Coward, was … a horse-dealer and he married this gypsy woman called Queenie who was in the same line of trade. They had rows and a baby who was my great-grandad …, then her real husband, another gypsy man, turns up. And Snowy, being a Coward, chucks him out of the window and he lands on his head, dead. Snowy was hanged at Lancaster Castle. The baby was brought up by neighbours and I expect Queenie went back to the gypsies. I'm not sure.

> Dad and Chunder don't really like me talking about this – having a streak of gypsy blood. But you can see it, especially in my dad. He's got black curly hair, and blue eyes that go black when he loses his rag, but just before he goes mad, his eyes go sort of milky, calm and milky. (Janni Howker 1985: 13)

Such a passage draws upon a long history of representations of Gypsies without which it would not make a lot of sense. In order to understand it the reader needs to know what is meant by a 'gypsy' and the need to be able to relate this to ideas about Gypsiness being carried in blood, being associated with some kind of latent violence and manifesting in physical attributes such as black curly hair.

Of course, the typifying representation of Gypsies is not confined to literature; it permeates the whole culture and similar examples of the characterisation of Gypsies can be found throughout folk tales and songs and nursery rhymes. Imagine the impact of such representations as those above when put together with traditional skipping rhymes such as:

My mother said I never should
Play with the Gypsies in the wood
If I did
She would say
Naughty girl to disobey (Trad. skipping rhyme)

The impact of such portrayals leads to a deep-rooted acceptance of the nature of Gypsies. We have had passed down to us an idea of the Gypsy as a type, a type that populates the mainstream culture and that we come to believe (as we come to believe that characters in books can be mapped on to real people in the experienced world) has some basis in what individual Gypsies really are like. It becomes a kind of self-evident truth that Gypsies are violent, or at least threatening, that they aren't to be trusted, that they have dark curly hair, that there is something mysterious about them. Such associations create a schematic understanding about what a Gypsy is.

We have already seen schematic understandings in operation with the conversation of James and Rosaleen in chapter 7 and their depiction of the relationship between Gypsies and gorgios and all the possible variations, including contradictions, that that can entail. The schematic understanding of Gypsy amongst the mainstream operates in a similar sort of way, again incorporating contradictory depictions and points of view, and again enabling an inflected (rather than oppositional) relationship between Gypsies and non-Gypsies to be played out in interactions.

As we have seen from the exchanges with the minister at the Yarm christening, both Gypsies and non-Gypsies need to have ways of taking into account the fact that there are people around who do things differently. For the Gypsies that I worked with, this is done, at least in part, through building up a vision of the world whereby those outside the immediate face-to-face group are characterised as being in (and coming from) a strange, unaccountable and potentially dangerous world, and this forms part of their schematic understanding of what a non-Gypsy is. For non-Gypsies the mainstream print and broadcast media draw upon a schematic understanding of 'Gypsy' and thereby reinforce its influence and perpetuate its use in describing and understanding Gypsies as a type – people who exist in the world of contemporaries and ideal types but who are not known in any relationship of direct communication. In this way, most people's understanding and knowledge of Gypsies are mediated by the media, both in the sense of having an 'go-between' and in the sense used by Wertsch (1991) concerning tools and the processes of pedagogy.

I have shown how we learn patterns of expectation that, like the stories with which we learn, are open and unpredictable by nature but from which we can internalise a sense of 'rightness' or 'fit'. These patterns of expectation are connected to the world that we live in. So we learn about Gypsies from stories we are told about them, and this teaches us what to expect from Gypsies and also what we might expect to do – how we might expect to react (and expect others to react) to them. Let us see how these stories are implied and put together in newspaper reports in order to generate expectations about the 'right' things that should happen about the situation that led to the meeting with which I began.

An Unfolding Story

Towards the end of 2001, a month or so after we had returned from Whitby but before Yarm Fair, a situation began to develop concerning one of the local authorities, members of the housed (non-Gypsy) community, owners of local businesses and a small group of Gypsies. The Gypsies were trying to find somewhere to stay; the local official site was closed but they still wanted to stay in the area as they had family living there and there was also the promise of some work. At first, the Gypsies moved on to the council car park, as they hoped that the nearby site would soon be opened. The site was indeed opened, but some families moved on whom others didn't get on with; those who didn't want to move on to the site moved further afield to a patch of land that had been used by their families as a stopping place for many years.

Whilst this was happening the council was trying to identify some land that could be allocated for use as a transit site; they had already accepted that there needed to be more than one site in the area because different groups of travelling people didn't necessarily get on with one another. The piece of land that the Travellers moved to who didn't want to settle on the official site was one of those up for consideration as a transit site. A council subcommittee was established to deal with the situation and decide how to proceed, and this subcommittee decided that it would pilot the idea of using the land as a transit site and provide portable toilets, water and rubbish collections. Before this decision could be implemented, however, it had to be agreed by the council's executive committee, on which sat representatives of departments that had few or no direct dealings with Gypsies, along with elected members whose constituencies rarely had Travellers in evidence. Instead of being agreed at the executive committee, the decision was deferred pending the establishment of a larger working group on which would be representatives of all departments potentially concerned with the situation. In the meantime, the Gypsies stayed on the land without water, toilets or rubbish collections.

Eventually, at the beginning of 2002 and after a number of meetings, a compromise was reached whereby the Gypsies would be allowed to stay on the land. Facilities and services would be provided in return for the Gypsies signing an agreement of 'good behaviour' that would last for fifty-six days after which the decision would be revisited and possibly revised. Non-Gypsies who owned businesses, or rented allotments, or lived nearby got wind of the council's decision to provide these services. They also discovered that the council was considering making the piece of land into a transit site to be used by Gypsies and Travellers passing through the area – in many ways formalising the situation that already existed as the land was regularly used as a stopping place anyway. This is how one local newspaper reported the decision:[3]

Gipsy camp anger vented

Angry opposition has been fired at a Teesside Council over an illegal gipsy site.

Residents and firms want a reassurance from Redcar and Cleveland Council that the camp site, set up illegally by gipsies at Sandstown, near Redcar, will not become permanent.

The council's executive board heard that gipsies had set up camp despite there being an official site at Bankside. Now residents and businesses have fired a protest letter to the council, along with a 280-signature petition, expressing their 'absolute disagreement and total disgust' about the site.

'A properly constructed and wholly adequate site already exists in Bankside and the council has therefore met its legal obligation,' adds a letter accompanying the petition. Residents say they have heard 'a suggestion' the site could become permanent.

A partner in one of the firms in the area, who asked not to be named for fear of reprisals, said they recently lost a contract due to the 'condition' of the surrounding land.

'This contract was worth approximately £300,000 per annum and it is unlikely we will be able to win it back, which may result in us having to lay off five staff,' he added.

One resident, who asked not to be named, said: 'Now the council has provided all the amenities, including cleaning up the site, there is absolutely no reason for the travellers ever to leave.'

But a Teesside Council spokesman said: 'The official site at Bankside is full and there are a number of families who have set up at Sandstown. We are in dialogue with them and we will be providing water, toilets and organising refuse collection. In return they are signing an agreement on their behaviour.'

He added if they fail to comply with the agreement, the authority would seek enforcement action against them.

The spokesman added: 'It's not going to be a permanent site.'

Councillors ... are now planning to visit the site to meet the gipsies next week.

Cllr … said councillors are trying to arrange a public meeting to discuss the situation.

'We will be asking them to be good neighbours,' said Cllr. (*Middlesbrough Evening Gazette*, 29 January 2002)

Let us consider the various positions of the people the report is about – the Gypsies, the council (both elected members and officers) and local (non-Gypsy) residents and business owners. The aim is to catch a glimpse of the inchoate situation behind the story and also catch a glimpse of the ways in which people try to grab hold of that inchoateness and give it some sort of form that will render themselves and others mutually intelligible.

At first sight, we have three perspectives ranged in relationship to one another in the description of a situation where, on the one hand, there are the Gypsies, on the other, there are the non-Gypsy residents and firms, and trying to reach some kind of accommodation between the two is the council. The report then outlines some of the background to the story – the camp at Sandstown, the petition and letter of protest, the 'suggestion' that the site may become permanent. In the first instance, the fact that this story centres on the presence of 'gipsies'[4] is of fundamental importance, and without an understanding of all the possible implications of 'gipsy' the report would not make much sense. Schematic understandings about Gypsies put the report into a wider context, framing the residents' 'absolute disagreement and total disgust' and the 'fear of reprisals' of one of the business partners, for instance.

Examining in more detail the reported words of the resident, we can see the ways in which a schematic understanding of Gypsiness can be used both to make sense of a situation and to allow for what seem to be contradictory understandings. When the resident says, 'Now the council has provided all the amenities, including cleaning up the site, there is absolutely no reason for the travellers ever to leave.' they are in fact drawing on conflicting ideas that are contained within a single schematic understanding. For a start, the implication is that Travellers are a nuisance and that the council should not be helping them – it should not be providing amenities and clearing up for them. This draws upon notions about Gypsies being undesirable, being lawbreakers, being people who want something for nothing and so on. The second part of the statement voices a belief that, now they have got what they wanted, they will stay. If we look at this in the light of schematic understandings about 'real' Gypsies and so on, we can see that there is an implicit suggestion that these people are not 'real' Gypsies, because 'real' Gypsies travel and these people will want to stay. These conflicting points of view can be used to construct an understanding of the situation and what should be done about it without ever having to deal directly with the assumptions about 'real' Gypsies and their desirability (or not), which remain implicit – it is up to each reader to draw these conclusions themselves. So it is that the reported words of the unnamed resident are charged with little extracts of schematic understandings.

It would seem, at first glance, as if the newspaper is merely and matter-of-factly reporting the situation – the perspectives of the newspaper and the reporter aren't obviously present in the report at all. However, the reporter is choosing to write the situation, drawing upon a stock of stories, which, combined, provide a schematic understanding about Gypsies and what happens when a story has a Gypsy in it – and in doing this they also serve to reinforce such schematic understandings. For a start, by the time we read what the anonymous resident said, the report is already framed – first by the choice of headline and, secondly, by the opening sentence which reads: 'Angry opposition has been fired at a Teesside council over an illegal gipsy site.' From the outset the report places non-Gypsies in opposition to the council. This position can then be expanded to show how the council have sided with the Gypsies and are allowing those Gypsies to break the law. Indeed, the Gypsies are presented as being on the wrong side of the law, a portrayal that reflects many stories about the nature of Gypsies. This last is, however, evidence of the way the reporter uses schematic ideas to make a story (rather than simply reporting 'facts'), as the unauthorised camp at Sandstown is not as yet illegal in that no moves have been made to ask the Gypsies to leave.

So here we have an unresolved situation that is formed into a story through the use of story seeds or minimal narratives. As Carrithers notes, 'when a minimal narrative finds resonance in listeners, it is because it calls up familiar information, familiar motives, familiar story lines' (Carrithers 2003). Telling a story in this way allows this same situation to be taken and told by the newspaper's readers in a way that connects it to the knowledge they already have about Gypsies and councils and so on, thus both deploying and reinforcing the schematic understandings that the newspaper's readers already have.

We can relate this telling of an inchoate situation to ideas we have previously explored about the link between stories and the ethics in which we ground moral decisions. This report concerns a situation that is being told for the reporter's contemporaries, not consociates – the writer does not know who will read the story. This being the case it is couched in terms of an 'ethic of right' – an ethic that, as we have seen, applies to an imagined community. In these terms, the idea of 'the law' has considerable influence – the idea that there is a moral code that everybody should subscribe to. Drawing upon what is known about Gypsies as a type enables the portrayal of these particular Gypsies as going against the accepted code of ethical or moral behaviour. This reinforces what might already be expected by a readership who have been taught to understand Gypsies as people who do indeed break the law –again part of a socially distributed schematic understanding of what a Gypsy is.

Of course, the way snippets of schematic understandings are used to help form the situation into a story is only one part of how the situation becomes moulded into something that can both explain past actions and inform future ones. The story as initially formed does not reflect how the people who represent the council see themselves, as becomes apparent later in the report when the words of a council representative are quoted: 'The official site at Bankside is full and there are a number of families who have set up at Sandstown.' Here the council officer doesn't mention Gypsies (at least as he is reported) instead he talks about 'families' thus drawing on a schematic understanding that refers to ideas about family life and responsibilities, care and so on. If his word 'families' was replaced by the word 'Gypsies' the sentence would carry a very different kind of moral tone and the expectations associated with his words would also be different. By using the word 'families' the tone shifts to suggest that there might be a reason for the Gypsies to be there and – probably more importantly for the purposes of this scenario – that there might be a reason for the council to allow them to stay there. We have already seen that the idea of 'family' is one that is used to carry ideas about morality and moral responsibility. In the words of the council officer quoted in the newspaper report there is a suggestion that the council is trying to do 'the right thing' in supporting 'families'.

Mention of 'families' carries with it a suggestion of a possibility that the Gypsies in question are human beings who care for one another, who build up family relationships and who have feelings and emotions that can be attached to the establishment of such relationships. This is recognised by a councillor who becomes included in the story as follows:

Councillors ... are now planning to visit the site to meet the gipsies next week.

Cllr ... said councillors are trying to arrange a public meeting to discuss the situation.

'We will be asking them to be good neighbours,' said Cllr ...

So the councillors are actually going to try and get to know the Gypsies on a more personal basis. There is an assertion that one possible way to resolve these problems lies in face-to-face contact, with the implication that the Gypsies' behaviour might be influenced by meeting with them in the intersubjective realm rather than leaving them known only as representatives of a type.

As if this situation isn't complex enough, the reporter has preceded the residents' words with those of someone who has a different, though complementary, perspective and associated moral ideas – the point of view of a 'partner in one of the firms in the area'. Apparently this firm has lost a contract worth approximately £300,000 because of the 'condition' of the surrounding land. What exactly this 'condition' is the report does not say – it is implied that the land is dirty and unkempt because the Gypsies have made it like that. Of course the associated suggestion is that before the Gypsies arrived the land was in a clean condition – whereas it was a semi-derelict, semi-industrial wasteland that was regularly used for fly-tipping. At no time is it explicitly claimed that the contract was lost because of the actions, or even the mere presence, of the Gypsies. This claim is implied by including the businessman's statement in the context of a report about the problem of Gypsies being on an illegal camp. This partner is reported as saying: 'it is unlikely we will be able to win it back, which may result in us having to lay off five staff'. As with all the other statements in the newspaper story, this comment carries a number of unstated expectations and suggests a number of stories that can be built upon by the reader in order to understand the moral values that are being threatened by the Gypsies. In this instance, these stories include those of the workers who might have to be laid off by the firm that lost the contract; by placing the stories of these workers in a report about Gypsies camping illegally on a piece of land, the suggestion is made that it is the Gypsies that have caused (or will cause if nothing is done to stop it) the redundancies of workers. In this way, ideas about how Gypsies' behaviour threatens 'ordinary people' from the mainstream is both drawn upon and reinforced.

What we have, then, is a variety of perspectives and an associated assortment of possible stories that could be told, depending upon which point of view you adopt – and, as we have already seen, stories carry ideas about ethics and the possible and proper moral decisions that can and/or should be made.

We can see that what the newspaper's report is doing is drawing upon an assumed knowledge of 'types' of people and an associated understanding of the motives and intentions of those types in order to present a story to a mass and anonymous readership. In order to do this, the reporter needs to draw upon a knowledge of types that she shares with her imagined readership. It is this shared understanding of the 'typical' world that makes the mainstream with which I have so far juxtaposed Gypsies. In order to reach this level of assumed (or imagined) sharedness, people need to share an education that teaches them the same things about the various types of people there are in the world. The stories we are told about Gypsies form part of this education – whether formal or informal – and provides a basis for knowing about Gypsies without necessarily knowing any Gypsies.

One thing stands out: the perspective the reporter has as concerns the Gypsies is very different from any of those we have looked at so far – whether residents, businessmen, councillors or council officers. Whilst the report is about the effect of there being Gypsies in an area, the Gypsies themselves are not represented in the report. This being the case, we can only guess what their story might be as it is told 'between the lines' of the other stories that are being told by the reporter. The Gypsies are both excluded from and unable to exert any control over the ways that they are represented in this story. Such a lack of control comes less from an inability to engage in the making and broadcasting of such stories and more from being placed in a position whereby all individual Gypsies' behaviour (and indeed their mere presence) is always already defined and interpreted. Gypsies are already 'framed' and such framing is replicated and reinforced by the framing of particular situations including the reporting of 'facts' by newspapers.

The Story Continues

This is how things stood in January 2002. Let us now catch up with it a little while later and see how the various stories have panned out. By March the developing situation around the unauthorised encampment was beginning to develop into something of a saga. On the face of things, it seemed as though very little had happened since January: the Gypsies were still on the patch of land, the neighbouring residents and businesses were still complaining. Council departments were at an impasse, being unable to agree between themselves on the best way forward: was their responsibility to the residents, the businesses, the Gypsy families or what? In fact, whilst little had actually changed in terms of who was where and doing what, there had been a great deal of fevered activity behind the scenes in the council and amongst the local residents. Council protocol meant that the petition referred to in the report had to be acknowledged and a plan of action for dealing with the complaint had to be agreed upon. This decision again had to be heard by the council's Executive Committee at a meeting where both petitioners and the press would be present. The day after this meeting was held, the *Evening Gazette* carried a report under the headline: 'Residents happy as illegal site faces closure: GIPSIES MUST GO'.

As with the report discussed above, the first sentence frames the context of the report: 'Gipsies are living on borrowed time at an illegal Teesside site after councillors ruled they must move out.' When we compare this first, framing, sentence of the report with that of the earlier report, we can see that the perspective has shifted. In the first report, residents and firms are angry with the council because they have been perceived as doing the wrong thing regarding the 'illegal' site. In the second report, the council seem to have shifted their stance to move into a position that is pitched against the Gypsies. It appears as if the residents and firms – perhaps partly through the ways their stories have been told by the newspaper – have won the council round so that it is now allied with the residents and firms against the Gypsies and their 'illegal' activities.

The report goes on to detail the story as it developed from the point of view of the two main groups in this particular frame – the petitioners (residents and business owners) and the councillors, who had overturned the earlier decision to allow the Gypsies to stay while things were sorted out regarding the official site and a potential transit site. Again, the perspective of the Gypsies is absent from the report, which only notes comments made about the Gypsies.

There had, however, been a good deal of talk amongst the Gypsies who were at the unauthorised camp, and who were trying to figure out how they wanted to act in this particular situation. We have already seen how Gypsies aren't simply passive members of an unreflective community and we have also seen how they are portrayed by the mainstream culture. Gypsies are aware of how they are portrayed and they are also well practised in resisting such portrayals when the opportunity arises, as we saw with the heckling at the christening. Friedrich (2001: 232) points out how Gypsies and other marginalised groups are particularly sensitive to the irony of their situation and how such irony involves an asymmetrical and contested power relationship that is played out in actions unfolding in time. As the story about the 'illegal' camp developed, the resisting voice of the Gypsies became more obvious and the irony inherent in their own 'framed' situation was acted out in the public world of newspapers and the events that they report.

A week or so after the second report above was printed one of the group of Gypsies decided to enter the game and contacted the newspaper. This time the story had the headline: 'Gipsies' fury over site state: WE'VE BEEN DUMPED ON'. This headline immediate underlines an ironic perspective, having for the first time actually spoken to some of the Gypsies that the whole story is about. The suggestion is that it is not the Gypsies who 'dump' (and it is very significant that this word has so many meanings associated with rubbish, waste and excrement (see Sibley 1995)); it is the non-Gypsy world who do that, whilst the Gypsies have to put up with the mess that the mainstream world leaves behind.

The opening sentence of this article states: 'A gipsy family living on an official site is claiming their new home is a rat-infested disgrace.' In the first report discussed where we saw both residents and firms (and the newspaper reporter) referring to 'gipsies' and then a council spokesman referring to 'families'. In that first report ideas about 'gipsies' and 'families' were used to delineate different sets of moral action – the first illegal, the second responsible and caring. In this report, these two moralities are linked together and so afford a move of 'Gypsies' from their separate and mysterious, 'illegal' world, to the mainstream world of families and associated family responsibilities. The report suggests that these Gypsies are going along with the legal obligation to live either in houses or on an official site. Compare this opening sentence with those of the previous two articles, which both noted the 'illegal' nature of the Gypsy camp they were referring to. This movement is one that has been generated by the Gypsies concerned. Aware of the newspaper reports and drawing upon their knowledge of the non-Gypsy world, they decided to become involved in having some say over the way the situation was formed into a story and so the way in which decisions will be taken and actions implemented. Hence a further difference between this report and the previous two is, of course, that this time the Gypsy story is presented directly in the same way that the points of view of the residents and so on were presented in the previous reports.

This move from one schematic understanding (that of 'gipsies') to another (that of families) is accomplished partly by the juxtaposition of 'gipsy' with 'family' and it is also reflected in that juxtaposition. However, given their sophisticated sensitivity to the way the mainstream world frames their Gypsiness, it is not surprising to know that what is going on is a great deal more complex and sophisticated than that. The larger family group – of which this particular 'gipsy family' was a part – was still living on the 'illegal' site and those who had moved on to the official site still went back and spent a great deal of their time at Sandstown. They had decided to appear to move to the official site in an attempt to force the council's hand, as they felt that they might actually be provided with more services and the transit site they wanted. With this in mind, they approached the newspaper to tell their side of the story.

In the story, there are two different perspectives being positioned in relation to one another – the Gypsies on the one hand and the council on the other. The movement in the story shows how these two, whilst not being polarised, are somehow antipathetic to one another and the route to reconciliation lies in the actions and choices of individual Gypsies – in this case Joseph Farrow – who chose to cross the divide. The council in return is represented from the Gypsies' perspective as owing something in exchange for the Gypsies' cooperation. These two perspectives are shown, for instance, in the following statements from the story:

'The council asked us to move from Sandstown and we were told it was a lovely site but we were wrongly led – I wish we'd never moved now. We shouldn't have to live like that.'

Mr Farrow has promised to sign a council contract but is pressing for the site to be cleared up: 'We've done as they've asked and moved here but it's not fit for anyone to live here at the moment.'

Telling the Story 'Our' Way – the Various Faces of 'We' and 'They'

When we looked in detail at the exchanges at the christening on Yarm high street in chapter 7, we saw how shifting pronouns, such as 'we' and 'they', are used in order to try and move the thoughts, opinions and ensuing actions of people in a particular, desired direction. We also saw that the effectiveness or otherwise of such strategies depends upon a certain level of shared and taken-for-granted understandings of the world. Here again, we can see a similar process in operation, this time not only directed at the people who are involved in the interaction but also projected out (via the newspaper) to an imagined community in an attempt to influence particular political decisions. This is important as it is the political institution of the local authority that is able to make the necessary decisions and it is also the opinion of a non-face-to-face public (expressed, for instance, in the form of a petition) that needs to be changed in order for the Gypsies' preferred results to be achieved.

The extract above could be read as referring in the first instance to a 'we' that includes all the Gypsies at Sandstown, and in some ways Mr Farrow does seem to have assumed the role of a spokesperson for all the Gypsies involved. He is also using himself and the 'we' of the group who moved away from Sandstown with him in order to highlight the shabby way they have been treated by the 'they' of the council: Mr Farrow speaks for a 'we' that have acted in response to the council's requests and have thereby been somehow deceived – 'wrongly led' – by the council's 'they'. Carrying this point further, Mr Farrow represents both a particular individual's experience and a more generalised human experience of being let down by an institution that has a moral obligation not to let him (or others) down; thus he reflects the same kind of perspective initially attributed to the residents at Sandstown, who were angry at the way they had been let down by the council.

This scenario also fits the stories that Gypsies have learned and that we explored in the previous section – people outside the 'we' group have behaved in a duplicitous way and exposed the Gypsies to danger. As the report quotes Mr Farrow earlier:

> But Joseph Farrow, who moved to the Bankside site on Tuesday with his family, claims the area is not fit for humans.
>
> He says the place is full of vermin, there is human faeces on the ground and hanging wires from electricity boxes are posing a danger to children.

Whilst reports in the newspaper about the illegal activities of Gypsies, the ways they make problems for people and so on reinforce the stories about Gypsies that are taught in the mainstream, this account reflects and reinforces the kinds of stories that Gypsies tell. For instance, it fits with ideas about the questionable and threatening moral nature of the non-Gypsy world. Here Mr Farrow is also using the same kinds of associations and devices as the non-Gypsy world – the association of faeces and danger, for instance – in order to place himself with his family in a particular position, with moral overtones, in relation to the world of non-

Gypsies. Here we get a perspective referring to a storytelling tradition that diverges from that of the mainstream and hence has a different slant on the events that have led up to the story – including the conscious and deliberate actions of Joseph Farrow. This leads to a difference of view that is not diametrically opposed to the other points of view, but that does differ from it in substantial ways.

Whilst Mr Farrow orients himself and his actions (at least as they are reported by the newspaper) towards his known 'we', which is contrasted with an unknown and untrustworthy 'they', the other perspective – that of the council – refers to an institutional and imagined 'we', which is contrasted with the lumped together 'they' of the Gypsies. This is the first time that these two perspectives have been juxtaposed. As we have seen, the Gypsies' story and the associated tradition of stories and storytelling have been absent from the reports so far. What we then get to see through the means of this report is a picture of far more complicated goings-on than we might have first thought. This is not simply a story about the rights and wrongs of Gypsies occupying a particular piece of land; this is about the various kinds of rights and wrongs there can be, the associated responsibilities and expectations, and the actions that ensue from the different perspectives and how they come together in a complex and intricate 'dance', which is then reported by the newspaper. The council's role (and therefore that of both council officer and councillor) is to navigate a way between many potentially conflicting responsibilities and come up with a solution that will satisfy all. The following statement outlines some of the responsibilities and expectations associated with the council: 'A council spokesman said the authority had to strike a balance between maintaining good relations with the gipsy community and adhering to responsibilities as a landlord and public authority.' And later:

'We want good relationships with the gipsies but there's a balance to be struck and we also have to maintain our responsibilities as a landowner and as a council.

'We hope to liaise closely with the gipsy community to make sure we can develop policies which help us work together effectively.'

Such positioning and reporting of the story only really make sense if the anticipated readership of the story shares the accepted understandings about what a Gypsy is, what a council is, where moral responsibility lies and so on. This sharing of understandings about the world has been referred to as a 'community of interpretation' (Schrøder 1994: 344); in other words, the readership shares an interpretative scheme (Schutz 1972: 122), whilst those who speak to the newspaper reporters and the reporters themselves share an expressive scheme (ibid.) and these schemes combine in, for instance, shared schematic understandings about what a Gypsy is. What is particularly notable here, however, is that, in reporting the Gypsies' side of the story, there is evidence not only of different and contrasting schematic understandings in operation, but that in drawing upon their schematic understandings Gypsies can still be aware of and take into consideration the shared understandings of the non-Gypsy world. So here again we see a situation whereby Gypsy and non-Gypsy inflect one another, implying a mutual awareness, and not necessarily an opposition. This suggests something more of a 'community of improvisation', whereby there is a shifting of ideas and perspectives within a shared cultural landscape (Machin 1994; Machin and Carrithers 1996).

Discussion

There are (at least) two ways to analyse this sequence of events. First, we can look at the way that the newspaper reports what is happening and analyse it with regard to the ways that the modern media produce and construct events and so influence the actions and ideals of people in society. Secondly, we can look at the events that are being reported and see how these are affected by the attitudes of society at large, or how they are influenced by different attitudes held by different communities of practice within the society.

The first views the press as it relates to a 'community of interpretation', expecting that the reporters in the newspaper are directing their writing towards a particular imagined community that shares sets of understandings about how to interpret and understand what is being written. In many ways, this would seem to accurately reflect what we have seen: the newspaper reporters are quite clearly able to draw upon sets of shared understanding about the nature of Gypsies, expectations about the responsibilities of a council and so on. However, this is not enough; in this story the press is itself, along with the reporters, drawn into the sequence of events when Joe Farrow decides to go to them to tell his story the way he wants it told and with reference to his understanding about the nature of the world and the immoral character of non-Gypsies. Here we can see that the press, and specifically the reporters writing the stories, are participants in a 'community of improvisation' (Machin and Carrithers 1996), whereby shared landmarks – for instance, dirt, responsibility, law – are improvised around. This improvisation is carried out, at least in part, by the deployment of shared schematic understandings – understandings that are used by individuals and the media, and in so being used they become reinforced. In this way schematic understandings are perpetually distributed amongst an imagined community and are also internalised by people who either experience the situation that is being reported or who can relate the reported story to their own experience and knowledge. All these various interests and perspectives – both individuals and institutions, both experienced and imagined – are drawn together into a single storyline that has no clear beginning and no clear end and no suggestion of ultimate resolution.

In conclusion, we can see an incredibly complex interplay of processes involving ideas and actions, which, while providing some common ground –a shared cultural landscape – do not in themselves determine any specific course of events. Rather, such a cultural landscape provides a resource that people draw from in order to perform their actions within unfolding and open-ended storylines. In order to do this people also draw from shared sets of social aesthetic standards, which include schematic understanding about types of people (for instance, Gypsies), institutions (for instance, councils) and ideas carrying moral value (such as 'family'). Such understandings are especially important when the storyline is projected into, or told to, the world of the 'imagined community', whether that be a newspaper's readership or a councillor's electorate. There is, however, an underlying awareness that these schematic understandings cannot account for or determine people's behaviour, their actions and interactions in the face-to-face and intersubjective realm of consociates. Hence the councillors are aware that the situation might change if they talk to actual, individual Gypsies. Also, the way the overall story is reported changes when Gypsies talk to reporters. Similarly council officers point towards the actions of particular Gypsies when they feel a need to challenge the way their responsibilities are 'typically' seen by an imagined community of residents or businesses.

In this chapter, I have shown how schematic understandings can be carried in printed stories and so help to create and confirm a kind of 'general consciousness' about, for instance, what a Gypsy is. This schematic understanding of Gypsiness consists of themes and ideas that are used creatively in the construction of new stories, where whoever is doing the telling is trying to encourage a particular result to come about (the Gypsies might be told to leave by the council, the council might provide a better site for the Gypsies, etc.). So far, we have seen this happening through the pages of a newspaper and, through this, I have documented the situation the council was faced with when it called the meeting with which I began this book. In the following chapter, we shall see even more explicitly how schematic understandings about Gypsiness are used in face-to-face interaction. The illustrations of a schematic understanding with which I began this chapter appear in many ways to be fixed – we cannot rewrite the stories – and indeed the ways that the themes were used by the newspapers seem to reinforce a fixed idea about Gypsiness. In the next chapter, we shall see how the apparently static understandings of the printed word become vital and malleable as they are used by people in face-to-face interaction. I shall examine one such interaction in order to cast more light into that 'dark' (and ultimately inchoate) world within which the Gypsies maintain their close and intimate relationships with one another. In order to do this, I shall reel back time from March 2002 to November 2001 and the first of the meetings called to respond to this situation.

Notes

1. Such an argument has been effectively used by black rights campaigners to argue for fairer representations of black people in children's storybooks.
2. A particularly evocative poem for anthropologists studying Gypsies perhaps; an excerpt from the poem is printed at the end of Okely's (1983) *Traveller-Gypsies*.
3. See appendix II for articles reproduced in full.
4. Although the correct spelling, according to guidelines laid down by the Race Equality Council, is Gypsies and should be capitalised as it refers to a minority ethnic group, the paper persisted in using 'gipsies' and I repeat that usage when I specifically refer to the contents of the newspaper report.

Chapter 9

A Meeting of Minds?

One evening in November 2001 I was called to an emergency meeting in the offices of one of the local authorities on Teesside. The reason for the meeting was the arrival of an unauthorised encampment of Gypsies in the area; as development worker with Gypsies and Travellers, it was felt that I would perhaps know something about who was on the camp, why they were there and how long they were intending to stop. As is common when an unauthorised camp appears, there had been a number of complaints, both from residents of houses close to the camp and from people running businesses in the area. Local authorities are obliged to investigate any complaints they receive from the public and had accordingly sent officers down to the camp to find out if there were any grounds for the complaints or not.

By the time the meeting was called, there had been a number of visits to the site following an increasing number of complaints. Different officers from different departments of the council had been down to visit and had received very different treatment. The crucial problem as far as the council was concerned was that there was no simple way of dealing with the situation. On the one hand, there were complaints about people using bushes as toilets; on the other, there was no evidence that this was actually happening. One officer said that the people on the camp were threatening, other officers reported no such problems. There had also been some problems with bonfires and burning copper wires and tyres, but that seemed to have been sorted out. A further complication was that there was nowhere else for the Gypsies to go; the local official site was full and, with the adoption of the Human Rights Bill in October 2000 (Kenrick and Clark 1999: 181), they could not simply be evicted without taking into account various legal issues regarding their rights to their culture, their way of life, etc.

Whilst the number of complaints grew and became more vehement, the council remained at an impasse, and so it was decided to call a meeting of all those who might become involved in sorting things out (except for the Gypsies on the camp and the complainants). The meeting took place in two parts – one in the morning and one in the evening – because it was impossible to get everyone together in one place at one time at less than a day's notice.

So it was that one November evening I found myself at the later meeting, sitting around a table in the offices of a local council in the company of two development officers, an estates officer, an equal opportunities officer and a local councillor. I was the only person in the room who was not directly employed by or working for the council and, as far as I was concerned, I was there on an advisory basis to represent the needs and interests of the Gypsies on the unofficial camp and suggest possible ways forward for the council. The offices – a hulking brick building, the old offices of British Steel – overlooked a main road and the edge of a minor industrial area that backed on to a run-down housing estate. In the distance, I could see the blue-orange flame from the flare stacks at the chemical works in Grangetown, which shared the darkness with the intermittent bursts of light from fireworks – it was nearly bonfire night.

Introducing the Characters

Inside, the meeting room was panelled with wood and lit with a yellowish fluorescent tube. Six of us sat round the large committee table. One, Mark, had been equal opportunities officer for the council, responsible for ensuring that all the council's policies and implementation of policy accorded with both equal opportunities law and the council's own equal opportunities policy. Mark had been involved with Gypsy Traveller issues for many years and it was to him that the council had got used to directing complaints or queries regarding Gypsies – anything from questions regarding unauthorised camping to concerns about the well-being of horses. Recently Mark's job description had changed from being concerned with implementing policy to overseeing implementation. This being, so he was trying to distance himself from Gypsy Traveller issues that he regarded as being fundamentally unresolvable.

Next around the table was Fiona, head of the council's estates office and responsible for ensuring that the council's return for their investment in land was maximised. Fiona had previously had minimal experience of Gypsy Traveller issues and had become caught up in this case because the camp was close to some small business units let by the council. The tenants of these units had filed a number of complaints to Fiona and were threatening to revoke their contracts with the council. She came to the meeting concerned to represent their interests and to ensure that the value of the tenancies and the land the camp was on was safeguarded.

Trish, sitting next to Fiona, was taking the minutes of the meeting. An officer for the Development Department of the council, Trish had been connected to Gypsy Traveller issues for a while as she had been involved in the initial designs for the official site at Bankside. Over the past year or so, she had become more involved, working with me and members of the Gypsy Traveller community to redesign the official site. In the process, Trish had met some of the local Gypsy families a number of times and had got to know some of them quite well. A year previously, Trish would not have dreamed of going on to a camp unaccompanied; now, more aware of what to expect, she is quite happy to do so. Trish also has something of a passion for maps and plans and would come to each meeting armed with a number of these so that people could see where things were. This occasion was no different and Trish had a plan on which all the trailers on the unofficial camp were marked.

Sarah, Trish's boss, was chairing the meeting. Second in command of the Development Department, Sarah had only fairly recently become involved with Gypsy Traveller issues, when she had been invited to chair the working party. As chair of the meeting and of the working party, Sarah's task was to identify courses of action that would meet the needs and wishes of as many members of the group as possible, whilst still maintaining a responsibility to the council to ensure that its future plans (e.g. for the use of land as development sites bringing in employment, or housing sites, or leisure sites, improving the quality of life) were not compromised.

I was sitting next to Sarah, opposite Mark. I was the only person there who was not directly answerable to the council and whose interests lay first in representing the needs of the Gypsies. I was not wholly independent, however, as my post was funded by regeneration money, some of which was routed through the council. This brings with it expectations; at the meeting in question, the expectation was that I was there as a conduit of information – conveying to the council what the Gypsies' intentions were, and in turn conveying to the Gypsies what the council wanted them to do. Importantly I was seen as someone whose connections to Gypsies and Travellers could make it easier for the council to achieve its wishes.

Finally came Len, local authority councillor who had had a long-term interest in Gypsy Traveller issues. Len is a resident of Bankside, his politics are fairly traditionally socialist and he is quite vociferously anti-discrimination of any kind. Len's agenda in the meeting was to identify the fairest way forward for all concerned, whether residents, business tenants, Gypsies or council officers – and to ensure that any decisions made could be justified to the electorate. As a councillor, Len is in a position to take responsibility for any decision made by the group and can effectively override any of the officers there. Len can both make life easier (by taking responsibility for an unpopular decision) and harder (by insisting that decisions are made that are difficult for officers to understand or implement) for officers who are there with a particular job to do.

Conflicts and Contradictions – the Meeting's Internal Processes

The November meeting began with an outline of the events that had resulted in its being called:

> Sarah: I've called the working party together, but nobody could meet at the same time so this is why we've decided to do it in two rounds really, with Trish and myself being constant so we can piece all the bits together. Basically, um, Gypsies at Sandstown. Which we were investigating at our usual pace until mid-week, um, by Harry going out really because there's been (*quietly*) complaints about defecation and so on (*normal voice*) but it sort of gained speed towards the end of the week because we were getting more and more complaints. Fiona will be able to tell you about them because she's been receiving them. But basically as I understand it, Fiona, from the tenants?
>
> Fiona: Yes.

Here the complexity of the situation is summed up by Sarah when she states the need to 'piece all the bits together'. The hope is that from the meetings a way forward will become clear and decisions can be made that will be acted upon. In terms of the council institution Sarah occupies the position that is invested with the power to enforce whatever decisions are made in the two meetings. Sarah goes on to explain why the meetings have been called at such short notice, why the matter has reached such a pitch of urgency. This is where the basis of the following discussions and the decision-making ground is laid, with a description of conflict between Gypsies and residents and complaints that have been received. The undesirable habits referred to in the above statement are not the only grounds on which housed residents have complained; however, they are considered significant enough to be illustrative of why people have complained about the presence of Gypsies and also why those complaints should be dealt with as a matter of urgency. So, in this opening statement, an association is made between Gypsies and undesirable or unacceptable habits – 'defecation and so on' – which is signalled by the change in the pitch of Sarah's voice, a change in pitch that also signals an awareness of the potentially offensive nature of what she is saying. In her understanding of the situation, Sarah draws upon a schematic understanding about what Gypsies are; part of this includes an understanding of how people feel about Gypsies and part includes a recognition of the possibility of causing offence. This use of schematic understandings allows Sarah to explain why the local authority should act quickly to sort the situation out without having to explain in excessive detail. Further, Sarah brings a schematic understanding about 'types' of people into a face-to-face situation and so links the decision-making process to an understanding of herself as a human being amongst other human beings, who have in common an ability to feel offended.

A significant dynamic of the meeting involves a need to consider the people present as both individual human beings and as members of a shared group or team with associated institutional roles and responsibilities. This issue, first seen in Sarah's sensitivity to the possibility of causing offence, is that of a need to achieve a balance between the individual and their role in the group. This balancing act is also indicated by Sarah's inclusion of Fiona at the end of her introductory statement:

Sarah: … we were getting more and more complaints. Fiona will be able to tell you about them because she's been receiving them. But basically as I understand it, Fiona, from the tenants?

Here Sarah introduces another person – Fiona – as somebody who is both institutionally and individually central to the processes the meeting is concerned with. Because of her institutional position, Fiona is the person who has been receiving the complaints and is thereby perceived by the complainants as the person responsible for sorting them out. Fiona has also had to deal with the personal pressure of listening to people who are upset by the presence of Gypsies and who expect her to do something about it – a situation that can become quite verbally abusive. Fiona's attitude in the meeting suggests that she is finding the situation very difficult: she adopts a 'small' posture and speaks with a similarly small voice. Once more, the need to carry out a balancing act between considering the feelings and needs of a particular human being (in this instance, Fiona, who is visibly unhappy) with the roles of members of an institution is apparent. This need is further underlined and elaborated on in the following statement made a couple of minutes later:

Sarah: … clearly, Fiona's very upset, um, she's been telling me that, um, some of the tenants are talking about walking away and some conversations have been that maybe somebody considering investing being put off by this. So we really need to do something.

The point about Fiona being upset is a personal one; it concerns Fiona as an individual with emotions and needs that might be caused by, but are not a necessary part of, her role in the council. However, Sarah justifies her concern at Fiona being upset by referring to Fiona's work responsibilities – consideration of the needs of the tenants. It is these work interests that are used to justify the need to do something and thereby address the fact that Fiona is upset.

This statement that Fiona is upset can be viewed as a story seed that relates to a whole schematic understanding about what upsetness is, what it means and so on. The fact that Sarah points out that Fiona is upset brings it into the situation that the meeting has been called to deal with and so has to somehow be incorporated into the way that situation is moulded into a story that makes sense of the actions of the past and uses them to decide upon actions to take in the future. The suggestion here is that Fiona is finding it difficult to fulfil her role within the institution, and this is felt by her on a personal and emotional level. Sarah proposes that the meeting must become concerned with a plan of action that balances the needs of individuals with the responsibilities of institutions. This is focused in Sarah's concern with the personally and individually significant point that Fiona is upset, combined with the institutionally important factors regarding the council's responsibility to manage the land and potential investors.

Balancing Individuals and Institutions – How Groups are Made and Remade

The crucial point is that there has been introduced into the meeting concern with a particular person's feelings – a person who is known to members of the group. This has a different motivating force than the needs and possible feelings of a group of people who are not known as individuals, whether residents, tenants or Gypsies.

Sarah continues her statement:

Sarah: ... and on the tyres they couldn't actually prove who was doing it because as we all know the fact that Gypsies are there, it could actually be somebody else setting light to the tyres there and they're getting the blame for it.

The theme of balancing the needs of individuals and groups is given a new direction here in the separation between what the Gypsies (as a group) have been blamed for and what they may or may not actually have done (as individual human beings) – were they or were they not responsible for the tyre burning? The distinction between groups and individuals seems to allow for a split in the way the people in the meeting perceive them – on the one hand, as individual human beings, on the other, as members of a group of unknown people that poses a threat to the way the council manages things. This adds to the complexity of the situation: not only do we have the tension created in the various needs of individuals and group, but also the potential conflict between different groups.

Such a splitting is again indicated a little further into the meeting. The following is an excerpt from near the beginning of proceedings – after approximately five minutes – and following the introductions and background so far discussed.

Mark: If we disassociate behaviour which is associated with the residents and behaviour which is associated with the carrying on of business ... What we are saying is that this is an area of toleration, it's an area where the residents of Gypsies' trailers can dwell.

Mark's statement draws a distinction between different sorts of behaviour – that which is associated with the everyday needs of human beings and that which is associated with carrying out business activities. The sort of behaviour that is associated with human residence is simply the behaviour that is necessary to meet human needs – e.g. the need to go to the toilet. The sort of behaviour that is associated with business activities is, for instance, that which results in burning cable to extract copper wire. Mark's suggestion is that the council might be prepared to 'tolerate'[1] Gypsies residing in an area but not carrying out their business there. At its root this is a split between human beings as individual organisms with associated needs, and human beings in groups. The business of Gypsies is an economic activity that is not confined to single people acting in isolation; it is a manifestation of the Gypsy group and as such is unacceptable to the council, which has been positioned as an opposing group.

This situation is analogous to that played out earlier between Fiona-as-person and Fiona-as-officer, but here the implicit burden is about the person as a bearer of rights as opposed to the person or group as an object of positive law. The hope is that some kind of resolution can be arrived at that will resolve the current situation by recasting Gypsies as, on the one hand, human and therefore in need of somewhere to live; and on the other hand, as behaving in ways that are not allowable and that need to be changed. As suggested above, this distinction is based on an understanding of living and working being separate activities; and, whilst being human is something that cannot be changed, certain forms of behaviour can and should be changed. The expectation is that the Gypsies on the unauthorised camp will be able to separate their human beingness from their ways of making a living and their associated roles within their group. This is, however, quite different from the attitude shown by Fiona earlier, which suggested a very crucial link between her understanding of herself as a person and her ability to fill a position in a group. Whilst with Fiona it was recognised that an inability to fulfil her role within a group was both grounds for her being upset and grounds for the group to base a decision-making process, for the Gypsies there is no suggestion that they might be upset by not being able to fulfil their roles within their group. This difference of understanding reminds us that the people in the meeting know the Gypsies as members of a type –people who are in general not known on a face-to-face basis. This suggests a series of conflicts within the meeting situation regarding the simultaneous use of 'ethic of right' and 'ethic of care' grounds for basing decisions. But let us return to the action.

Mark elaborates on his point in the following passage:

Mark: Our view of the situation is that the official site is virtually full and certainly couldn't accommodate this number of new residents. … So could we reach a position where we could tolerate residence and provide for that – i.e. waste collection and some form of toileting services and then invoke on top of that a contract which said you can reside here, we have provided the use of services … but what we cannot tolerate is this business practice …

Here the conflict that is making itself felt is that of tension between groups (Gypsies and the council) rather than tension between individuals and their group roles. At the start of this complex statement, Mark places himself as representative of the council group – hence he speaks of 'our' view of the situation and the position 'we' could reach. By doing this he attempts to produce a sense of consensus that then creates a cohesive sense of group identity.

Mark manages to shift the focus of the meeting, disassociating individual needs, which the council can accommodate, from group activities, which threaten the preferred activities of the council group. Mark splits the portrayal of Gypsies into individual persons with associated rights, on the one hand, and on the other hand, a group that is subject to the action of law. He focuses on a tension between groups, but denies a conflict between individual people.

Mark makes the point that in previous meetings the working party had already suggested that the land in question could be designated as a suitable area for an area of toleration. Now events have overtaken the decision-making process of the council, though with essentially the same outcome – land that is currently used by Gypsies to camp on will be shown as land that Gypsies use to camp on. According to Mark, the point that would make the difference is that; if the land is accepted as an 'area of toleration', then the council would claim some rights over regulating the behaviour of people on the land. At present, this is not the case as the Gypsies are designated as unauthorised campers who need to be evicted. The implication of this would be that those people who are camping on the land could be expected to 'play by the same rules' as the council, the tenants and the residents – which in turn suggests that at the moment they are breaking the rules. Of course, to the members of the council group this is quite obviously the case, as the Gypsies are camping unlawfully and the law could be invoked in order to evict them from the land.

Adopting Roles, Assuming Responsibilities and Assessing Behaviour

So far the understanding of what is going on has been unchallenged: the group is there to decide what the council should do about the problem of the unauthorised camp. As every individual present is expected to share a responsibility to the council, so all those in the meeting share a responsibility to jointly come up with an understanding of the situation that will allow them to implement future actions to move the situation in the direction they agree upon. However, this assumption is about to be challenged:

Sarah: I mean all we would ask you to do, Sal, is say that council officers need to come to, you know …

Me: No, sorry, my role is nothing to do with the council officers at all.

Sarah: No, it's, well …

Mark   I, I would support that, there's a long history of development officers not being involved in evictions.

Me: Yeah.

Sarah   Well, no no, we're not at the eviction stage, it's just to get information.

Me: Yeah, but, no, I don't provide information on that basis either.

Sarah: No, no.

In this exchange Sarah was effectively asking me to identify and support the aims of the group in the meeting, which I did not and could not do. The agenda that I took to the meeting was not to find the course of action that was best for the council but to represent the Gypsies on the camp, most of whom I knew personally. Being in this position meant that I felt very keenly the potential conflict involved in approaching the situation as a personal acquaintance or friend of some of the people involved, as opposed to having, or being expected to have, a particular institutional role with associated duties and responsibilities. I had to tread a fine line between refusing to have anything to do with what the council was talking about (and so risk being seen by the council group as so much on the 'side' of the Gypsies that I was not worth talking to) and the converse happening (and the Gypsies seeing me as another council worker and not really worth talking to). I tried to resolve the issue by making clear what I could and could not do – or would and would not do – what my role could be:

Me: What I can provide is information to the Gypsy Traveller community that the council is very unhappy and that they are intending to do that, but I wouldn't do that by going out and saying that officers have got to come – no. Y'know, I'm quite happy to tell people that this meeting has taken place and that people are discussing the various options and what they think they ought to do.

In outlining my position in this way, I also draw upon schematic understandings in order to gain acceptance for the way I want the situation to be understood, the way I want my role to be understood and (hopefully) the way the situation will develop in the future; for instance, I juxtapose 'Gypsy Traveller' with 'community'. In this usage, 'community' can be seen as having similar qualities to 'family', in that it seems to denote a cohesive group of people who have in common feelings of responsibility for and care towards one another. It is also a term that can be used to carry moral value – and the way it does this is illustrated if you change 'Gypsy Traveller community' for 'Gypsy camp'. I try to point out that I understand and accept and sympathise with the feelings of the people in the meeting and acknowledge their sense of where their responsibility lies by recognising the way that they are, as a group – 'the council' – unhappy. By doing this, I attempt to bridge a gap between the two groups of people – members of which are known to me personally. I also try to open up the possibility that I could do something to help the council but that wouldn't compromise my position with the Gypsies – and it had taken me a number of years to build up their trust, I didn't want to jeopardise it. To make this point clearer, I also refer to my own feelings about the situation – what I am happy to do. In fact, I try to play both by the rules of the meeting and the rules of the Gypsies and to do this I choose to focus on emotional and relationship issues (and note that these have already been accepted by Sarah as relevant), rather than the rights and wrongs of particular actions. In other words, in an attempt to play by rules acceptable to both groups, I choose to operate within the terms of an ethic of care rather than those of an ethic of right.

We can see that various roles and responsibilities (for instance, chair of the meeting, representative of the tenants, representative of the Gypsies) are assigned to individuals in order to address, as a group, issues that are causing an upset. We can also see that these roles are attached to expectations of responsibility to the council – an organisation that is 'imagined' in that it is too large for all those in it to know one another on a face-to-face or experienced basis. This being the case, they are roles that are expected to generate actions appropriate to an ethic of right. The various roles and responsibilities have attached to them powers to act to enforce decisions and ensure that any decisions that are made become enacted in the material and social world. The assumption is, further, that the assigned roles and responsibilities and their associated powers are generally accepted and it is perceived as a problem when this isn't the case, as can be seen when I refused to accept the role that Sarah tried to assign to me.

This issue of assigned group roles and associated powers is also addressed in the following excerpt. At this point in the meeting, the conversation has become concerned with how, if a particular use for the land is agreed upon (e.g. an 'area of toleration' for Gypsies), it can be policed in such a way as to ensure that it is used in the way prescribed by the council. The intention is to try to ensure that the people on the land – the Gypsies – play by the same rules as those in the meeting and accept the powers invested in the council and its enacting officers.

Len: Once the wardens are in place, it can be part of their job, not to have surveillance of the site but at least to patrol around occasionally because we are aware that these things arise from time to time and it's in Gypsies' own interest, isn't it, to make sure that they're ... behaving acceptably.

The wardens referred to are 'Neighbourhood Wardens'. The idea of having 'Neighbourhood Wardens' had arisen from a central government guideline that advocated employing members of the local community to patrol a certain area and try to ensure that everything was quiet and that (as far as the eye could see) the law was being obeyed. The thinking behind this was along the lines of it being easier to accept being told to behave by someone you know and who knows you than by a stranger; it was also inspired by some residents' stated desire to see 'more bobbies on the beat'. At the time the meeting was held, there were no Neighbourhood Wardens employed in the area; however, the council was looking forward to their appointment in the near future.

Len's statement reinforces those made by Mark earlier that emphasise the belief that behaviour can and should be controlled and modified to fit with the accepted standards of the mainstream and that Gypsies' behaviour as a group should accord with those accepted standards. Len's last point about 'behaving acceptably' brings issues of morality into the foreground and what sort of behaviour should or should not be practised. We can begin to see clear links between the way that land is assigned to certain activities, such as sanctioned business, and the moral acceptability of those activities as opposed to 'unacceptable' activities, such as unsanctioned business. A moral judgement comes to be passed on the activities of the Gypsies who aren't playing by the rules and so are challenging the understanding of the world held by those in the meeting. Is the Gypsies' behaviour 'acceptable' or not? This begs the question: acceptable to whom? The suggestion is that there is some universal standard of acceptability and the council is the arbiter of whether any particular behaviour is acceptable or not.

Making a Metaphorical Wasteland

It might seem that we have strayed some way off our original course – after all, what has all this council business got to do with the real lives of Gypsies? – and so it is appropriate to mention that what I am concerned to examine here is the tension between the face-to-face and the imagined realms of experience. In the interactions in this council meeting we can see the ways in which people who live in 'the dark' world outside the Gypsies' 'fire' learn to manage interactions in order to carry a storyline into the realm of imagined communities – the realm that organisations such as councils belong to.

The meeting now begins to oscillate between different perspectives taken by the various participants – between consideration of what is going on within the meeting itself and consideration of what is going on at the piece of land in question. The decisions that have to be taken need to take into account both perspectives. The following exchange highlights conflict within the meeting itself as regards appropriate use of the land in question. At this point in the meeting, the suggestion has been made that the land be officially designated an area of toleration. Official recognition of its status in this way would, it is believed, make the activities of people on the land easier to police. The assumption is that accepting the presence of Gypsies entails that those Gypsies in turn agree to play by the same rules as the council. The problem as it manifests within the context of the meeting now becomes that there is no agreement as to which rules the council is playing by. In the following excerpt, Fiona is working on the assumption that the council can impose its will regarding what happens on the land; she is operating from a position assuming total acceptance of the council's authority. On the other hand, Mark and Len know from experience that this isn't necessarily the case and that there are still a lot of issues to negotiate and find a solution to.

Fiona:	... putting aside the implementation problems I'm just wondering if this is the best way forward.
Mark:	It's the least worst option.
Fiona:	Well, what I would ask is for a couple of you to, er, have another think about alternative sites. There seem to be conflicting objectives here and putting aside all the, the behavioural things, a contract is a contract, how do we manage this land?
Mark:	If people are signed to this contract then we will do it.
Fiona:	The physical presence is quite a barrier to ... businesses ... it makes a hard job.
Len:	Well, you know, at the end of the day Fiona you get, if we got down to a situation, for instance, where we had, um, and as Mark says de facto we've got a toleration policy now, I think that's the attitude that the council is generally taking, I mean Gypsies traditionally come to this part of the woods and particularly where we are now in Sandstown, but if we've got to a situation where a group have settled there, I mean we've allowed them to settle there so we're going to have some difficulty, even if they behave themselves and clear off, but if they settle themselves and behave themselves and there's nowhere else in the borough for them to go, there are questions as to whether we can shift them under those circumstances, even if there's somebody wanting to come in that might actually provide jobs. Emm, because that then would be their home and we wouldn't think about doing that with any other group of people, the fact that they happen to be living in homes that are on wheels, I'm not sure that in the context of human rights alone umm, it's a, it's a justifiable position to take. But there's a debate to be had there, I mean, that much I would concede.

Len's lengthy statement incorporates all the themes discussed so far and attempts to pull them together in a way that would make it easier for any decision to be made. His statement is preceded by Fiona's revisiting the theme of the interplay between people's understandings of themselves and others, both as individuals and as actors with an institutional position that endows them with certain rights and responsibilities: 'The physical presence is quite a barrier to ... businesses ... it makes a hard job.'

Fiona is not simply saying that the presence of the Gypsies is making a difficult job harder, but that it is making it harder for her to do her job. As we saw earlier, when Fiona feels that her institutional position is threatened, she also feels threatened as a person. Whilst the apparent cause of this conflict is Gypsies on a piece of land, the real arena of conflict is not only 'out there' and between opposing groups (Gypsies, housed residents and the council), it is also 'in here' and between people with different conceptions of whose decisions should carry the most weight and hence become enacted. As Fiona points out, 'There seem to be conflicting objectives.' So an argument develops within the meeting between Fiona, who feels that to designate the land as an area of toleration would effectively, and for the foreseeable future, make it difficult for her to do her job, and Mark who feels that it is his job to ensure that the needs of all the people involved are met. This attitude is not made any easier to bear by Len, who is effectively Fiona's boss, suggesting that she has to put up with it:

Len: Well, you know, at the end of the day Fiona you get, if we got down to a situation, for instance, where we had, um, and as Mark says de facto we've got a toleration policy now ...

Fiona's, Mark's and Len's roles, as they perceive them, are now coming into conflict. Fiona wants to safeguard the council's investment in the land and wants to keep the tenants happy so that the rent keeps coming in. Mark wants to ensure that everybody's needs are met, though his main focus of concern is with the needs of the minority as his post is connected to equal opportunities issues. Len's position as an elected councillor, rather than an appointed and employed officer, is somewhat different; Len seems to view his main role as the overall mouthpiece of 'the council' as is indicated by his use of 'we'. This 'we' is used in a rhetorical way to draw those in the meeting into a particular and inclusive point of view (that of the council) which is placed in opposition to Fiona. The suggestion is that 'at the end of the day' 'the council' (rather than those actually present at the meeting) is not concerned with the needs of Fiona as an individual person. Len is concerned to ensure that any decisions made are 'justifiable' – in other words, he needs to feel confident that he can explain those decisions to the electorate.

Just as the group roles are coming into conflict, so too are the individual people who are performing these roles. This becomes evident in the following exchange, which takes on a more emotional tone than those so far:

Fiona: But I got the impression that once it was an area of toleration then it would have been given over to Gypsies.

Mark: No, we would have tolerated people there (*then talks about other uses and policies and what they would do if there were other users (investors) that came forward but much of it is barely audible on tape*) ... there would be no right to carry on with it beyond where the council will tolerate it.

Fiona: Can I just come in, because, looking at the message that goes with it being an area of toleration, if I came into the area and saw that I would immediately turn round and take my business elsewhere – it does actually look as if

Mark: Well, that, that's the message that we need to get across to the business community, that we're not just dealing with the likes of business, we're dealing with human rights and these people have legs and arms, and their horses have legs and their vehicles have wheels

Fiona: Well, I'm not talking about that, we're talking about the message that it gives and that this land is for business and that you're talking about giving it over as an area of toleration

Mark: Well, I come back to my original point – find another area within the borough which isn't designated for other purposes and we'll happily advise the Gypsies to stop there.

That the meeting has taken on a more confrontational feel is evident from the way that Fiona and Mark keep interrupting one another (marked by dashed lines —). In many ways, this is an enactment of the conflict that is happening in the 'real world', with Fiona representing the tenants and residents and Mark representing the Gypsies. At the same time, it is also an enactment of the experience of individual versus group conflict – this time it is Mark who uses 'we' as a rhetorical device with which to persuade Fiona to accept his point of view. Fiona, however, feels in opposition to Mark and his 'we', as is underlined by her use of 'I', and she proceeds to shift the alignments in order to place her view as central to the council and make Mark's view the opposing one. Hence she turns her 'I' into a 'we': '... I'm not talking about that, we're talking about ...' and shifts Mark's 'we' into a 'you': '... you're talking about giving it over ...'

This excerpt demonstrates how areas of conflict are articulated and worked through, though not necessarily resolved. To begin with, Fiona counters a previous move to designate the area of land in question as an official area of toleration by claiming that the land has already been designated for something else – business development. This argument, whilst being relevant to the discussion taking place at that precise moment, seems to contradict what was said earlier about not being able to tolerate the Gypsies' business practices on the land. Evidently, then, the difficulty is not with the carrying out of business per se but with acceptable and unacceptable business, or between sanctioned and unsanctioned business activities. In other words, the exchange needs to be understood as about control over the land and who decides what rules to play by. Understood in this way it is not contradictory although it is a site of conflict.

One aspect of the schematic understandings people hold about what Gypsies are is the idea that they are threatening. In chapter 3 I examined an excerpt from a meeting where under discussion was whether a group of people were or were not Gypsies. In that exchange, Greg noted how when they were asked to move on they did: '… British Steel come along and ask them to move and they moved straight away.' Len noted, a little later on, '… if people generally don't cause a nuisance'. In doing this, Len suggests that the people in question hadn't caused a nuisance and so agrees with Greg that they probably weren't Gypsies. In other words when Gypsies are visibly not 'playing by the rules' – that is, not behaving in ways that the dominant groups find acceptable – then they are perceived as a threat. Those people who have to deal with the situation experience this threat and so the threat becomes materialised in the relations between people – i.e. the council officers and the Gypsies involved. This theme is picked up by Sarah at the beginning of the November meeting when she speaks of complaints about 'defecation and so on'.[2] This threat is, in fact, part of what it means to be a Gypsy according to members of the mainstream society – if they are not threatening, then they are probably not Gypsies.

In the context of the meeting, the assumption is that it is not in the best interests of the council to allow activities that threaten its territorial and moral claim to the land and to control the activities that take place on that land. Fiona's position, in defending the interests of the council, is that the competing activities of another group playing by different rules should not be recognised or allowed. Fiona seeks to strengthen her point by suggesting how the council might be perceived as a group if they continue to allow people to be there who do not accept the council's authority: 'the message that goes with its being an area of toleration'.

Mark's way of dealing with this is to stress the ways in which Gypsies as individual human beings are not a threat:

Mark: Well, that, that's the message that we need to get across to the business community, that we're not just dealing with the likes of business, we're dealing with human rights and these people have legs and arms …

This, however, was not Fiona's intention: 'well I'm not talking about that.' There is now conflict in the meeting not only between different alternatives as regards designation of land use, or only between the needs of Gypsies and residents, or simply between institutional roles and individual needs. The conflict is between all of these. What happens next is that Sarah attempts to bring a resolution forward – a way of keeping the meeting on track and not developing into an argument about the merits of one point of view over another. This is in keeping with her role as chair of the meeting, on whom the final decision is seen to rest. Sarah's aim is to somehow resolve all the different layers of conflict that are being articulated in the meeting and arrive at a decision that will then be enacted in the 'real' world.

> Sarah: Get somebody out there saying look, you sign this contract with us, you sign this agreement and there will be a policy of no harassment, but it's on the understanding this is a temporary situation ...

Sarah returns to the idea of the contract – asking the Gypsies to agree to play by the rules. Implied in this suggested solution is the belief that by signing the contract the council has something that it can use to justify its actions – something signed that shows that the council has persuaded the Gypsies to recognise its power over deciding who does what on the land in question. However, Sarah is aware that this solution won't satisfy all members of the group and so qualifies the suggestion by saying that it need only be temporary. The problem is that, whether or not the Gypsies involved do sign the contract, do play by the council's rules, do accept the authority of the council, there will always be those to whom the very presence of Gypsies is undesirable and should not be allowed. This acknowledges Fiona's point made earlier about the message that is given if the council allow Gypsies to stay on their land. In many ways it is a problem of appearances and is addressed as such by Sarah in her remarks immediately following those above:

> Sarah: We've had talks about a site search and – it may be that in design terms an effective solution may be some way whereby both parties can live side by side, it may mean coming up with whatever practical means of screening there are, but, if we make it clear at the moment this is just a temporary solution whilst we look at something else ...

This time Sarah's suggested solution is a possible compromise should the situation remain unchanged (i.e. the Gypsies stay on the land and the residents and businesses in the area keep on complaining). The idea is that of 'screening', of making invisible the challenge that is created by the presence of Gypsies. In effect, the meeting has been unable to come up with a clear way forward – there are too many conflicting concerns for a single course of action to be agreed upon. What is decided is that the situation will be monitored; it is hoped that it won't get any worse and that it might get better because people might move off to other places. What this means is that a piece of land that is contested remains contested and marginal – it remains a physical place where conflicting ideas and actions vie for dominance, including those of the Gypsies currently occupying the land. At the same time, the conflicts that were internal to the meeting – those between people who felt more or less empowered and valued as individual people and the roles they were playing out – were also left unresolved. In the creation of a metaphorical wasteland through the various tensions arising in interaction, we can see echoed the physical wastelands where Gypsies manage to make their camps and live their lives.

Discussion

If enacted, such a solution will have an impact on the world outside the meeting; it will not remain as talk. The rendering invisible of behaviour and people that challenge dominant ideas is a common course of action taken by councils dealing with Gypsies. That the mere presence of Gypsies is sufficient to cause such conflicts to arise is a consequence of people using what they know about the type 'Gypsies' as a basis for their actions and understandings of what is going on. In the meeting, this is challenged by people who know particular Gypsies and understand Gypsies in a different way. We are reminded of Greg's idea in the earlier discussion about whether people 'look like' Gypsies. Greg's earlier comments are reflected in the note on which the November meeting ended – that the problem was not resolvable except by keeping different areas of conflict separate, by effectively compartmentalising the different issues to be considered, screening off and rendering invisible.

From the above study of the Gypsy and Traveller Working Party meetings, it is clear that there is no single dynamic at work in the relationships between the Teesside landscape, institutional practices and the needs of the individuals, including Gypsies, who live and work in that landscape. It is not simply a matter of an institution (such as a local authority) acting as a unified entity and imposing its will upon the land and the people in that land. A view that considers institutions as entities that act as an undifferentiated whole is a theme that runs through much of the literature regarding both Gypsies and the production of urban space (Sibley 1981, 1995, 2001; Okely 1983; Shields 1991; Hawes and Perez 1996; Kenrick and Clark 1999; Morris and Clements 1999). Such a view is, however, only one part of the story, as is illustrated by the goings-on in the Gypsy and Traveller Working Party meetings.

A major motivational force in the interactions of the meeting comes with the interplay between individuals and groups. It is the feelings of individuals that spur the group into action, as is illustrated by Sarah's consideration of Fiona's feelings and her awareness of the need to take these into account.[3] A similar tension was seen in the various participants' perception of their roles and the significance these roles bear in relation to each person's sense of self – as we saw with Fiona's strong identification with her ability to perform a role. We also saw how it is through the enactment of group roles that any decisions are concretised, that people are invested with power to do what has been decided. In the interplay between individuals and the group roles they act out are focused an enormous number of processes, which, taken together, produce an impetus towards change through the desire to reach some sense of resolution or balance.

For all of the people discussed, it is their particular sense of dissonance that counts as sufficient grounds for action and is used as a consideration for the group to act upon. Fiona's perspective is that Gypsies are threatening and should be got rid of – removed from that piece of land. Interestingly and very importantly Fiona doesn't know any Gypsies on a personal basis; she has no basis from which to question the understanding of what Gypsies are that she has at present. For her, the dissonance comes from the tension between her understanding of what Gypsies are – that is, a threat to be got rid of – and the way the council is acting in possibly allowing them to stay. Len, on the other hand, has had some person-to-person dealings with Gypsies and knows from first hand experience that they don't all behave in the same way all of the time. For him, the dissonance is found in the tension created by groups who don't behave acceptably, or the possibility that there are different standards by which to judge the acceptability of behaviour. Similarly, Mark is concerned with differentiating between, on the one hand, humans as equal beings and, on the other, with unequal and unequally acceptable ways of making a living. In other words, to Mark the various groups are not of equal standing, although the individuals that make up those groups are. Importantly, Mark has had a lot of contact with Gypsies and would count some of them as friends and this gives him a basis from which to challenge part of the knowledge schema about what Gypsies are that is shared by the group.

So we can see that the different members of the meeting all have a slightly different orientation to a schematic understanding about what a Gypsy is, and this different orientation is influenced by the extent to which each individual knows Gypsies on a personal level. It would appear that, whilst the group as a whole may share an understanding of what Gypsies are, the ability to challenge and change that schema comes through person-to-person interaction.

Gypsies have been stopping on the site the meetings were concerned with for as long as people can remember – it's a good stopping place on the way to and from the North Yorkshire fairs. Teesside is a place that is home to Gypsies, and they are as involved in its making as the planners, the valuers and the settled residents. Like other residents and workers, they too have networks of relationships on Teesside and, as we have seen in 'The Fire', they have acquired frames of reference, including shared schematic understandings and individual experiences, with which to make sense of the world.

So it was, then, that, unable to reach a definitive course of action that would satisfy all parties, the working party decided to extend an invitation to the Gypsies on the unauthorised camps and members of their families who lived in the area. On 1 February 2002, the meeting took place and in the next chapter we shall see what happened.

Notes

1. 'Area of toleration' is a term used in official planning guidance and policy (Hyman, 1989: 58). These are areas where the presence of Gypsies is allowed for a certain period of time – in other words, where Gypsies will not, as a matter of course, be evicted. It is a term widely disliked by Gypsies; as they say 'you tolerate dogs, not people.'
2. Sarah specifically mentions threatening behaviour as one of the grounds for complaint a little later on in the meeting.
3. It may be that there are also issues concerning gender here; however, I have not examined this aspect of the conversation.

Chapter 10

MANAGING MULTIPLE PERSPECTIVES

In the 'Fire' section of this book, I described how Gypsies' sense of being in the world is informed by the stories they are told, the ways they are told those stories and the social world they learn to be part of as a result of being taught through the use of stories. At the end of that section, I described a scene from a christening that took place on the high street at Yarm while the annual fair was on. In examining the exchanges at the christening, especially those between the minister and the Gypsies present, it became clear that there were a number of differences in perspective concerning what the social world is, what shape it has and what values are expressed in and through it.

In the previous two chapters, I have set that understanding of the Gypsies' social world in a wider context – that of the unaccountable 'dark' in which the familiar 'fire' of the Gypsies' social world burns. It has become clear that these two worlds are not separable and able to be viewed as distinct cultural entities. Chapter 8 outlined some of the ways in which ideas about Gypsies and the idea of Gypsiness are integral to the wider cultural history (including folk history) of the mainstream world. I showed how such ideas build into a schematic understanding of what Gypsiness involves, of what Gypsies are, and how this understanding is reinforced through the continual recreation of that schematic understanding in the context of stories – for instance, in the context of news stories told by the media. In chapter 9, I looked more closely at some of the underlying processes that take place in the actions of people involved in the creation and interpretation of such stories – specifically people in a council meeting where the story that will be told by the press is being dealt with. In that last chapter, we saw how people project storylines in order to reach agreement about how to understand and react to (and thereby manage and influence) events in an unfolding story.

Throughout, I have shown how ways of telling stories and ideas about what a story is, what it is about, what kind of setting it has and so on – in other words, all the social aesthetic standards tied up with any particular way of articulating narrative thought in order to confabulate and confabricate the social world – can be compressed into small verbal gestures, metaphorical moves, ironic stances and so on. I have also pointed out that such tropes need to be placed within some sort of narrative structure – a storyline or plot – in order to convey values and associated judgements about what has happened and what might happen next, in order to have any motivational or intentional force and meaning. Such storylines need not be explicitly stated all the time. We learn different kinds of story as we grow up and they come to form part of our 'out-of-focal-awareness' sense of being in the world. In this way, such tropes encapsulate many taken-for-granted understandings about the world and provide a means by which to make that social world together in a joint enterprise; the tropes become 'story seeds' or 'minimal narratives' (Carrithers 2003). We have seen how the moves we make using such tropes inform not only the immediate, intersubjective context of making and telling stories but also the wider context, which includes the realm of contemporaries and recognises their potential input into an unfolding story. For instance, we have seen how ideas about Gypsies that are drawn from schematic understandings about Gypsiness influence the interpretation of events by the press and also the reaction to events by non-Gypsy residents, business owners, council workers and so on.

Now that we begin to see some of the understandings that are caught up in people's talk, we can start to look at what happens when they come together in an attempt to achieve a joint decision that will have an impact in both the social and the physical world. In the introduction, I described a meeting that was the original impetus for this particular investigation. I shall now return to that situation and apply the understandings outlined so far in order to see how far they can help me to understand what went on or what didn't go on. What I want to know is: how do people who draw on differing understandings of the world manage to communicate effectively and where and how does that communication break down? It is a question about dissonance and the resolution of dissonance, or not, as the case may be; dissonance being understood as differences that become apparent in the ways that people draw some sense from the inchoateness of the world they are interacting within.

What I describe next is a scene from a meeting that took place a couple of months after the November one described in the previous chapter. The situation regarding the Gypsies camped on the unauthorised site at Sandstown had developed slowly; however, as it came to the attention of those in the 'outside' world, it began to gather momentum, resulting in the press coverage detailed in chapter 8. At the time this meeting was held, the camp was still there, the council was still trying to find a solution that would satisfy everyone and the press had begun to cover the story, so giving the council some uncomfortable publicity. This meeting was a popular event; there were many people there from various council departments and local Gypsies, including some from the camp, had been invited too, although only two turned up on the day. The meeting was held in one of the council chambers in the modern town hall; approximately twenty people were sitting round a square of tables at one end of the room. Officers and elected members from the council were seated around three sides of the square of tables. Some of these people, for instance, Len and Sarah, I knew as they were regular members of the Gypsy Traveller working party. Others, for instance, from environmental health and social services, I had not met before. Along the fourth edge of the square sat Janey and Robert, Gypsies from Bankside. I sat next to them and on the other side of them sat Mark, who knew Janey and Robert through his previous role within the council, which had involved liaising with Gypsies – usually finding out whose horses had broken free and were running loose on the A66. Len, Mark and Sarah we have already met in the previous chapter; I shall briefly describe others who feature in the following passages.

Sue is a local authority officer in the housing department. She has worked in housing for over twenty years and has a great deal of experience. She has not, however, had much experience of or training for her role as supervisor of the official Gypsy site in Bankside, this responsibility was 'landed' on her when the person who was previously responsible resigned. In fact, it was something of an accident that the site came under the overall management of the housing department – the result of other departments refusing to take it on and the Chief Executive of the council then assigning it to the department he felt was most appropriate for it.

Janey is a member of one of the largest Gypsy families in Bankside. At the time of the meeting, she was spending most of her time living in a house, although she did maintain a plot on the permanent site. Many of the people camped at Sandstown were members of her family network, and the manager of the permanent site was her son-in-law. Janey is familiar with the way that the council assigns roles and titles to people; she had been working with me for a number of months and had grown accustomed to introducing herself as 'secretary of the Bankside Gypsies and Travellers residents' association'. Janey did indeed fill such a role but only found it important in her dealings with the non-Gypsy world, and she only identified herself as such if she was in a non-Gypsy situation, such as this meeting. It had proved to be important to establish some sort of officially recognised group in order for Gypsies and Travellers to get any kind of voice within council meetings – including any kind of funding to run some of the courses they wanted, such as hairdressing and driving theory. The structures of the corporate world of the council and other institutional bodies would not treat an individual as a representative of anything other than themselves unless they could claim they were also fulfilling a role within an organisation structured along lines similar to the council. In actual fact, the residents' association ran on much more informal lines than this would suggest, did not hold regular meetings, did not minute its meetings and preferred to carry out its business on a word-of-mouth basis. In fact, as far as financial dealings were concerned, any attempt to do things other than by word of mouth and on a basis of 'honour' was construed as an insult and a suggestion that people couldn't be trusted.

Robert is Janey's husband and he undertakes much of the day-to-day management of the site and other dealings with the council, although this is officially supposed to be carried out by his son-in-law, who had been appointed by the council as the manager. Indeed, this arrangement highlights some of the differences in working practices and understandings of the world between Gypsies and non-Gypsies, in that the Gypsies view the management of the site as part of their joint responsibility – at least, the joint responsibility of a particular family group. The council, on the other hand, wants to assign a single person to the post and hold that person responsible for all that needs to be done in order to run the site and maintain it.

Paul is another council officer – head of the housing department and Sue's line manager. He has been involved with the permanent site since its creation and is well acquainted with its problematic history. I first introduced Paul in chapter 1, when I described his refusal to meet with some Gypsies who wanted to get the site reopened and had ideas as to who could be manager.

Finding a Point of View – Placing People in Cultural Landscapes

The following excerpt is taken from near the beginning of the meeting, shortly after Sarah has outlined the reasons for calling the meeting. There had been a round of introductions as the number of people in the room meant that not everyone knew who everyone else was and what their particular interest in the situation was. At the point in the meeting when the following exchange took place, participants are trying to establish why people have chosen to move from the official site on to the unauthorised camp.

Len: Yeh, but why, I mean, following up Paul's point, why was Sandstown picked out as an alternative to Bankside, is it for a particular reason?[1]

Janey: I mean, if you go back over the years, there's always been Gypsies and Travellers staying in Sandstown, you know what I mean. I mean for me being a young girl, when I was fifteen or sixteen, my mother and father always stopped at Sandstown

Now, we already know from our previous encounter with Len that he is very committed to ideas and ideals of equality and fairness. Such ideals belong to a moral world grounded in an 'ethic of right'; equality and fairness are values that Len believes are 'good' in an absolute sense. Thus Len's attention and action are frequently directed towards an imagined community of people who have their existence in the world of contemporaries. In this, Len refers to the world of ideal types as the basis of moral decision making. However, in order to achieve his desired end of being able to explain to the electorate why the Gypsies are on the land and what the council is doing about it, Len needs to take another tack and direct his attention towards the people present in the meeting. What is more, Len also needs to ensure that they go along with him and support him – specifically by agreeing that the question he poses for Janey is relevant and appropriate. In order to do this, Len directs his attention towards specific individuals in the meeting, thereby rooting his current actions in this intersubjective realm of consociates. Len's starting point in this statement is to position himself alongside Paul, an officer of the council, by specifically referring to a 'point' he had just made. Len then directs his attention towards Janey in order to try to establish what would be, to both Paul and himself, an understandable explanation as to why the people in the unauthorised camp had chosen to pull on to Sandstown rather than the official site at Bankside.

In asking his question, Len establishes some kind of common ground between himself and Paul, in contrast to Janey, towards whom the question is addressed. Further, Len's question makes a move to extend a connection between himself and Paul to others in the meeting. He does this by requesting information that he hopes will help explain the actions of the Gypsies not only for his and Paul's benefit, but also for the benefit of all those present. Len's intention is to 'move' the people in the meeting into a shared perspective with him by persuading them of a need to 'follow' Paul's point. Len positions the people in the meeting as a group that can together 'follow' a course of thought and so Len creates a sense of cohesion and joint action through having people follow the direction of his own thoughts.

At this point, although Len's words are directed towards the particular people who are in the meeting with him, he is still making those moves bearing in mind the people not in the meeting (contemporaries) whom he will also have to 'move' into a position of understanding and agreement with him. This is made evident in Len's statement just preceding the one above and that led on to it: 'The council's getting an awful lot of objections for all sorts of reasons, and petitions.' Len's hope is that there is a single (and perhaps simple) explanation that will be both explainable to and understandable to those present at the meeting and, by implication, to the council as a whole and also to his entire electorate, and this is where he is trying to get the meeting to move to. Len's hope seems to be that he can link the two realms of action – one 'here' in the meeting, and metaphorical in that the move to 'follow' is a metaphorical move, and one 'there' and imagined in that it concerns a world that is not immediately present and experienced – into a single storyline.

Len does not expect to do this on his own with everyone falling in behind him. His question is a genuine question and at the same time hands the role of speaking and story making over to Janey; as such it is a cooperative gesture that facilitates the joint nature of the process. Len's question to Janey holds (at least) two requests or urges for action. One is in the immediate term, the here and now, and is concerned with relationships being played out in the intersubjective realm of face-to-face contact; he is asking Janey to explain why the Gypsies are there to those people present at the meeting. The other request is in the long term and connects happenings in the meeting to happenings projected into the world of contemporaries; it is a request that Janey provide him (and others) with an answer that is understandable and explainable.

Len is looking for a specific 'place' to lead the meeting to and this is the object those with him in the meeting follow him to reach. This 'place' is the story behind why Gypsies are camped at Sandstown rather than on the official site, or indeed anywhere else. To get there, Len relies upon the social aesthetic standards regarding stories that he has learned and taken for granted in order to articulate so few words such a complex scenario. For instance, Len's question implies that there was a structured sequence of events – that first the site at Bankside was considered as a possible stopping place but that it was subsequently rejected. Furthermore, the suggestion is that the land at Sandstown was specifically put forward – 'picked out' – as an alternative. This sequence of events only makes sense when viewing those on the camp as a discrete group who, as a collective unit, decided (1) that they didn't want to stay on the Bankside site and (2) that they would stay at Sandstown and that the reasons for both 1 and 2 are shared between all of them. This was not the case; the camp at Sandstown was made up of a number of smaller groups who had arrived at different times but mostly within a couple of days of one another. Len, however, expects that what he proposes is a storyline that makes sense to all the people in the meeting, including Janey and Robert. In Len's storyline, all the Gypsies on the unauthorised camp are grouped together into an imagined and homogeneous group that can be accounted for as a whole.

For the majority of the people in the meeting, joining with Len in this storyline would not be too problematic. For Janey and Robert, however, this is not the case, as they come from a storytelling tradition that relates stories to specific, known people and regards unknown people as unaccountable – both unaccountable for and unaccountable to. This situation is likely to give rise to a degree of dissonance as the various participants try to confabulate with all the others a storyline that will fit with all their learned sets of expectations and social aesthetic standards. Janey, however, has learned to 'do' intersubjectivity differently from Len and the result is that her response to Len is not quite what he was looking for. In part, this is because his request (as he understood it) was not the kind of request that Janey was either familiar with or expecting. But I need to explain this a little more.

Len's storyline about why the unauthorised camp was at Sandstown was one in which groups of people such as 'the Gypsies' could be viewed as units and attributed motives and so on, just as you would attribute motives to a person. In fact, English law does actually allow for groups to be treated as persons – i.e. in getting incorporated status, etc. Such an attitude rests on a notion that a group can act as a singular, cohesive and bounded entity, and this in turn allows for the appointment of a 'spokesperson' who can speak as a representative of the group as a whole. Whilst such an attitude is reflected in the general assumptions of the meeting – for instance, in having representatives of the various departments present – it does not reflect Janey's approach, which is informed by an understanding that you do not tell others' stories.

Len does succeed in producing a common purpose in the meeting – a search for the 'story' behind the Gypsies' arrival – and this common purpose is recognised by Janey who responds with her understanding, her 'story' as to why the camp is there. Janey's response to Len also begins with a metaphorical move, but her focus of attention is not on 'following' a point in search of an answer, it concerns 'going back' to find the roots of the present-day actions in the practices of the past. In doing this Janey intends to link the proposed storyline to known people acting in a familiar landscape – a basis for all the Gypsy storytelling that we have examined in the preceding chapters. Janey's response to Len shifts the orientation away from the Council and the need to explain to the electorate – a faceless and meaningless group to Janey – and towards the more familiar world of people she knows. Janey achieves this in a series of moves, starting with a position that will be fairly familiar to Len and also to the other people in the meeting – the idea of Gypsies and Travellers as a homogenous group: 'If you go back over the years there's always been Gypsies and Travellers staying in Sandstown.'

At the outset this response reverses the move attempted by Len in his previous question – now the movement is one of 'going back'. However, this statement does seem to place 'Gypsies and Travellers' as an 'imagined' group. Such a view fits with Len's request for a single explanation as to why the Gypsies are at the camp. It also fits with a storytelling style that makes use of schematic understandings of types of people – for instance, 'Gypsies and Travellers'. The land in question is also part of a tradition of practice with which Janey has direct personal experience and to which she moves the attention of the group by metaphorically 'taking them there' – and this is where the next step away from Len's perspective and into the more familiar and accountable world that Janey is used to comes: 'you know what I mean. I mean for me being a young girl, when I was fifteen or sixteen'.

Here Janey is attempting to take the people with her by appealing to their ability to understand her, to understand what it is she is trying to say. Part of what Janey seems to be saying is that she can remember stopping at Sandstown; this really has little to do with the kind of explanation that Len wants (why are they on Sandstown now and not on Bankside?) but achieves a great deal in terms of framing the situation in a way that is understandable and meaningful to Janey, and also taking the people in the meeting with her. Just as Len assumed his point of view was shared by Janey (she would 'follow' him), Janey assumes her point of view is shared by Len (he can 'go back' with her). Hence she expects that he will receive her answer as an appropriate response to his request. In fact, there does seem to be some common ground in that Janey can begin from a point of view that is familiar to Len and then move away from it, hopefully taking Len with her. So Janey moves from a perspective shared by Len to her own remembered point of view, which places the subject matter of the meeting in a frame far more familiar to Janey – that of particular people, members of her family network, who have previously stopped at Sandstown: 'My mother and father always stopped at Sandstown.'

This explanation is sufficient for Janey, it places current events in a chain of practice, a known history carried out by known people. What is more, Janey has fitted her contribution to the 'confabulation' of the meeting in a way that meets the expectations and social aesthetic standards that she has learned. Moreover, Janey's contribution introduces a different tone and focus as it directs attention away from a potential set of abstract values and towards the values enacted in the behaviour of a face-to-face group. Further to this, Janey moves away from Len's desired end of finding an explanation that will be explainable and understandable to residents, businesses and the like. To Janey no other explanation is necessary; it does not go against her expectations that a story should be brief and without what would seem to the mainstream world as a clear resolution. As an explanation, it does not really fit the kind of story that Len was looking for because there is no causal sequencing: the only reason why Sandstown was chosen to pull on to was because people have 'always done it' and, more specifically, Janey's mother and father used to stop there.

Enacting and Re-enacting Storylines

The fact that Janey's response to Len is an unsatisfactory explanation for many of those at the meeting is now picked up by Paul, who takes something of a different tack:

Paul: It's just that, Sarah went down yesterday, one of the points that she, umm, quoted back to us, one of the things people were saying was that they were looking to get the land on a, er, permanent basis.

Paul's initial tactic is similar to the one Len used earlier when he aligned himself with another person present in the meeting. Paul does this by referring directly to another person present, specifically Sarah. Paul's alignment of himself with Sarah is then connected to the larger group of council officers and elected members when he refers to 'us', a group of people whom Sarah spoke to as a whole. This 'us', whilst apparently being distinguished from 'Sarah', is opposed to those to whom Paul's statement is addressed – specifically Janey and Robert. What Paul describes is a scenario where one of 'us' went to talk to 'you' and now that 'us' is sitting around a table asking questions of 'you'.

Paul is telling a little story that could be complete in itself, a story about Sarah going to meet some Gypsies and hearing what they have to say. In his telling, however, Paul links this small story that took place in a different time and place into that of the current meeting. Specifically, he refers to an 'us' that was present when Sarah repeated what she had been told, and that is also present in the meeting. This 'us' is thus suggested to exist in both the imagined realm (in the past, somewhere else and comprised of unspecified people) and in the face-to-face encounter of the meeting. Further, this 'us' is set against a 'they' of the Gypsies on the camp – a 'they' that finds its representatives in the meeting in the form of Janey and Robert. Paul's story then provides an outline from which to work and is suggestive of a past event that can be carried into the present and enacted in the face-to-face meeting situation. As was the case with the meeting discussed in the previous chapter, the perceived situation 'out there' in the realm of contemporaries, along with all the toing and froing that goes with trying to ascertain and understand the various points of view, intentions and motivations, is re-enacted within the face-to-face situation of the meeting. This time, however, the party that was missing from the previous meeting and that existed only as a type that some people had more knowledge of than others (i.e. Gypsies) is now present and participating in the situation and the attempt to find a mutually agreed way forward.

As part of this active confabrication of the current situation and the joint confabulation of a projected storyline, it seems as though Paul needs some sort of confirmation that what he understands to be the case is indeed so. What Paul wants to know is whether what he and the others had been told by Sarah is true. To this end, Paul is quite particular about the words that he uses, and especially the one word that is emphasised by his hesitation immediately before he says it – 'permanent'. By hesitating before using the word, Paul draws attention to it and it becomes the focus of what he is saying. The significance of this will become more apparent when we consider the exchanges that follow, especially bearing in mind the schematic understandings and expectations many of those present will hold regarding Gypsies, part of which will be an expectation that they travel around and do not settle in one place. What we have is a situation in which Janey is being challenged to say either that they do not want to be on the land permanently, or that they do. If the first, then it would seem that what Sarah reported was wrong; however, Janey would not be completely correct if she said that, because the people at Sandstown had indeed expressed an interest in buying the site. If the second, the suggestion is that they want to settle on the land for ever.

This pans out as two possible storylines. One is where the Gypsies on the land aren't real Gypsies because they want to stay in one place, and the associated expected outcome might be that therefore the council need not provide them with a site – after all, they aren't real Gypsies. The other possible storyline is that the people at Sandstown are real Gypsies who travel around and who fit other schematic expectations that would make them real Gypsies, including the fact that they must be lying about wanting to buy the land to make a permanent site because, as they are real Gypsies, they won't be permanently around. The suggested possible action associated with this storyline is that the council need not provide the Gypsies with anything as they are either (a) liars and therefore acting against an idea of what is morally acceptable and ought to be upheld by the council and/or (b) not going to be around for very long.

Janey, and by association the entire camp at Sandstown, is put in a difficult situation by Paul. Although the full impact of what he says has yet to become apparent, it would seem that Janey is aware that some kind of position is being laid out, as she is unsure how to react to this, Janey appears to agree with Paul, though she doesn't elaborate on her agreement, while she waits to find out more about Paul's reasons for raising this issue at this point:

Janey: Uh huh.

Having got some semblance of an agreement from Janey, albeit a somewhat uncertain one, that the people at Sandstown were indeed looking to buy the land and establish a permanent site there, Paul continues to expand on the ambivalent situation in which he has placed Janey – and by implication all those Gypsies who were at the Sandstown encampment:

Paul: Well, I wondered about that because, it's that, you felt people
          will stay the winter there, then they go off and travel. And I'm
          just wondering about that because the land – they say they want
          to stay permanently on the one hand and lease the land from the
          council, and on the other it seems like a temporary issue.

Paul's 'wondering' is directed towards what he senses as a dissonance between his understanding of the situation, Janey's response to him and also Janey's earlier answer to Len where she stated that Gypsies chose to move on to Sandstown because they always had done that. From Paul's point of view, Janey's answer doesn't actually answer the question. The nub of Paul's puzzlement seems to come from a feeling that contradictory things are being asked for – permission to stay on the land permanently and the freedom to travel. To Paul these two desires are in conflict – either the Gypsies want to stay on the land permanently or they want to travel (and stay on the land temporarily).

So here we have outlined the basis of a misunderstanding that emerges from a sense of dissonance – Janey feels she is answering Len's question, but to Paul the given answer doesn't make sense. To Paul the Gypsies are in a contradictory and ambivalent position and the meeting needs to resolve this contradiction by finding a way of the Gypsies being somehow one thing (a permanent presence) or the other (a temporary presence). Janey, on the other hand, is attempting to place herself in a situation that acknowledges her own understanding of the world and how to be in it, and that involves being able to sustain apparently contradictory positions; it also involves referring events in the world to real and particular people as far as possible. Now, the meeting is concerned to sort out this tangle of perspectives and arrive at some sort of decision for future action. In order to do this, all those present at the meeting will have to agree on a projected storyline. In attempting to achieve this, the theme of permanence is returned to at various points as it becomes a central feature of the potential plot – are the Gypsies staying permanently or not?

Shifting Perspectives and Enacting Situations

In Paul's statement and description of the situation above, we have a clearly ambivalent statement regarding the Gypsies at Sandstown, and, as we have seen, being in an ambivalent position is not something that Gypsies are strangers to – in fact, it is something they are quite used to and have a number of strategies for dealing with. Janey's response to Paul – now that she is clearer about the storyline he is putting forward and her place in it, as well as the place of the Gypsies at Sandstown – is to try to resolve the ambivalence and show to Paul how Gypsies can do both things at once – be both permanently and temporarily present on the land: 'If they did rent the ground off the council, I mean the women would stay on the ground and the men would go away to work like they usually do sometimes.'

Here Janey does something quite unusual and unexpected – she goes against her own set of social aesthetic standards and enters into an endeavour to project a storyline into the realm of contemporaries or imagined communities. Janey is no longer talking about specific people in a specific situation; she is talking about types of people doing typical things. This marks a shift in Janey's perspective that at first isn't specifically attended to by others in the meeting, as Janey has moved towards operating within their more taken-for-granted sets of social aesthetic standards. Janey, however, struggles with this shift, as becomes apparent after a couple of short exchanges where the storyline isn't progressed very far.

At this point, Mark joins in the exchanges:

Mark: Business people were saying you tend to have different groups of people winter and summer. That in, in the winter period now you're getting people who normally travel around and then in the summer you're getting people who tend to have more kids around who are probably coming down from, er, Bishop Auckland area and using that for a summer holiday. Now, do you know anything about that business?

Mark's contribution specifically introduces another group – that of 'business people' – and this is a group that, as we saw in the previous chapter, can be portrayed as opposed to the group called 'Gypsies' and referred to here as a vague 'people' or 'you'.[2] What Mark does not only draws our attention to a group of people to whom decisions made in the meeting will have to be communicated and accounted for; he also suggests a group of people as characters in the plot – people whose actions, intentions and motives as a group will have to be somehow predicted and accounted for in the storyline that the meeting is hoping to come up with. Mark thereby reinforces that focus of the meeting that gives attention to the actions and accounts of types of people, and which makes use of schematic understandings of the world. On top of this, Mark refers to Gypsies as a homogeneous group who have particular patterns of behaviour, elaborating on the schematic understanding that most of the people present in the meeting already have about what Gypsies are. This move would not be unfamiliar or feel strange to those in the meeting who have been taught from an early age to relate ideas about stories and so on to types of people, and to expect these to bear some kind of relationship to characters and events in the world. To Janey, however, it may well feel quite incomprehensible and it does seem that she finds it difficult to sustain her previous move to enter into the understandings and expectations of the people in the meeting. There is some sense of hesitation or doubt in Janey's voice before she responds to Mark's question with:

Janey: Well, not really, I, I don't really know a great deal of them from Bishop Auckland. But then, a transit site, means that, I mean you stay there for a, a couple of month and then you move on.

Here Janey tries to relate the question Mark has asked of her to what she knows about specific people, about people with whom she can claim some knowledge having been included in face-to-face relationships with them at some time. However, Janey is not able to do this as she doesn't actually know people from Bishop Auckland on that basis.

Nevertheless, Janey does try to continue with the meeting's project of reaching an agreed understanding of the situation and associated projected storyline – i.e. what they are going to do about it – as she expands on her understanding of what a transit site is. Here Janey is in an 'in-between' role, trying to move back and forth between her own known world of particular people and her learned ways of behaving and those of the other people in the meeting. It is a position that enacts within the confines of the meeting the position that Gypsies find themselves in when they are placed in ambivalent situations by mainstream understandings of the wider world. Janey has moved, within the meeting, into a metaphorical 'wasteland', where conflicting points of view can be potentially worked out, resolved or left to conflict.

What happens next is that Sue, who knows Janey very well, joins her in this 'wasteland' and between the two of them they expand on the theme of permanence, drawing a distinction between permanent features of a landscape (e.g. the site at Bankside) and the lives of people who move around but who always (permanently) need to have places to stop. Sue does this by turning her attention specifically towards Janey and having a direct, one-to-one conversation with her, which the others present in the meeting can hear but in which they are not, at present, included. Sue has been closely involved with the running of the permanent site in Bankside for a number of months, she has also been to visit the unauthorised camp on a number of occasions, she knows the people that she and Janey are referring to as specific people, and they can carry on their one-to-one conversation on that basis.[3]

Sue:	There's nowhere else. Because that, that's the nature of, of the lifestyle. There's not many people who want to stay, even though it's a permanent site, who want to stay for fifty-two weeks of the year.
Janey:	Well, no, no because I mean they have to go away to work. There's not work round here for Gypsies and Travellers, so they're away half of the time.
Sue:	No so, even though we're calling it a permanent site …
Janey:	It's more of a transit site, you're right.
Sue:	Some people stay longer, but it, it's really a transit site.
Janey:	Yeah.

This is an act of friendship. Sue understands what Paul is asking for; she also knows that Janey is very unfamiliar with the situation she is in and is struggling to try and make sense of it, so she steps in to help. But Sue does not speak for Janey, she joins with her, thus breaking down the potential division that Paul had created in his 'us' and 'they' construction. Sue moves herself from Paul's 'us' and positions herself, within the context of the meeting, alongside Janey by holding a conversation with her without constructing an alternative 'us' of herself and Janey in opposition to most others in the meeting. In doing this, Sue joins Janey in the 'wasteland', moving from an understanding of the world informed by the social aesthetic standards of the majority of people in the meeting – including a desire for general, abstract understandings and values – towards an understanding of the world informed by the social aesthetic standards of the Gypsies and the need to focus on specific people.

In this passage, Sue and Janey run through, for the benefit of the others in the meeting, a number of issues that bear upon the question that both Paul and Len raised earlier. Sue's framing of the issues places them firmly within the context of Gypsy practice – their 'lifestyle' – rather than in the causal expectations of the council officers such as were articulated in Len's earlier questions. Sue's statement also questions the meaning of the term 'permanent', as she points out that even on the 'permanent site' people don't stay there permanently. This is the aspect of Gypsy practice that Sue feels is most salient in explaining why Gypsies don't stay on one piece of land all year round.

The fact that their lifestyle considerations are based on particular needs is the next theme that is taken up, with Janey building on the points that have been made by Sue. Janey points out the fact that Gypsies need to work and that there isn't much work around for them. This is a perspective that should be fairly familiar to the council, concerned as they are with the labour market, employment prospects, the economy and so on.

Sue and Janey's performance does not entirely succeed and a little later in the meeting Sue finds herself needing to return to the theme of permanence. In the passage that follows, Sue is far more explicit about her understanding of the situation and the different orientations to, and ensuing misunderstandings of, the world that have given rise to the dissonance felt by people in the meeting such as Paul:

Sue: But the word permanent. Permanent is our word, I mean at Sandstown, I don't think anybody, anybody's thinking of staying permanently, to be there all the time

Sue points out that there is more than one way of understanding what is meant by 'permanent' and that the root of the difficulty lies in assuming that all the people present at the meeting understand an agreed definition of 'permanent', including what that means in terms of expecting Gypsies to be always present – a fixture in the landscape. In fact, Sue is underlining that it is very probable that the Gypsies are expecting that if the site at Sandstown becomes permanent that means it is permanently available for Gypsies to stop on – whether they always do or not. To check whether this is the case Sue turns towards Janey and Robert, who confirm the point:

Robert: Well no, no.
Janey: About six weeks and that's their limit, moved on, haven't they.

This, however, does not solve the problem as far as many of those in the meeting are concerned. Whilst Sue and Janey have effectively spelt out an understanding of the situation as far as it can be understood by the people present, it falls short of one of the original intentions behind calling the meeting – and that is explaining a course of action to people outside the meeting, people whose knowledge of Gypsies is based purely on schematic understandings and not the more intimate face-to-face understandings that those in the meeting now have some hint of. Sarah, whose responsibility it is to make the final decision about the meeting's agreed course of action (i.e. the agreed storyline that they manage to come up with together), is aware of this and wants to take the conversation one step further – away from the 'wasteland' where the land in question and the Gypsies are neither permanent nor transient features of the landscape, where knowledge of particular people merges with and sheds light on knowledge of types of people. Sarah now shifts her attention, and that of the meeting as a whole, once more to the realm of contemporaries and all the possible 'imagined' interests there and how she is going to be able to explain something that might well challenge their expectations about what ought to happen:

Sarah: Yeah, when I've been up there people have expressed an interest in one or two plans and, but I think like you I'm getting sort of mixed messages as to whether we can let the site out long-term. You know, we have to explain this and whether there will be people on that site long-term.

This statement of Sarah's almost brings us full circle: we are back with a request to provide an explanation or 'storyline' that will fit with the expectations of various 'imagined' groups of people. We saw how, at the beginning of the meeting Janey met such a request with a description of the actions and motives of particular and familiar people in a particular and familiar landscape. Now, in response to Sarah's request, Janey provides the following explanation:

Janey: You see, the thing is with them families up there at Sandstown, I mean they've been here all their lives, you know what I mean? I mean, really you could call them Teesside people. Do you know what I mean – I mean they've always lived round here – their parents before them was travelled round here. See, when you come from a place you always seem to come back to it, through the generations and then you'll get the mother and them coming to stay and they'll think, Oh well, then, we'll stop here for a few weeks.

Janey has returned to her more familiar way of doing things, talking about specific people in a specific place – she knows exactly who she is talking about when she refers to the 'families' at Sandstown, they are people she has known for a long time, indeed she is 'family' with them.

Conclusions

In this meeting, we can see a range of perspectives and possible storylines being laid out. Associated with this range of perspectives is a range of people in a particular social landscape, i.e. they are all in a meeting together and there does appear to be some sense of agreement about what they are there for – in order to co-construct, or confabulate, a storyline that will then inform the future actions of the people in the room. By implication, this storyline will also be told to all the others (the contemporaries), whom each of those in the room will meet up with in the future, whether those are intimately known, specific people, as in the case of Janey, or whether they are representatives of interest groups who may be communicated with via the media or other means, as in the case of the council officers, who will be expected to provide some sort of account of the meeting to the electorate.

In the context of the meeting, various storylines were suggested and played out. This allowed for people to challenge and change storylines in an attempt to find a plot and associated positioning of characters that fitted their ideas and expectations – both about what was being asked for and what should be done. When there are differences in understandings, which are experienced as a sense of dissonance, then some suspension of schemas, of the patterns of expectation and understanding caught up in our learned sets of social aesthetic standards,[4] can take place, which allows people to move from their more accepted, taken-for-granted ways of 'doing intersubjectivity' into a metaphorical wasteland where they attempt to find some sort of common ground from which to plan out a storyline. For Janey, such 'suspension of schemas' means talking about 'types' of people, or talking about people who exist only as contemporaries who are imagined and who have never been known on a personal, face-to-face basis. For many of the others in the meeting, the suspension of schemas comes in doing away with their taken-for-granted expectations of what a Gypsy is or isn't and taking on board alternative understandings of what it might mean to be a Gypsy.

This process of suspending schemas breaks down when a resolution is attempted and Sarah tries to find a way of moving from the specific intersubjective understandings and agreements that have been arrived at in the meeting to a storyline that can be projected into the imagined world of contemporaries.

The meeting does, however, end on an appropriately ironic note of concurrence:

Sarah: Mm, I think we've probably explored this as much as we can do.
Janey: Yeah.

Notes

1.   Paul's 'point' was made a little earlier in the conversation and consisted of the simple question 'Why Sandstown?'
2.   In fact, as we saw in the previous chapter, the interests and concerns of 'business people' are something Mark likes to make his business, just as he makes it his business to find out about the 'business' of the Gypsies.
3.   This point is made more apparent later on in the meeting when Sue refers to specific people by name.
4.   Such an argument echoes recent research into cross-cultural music cognition (Krumhansl et al. 2000; Narmour 2000), which shows that people are able to suppress the musical schemas (aesthetic standards) of the cultures they are native to, in order to make musical predictions and judgements regarding the music of other cultures with other schemas the important factor being exposure of each individual person to the music in question, rather than any degree of musical expertise. If such an argument were to be applied beyond the confines of music to group schemas and social aesthetic standards, it would show how person-to-person contact with people who hold different schemas could challenge the schemas already held by any one person; in so doing, that person could come to challenge those schemas within the group situation.

This suggests that both schemas and aesthetic standards are determining whilst unchallenged – they are continually reinforced by the group. However, when challenged by contact with other schemas, they become permeable and fluid, open to suppression and/or alteration. Such research is complemented by social psychologists researching the dynamics of intergroup relations (Dixon 2001), though the focus here is on intergroup contact rather than person-to-person contact.

CONCLUSIONS

───⊗⊗⊗───

I would like to end on a reflective note, to consider what I feel I have achieved through producing this study. I began with a puzzle, a tangle of human interactions that apparently shared both motive and intent but that nevertheless did not manage to reach an agreed conclusion. I went on to unravel these interactions, in the process showing how they consisted (at least in part) of suggested storylines, possible stories that had their origins in various traditions of practice and that are projected into the future, linking into other storylines that stretch between people and that move those people through time and space.

The first section of the book challenges the grounds of more traditional anthropology; I looked especially at anthropological devices such as notions of 'boundary' and 'oppositions' and 'difference', in order to make the case for using different metaphors to describe various traditions of practice. In doing this, we can see that anthropological knowledge and understanding are structured in such a way as to encourage categorisation into types of people – in other words, traditional anthropological knowledge rests on the notion that people belong to one culture or another. I showed how such understandings have led to a difficulty in understanding the experience of being Gypsy when Gypsies experience themselves as being simultaneously on both sides of the boundaries that the non-Gypsy world constructs.

I then explored how different ways of describing culture can be useful in analysing the interactions of people from different traditions of practice. The particular distinction I emphasised was that of the intersubjective context of human interaction set against (or within) an 'imagined' context – i.e. not presently experienced. This set the scene for an examination of how it is we learn to 'do' intersubjectivity in different ways, depending upon the particular tradition of practice into which we are born. I outlined a distinction between two different kinds of 'knowing' that are associated with these different realms of experience, pointing out the difference between the 'knowing about' Gypsies that is associated with the 'imagined' realm of contemporaries and types of people and the 'knowing' Gypsies that is associated with the intersubjective realm of consociates. This lays out the main theoretical frame for the rest of the book, which is an examination of the ways these two realms of experience and kinds of knowing are worked with by both Gypsies and non-Gypsies, and how these different ways of doing things can lead to subtle but significant differences in understanding the world.

I went on to demonstrate some of the ways in which a place (Middlesbrough) is linked to the cultures of those who live there – including opportunities for work, education, training – giving a clear connection between the physical and moral environment as illustrated in the writings of, for instance, Florence Bell. What for Bell was a self-evident truth has been for social scientists much more of a problematic relationship, generating questions about the connections between individual, environment and society and the power of the social and physical environment to mould the physical and moral nature of people (Foucault 1977, 1980, 1986; Bourdieu 1990). The complex nature of the interrelationship between individuals, groups, space and morality was a theme that ran throughout the meeting I began and ended the book with. It is a complexity that materialises in the landscape – hence the ambiguity and ambivalence of the 'county of contrasts' that is Teesside. It is also a further demonstration, as with the 'kinds of knowledge' explored previously, of the ways in which human beings are caught up in interactions that pull them in more than one direction – reminding us of Bakhtin's (1981) and also Strauss and Quinn's (1997) centrifugal and centripetal forces (see also Emerson 1986).

These tensions in human experience become most evident in the later chapters, where I explore interactions in the council meeting. In these chapters, people find themselves negotiating situations that challenge their accepted, more habitual understandings and ways of doing things. In order to make this more evident, I first describe something of the cultural tradition from which people emerge as Gypsies. In order to do this, I take one particular aspect of cultural practice and examine it in detail – that of storytelling. We saw how Gypsiness was taught, at least in part, by a specific style of stories and by specific ways of using stories. We also saw how this compared with a different use of a different kind of story employed by the mainstream literate culture, which encourages an extension from the known world of direct consciousness into the 'imagined' world of contemporaries. So here we can see how we are taught in different ways to deal with the tensions created through the experience of being human, and how these differences of tradition could be equated to different strategies for dealing with the realms of contemporaries and consociates.

Of course, the 'Fire' that provides the context for Gypsy storytelling needs to be set in a wider context, so I turned my attention towards the 'Dark' – the social world that the intimate and experienced family world of the Gypsies exists within. I looked briefly at the way ideas about Gypsiness have been told in the literate and imagined culture of the UK mainstream. Again, we could see some of the differences in apprehension of the world that are experienced by Gypsies and by non-Gypsies – and we can also gain some sense of the dissonance that comes about as a result of interactions where these differences are made clearer than usual, where they come into focus rather than being out of focal awareness.

As the differences in learned experience and expression of the world become clearer and we see how a sense of dissonance arises in interaction, we can begin to focus more closely on interactions in the mainstream to see what is going on there, with particular reference to what is going on when people talk about Gypsies. In the chapter titled 'A Meeting of Minds?' I did just this. I showed here that there is not simply a sense of dissonance between Gypsies' and non-Gypsies' understandings of the world. Dissonance also becomes apparent in the interactions of people from the mainstream; it becomes apparent that people do not simply operate according to a uniform and set cultural pattern, a pattern that links them together and ensures that they all operate with the same purpose in mind. We began to see the way both Gypsies and non-Gypsies are caught up together in a world of their mutual making – they are at once members of a single culture and members of different traditions of practice. Again, this experience gives rise to tensions that pull people one way and another.

Finally, I returned to the initial puzzle and examined the interactions at one particular meeting where people from a variety of different backgrounds came together to try to reach some sort of agreement about a course of action. Drawing upon the ideas explored in the previous chapters, we can see more clearly how differences in expectation and understanding – differences in how we have learned to apprehend the world – are worked through. Throughout, I have focused on strategies of reconciling the realms of consociates and contemporaries; we see that we are able to suspend our schematic understandings about types of people in order to reach a greater understanding and some sense of common purpose. We also see how this can fall down when that common purpose is extended out of the immediate, intersubjective context.

All in all, I have given an account of culture and human interaction as something that is always dynamic and lived and that can never be completely determined by sets of rules or structures. I have also shown how learned patterns can help in generating a sense of belonging, but how these patterns are not in themselves determining. There is always the openness we have to one another as human beings, and through our acts of friendship and attempts at understanding we show ourselves to be greater than can ever be determined and we are enabled to join in projects that cannot be achieved by one person alone. Such openness generates its own problems, one of which is the degree of uncertainty and unmanageableness involved in entering into projects that extend between people and across time in such a way that we can never be completely in control and sure of the eventual outcome. This quality of human experience has been referred to as 'the inchoate', a term that usefully describes the sense of both possibility and insecurity involved in being human. I have used this notion to demonstrate the different strategies that have been devised in order to try and gain some greater control over situations.

In *Seeing Like a State*, James C. Scott (1998: 64ff.) demonstrates the ways in which large, complex, social forms such as states need to categorise people in order to maintain a sense of coherence and continuity. Whilst Scott draws upon the adoption of surnames as the way in which this categorising project might be carried out (a practice that is both relevant to and challenged by Gypsies naming practices, as we have seen in chapter 5) I have shown how such categorising is also enacted through viewing people as belonging to cultural types, such as 'Gypsy'. It is such categorisations that people in the meetings we have seen attempt to draw upon in order to reach a workable solution to a persistent problem – to control an inchoate situation. It is such categorisations that their notion of government and also their notion of law rest upon and through which these notions are enacted.

Scholars who have examined contrasting notions (or, rather, enactments) of ideas about law amongst Romany populations have demonstrated that there are other possible ways of seeing the world and organising communities (see, for example, Acton et al. 1997; Caffrey and Mundy 1997; Sutherland 1997). In these studies there is shown to be a tension, though possibly not an unresolvable tension, between these different understandings of 'law', 'justice', 'morality' and so on. Indeed, in their article, Caffrey and Mundy suggest that it is through an exploration of these tensions and possible resolutions that some of the seemingly intractable problems of contemporary society might be worked through. In their article they suggest that there is perhaps not a single solution, a fixed way of viewing and organising the world that will solve all possible problems. Instead, they suggest that there is room for an ongoing process of working things through – a process that accepts and encourages alternative views of the world and alternative ways of doing things. It also rests upon a commonality in human experience – that of intersubjectivity, a human capacity which, whilst accepting that we all learn to do it differently, also demands that we recognise our mutual humanity.

In my own experience, this has been a very helpful perspective to adopt in that it has allowed for an increased understanding and a dilution of the social antipathies that can come about through expecting all people to share the same perspective. I have been able to use the insights I have gained in the pursuit of an academic end to work with non-academics (both Gypsies and non-Gypsies) in an ongoing project whereby we all feel we have gained something. At the very least, I believe that we all feel we have an increased understanding of one another and an appreciation of our different points of view. Increased understandings do not provide the final solutions to various social problems – although I am inclined to say that is not a bad thing – they can provide enough confidence in one another to keep trying to find effective ways of living in the same world together. The kind of knowledge and understanding that can be generated through anthropological and ethnographic projects is enormously useful in this regard – provided it refuses the temptation to view people as types, which is the legacy it has borne from its inception in more colonialist times, when it was, in fact, the tool of categorising and constraining systems of government.

APPENDIX I

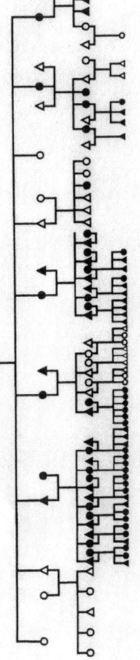

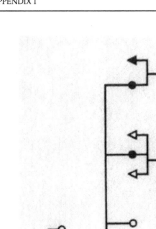

Janey's family chart

NB shaded symbols = those living on Teeside

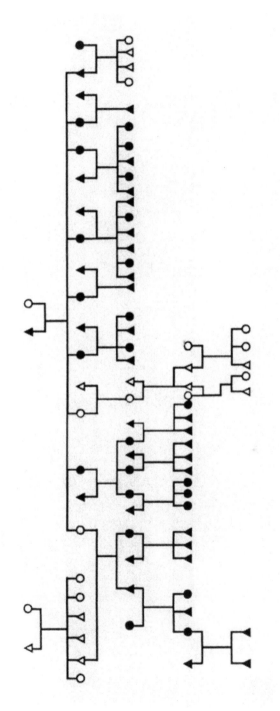

Maudy's family chart

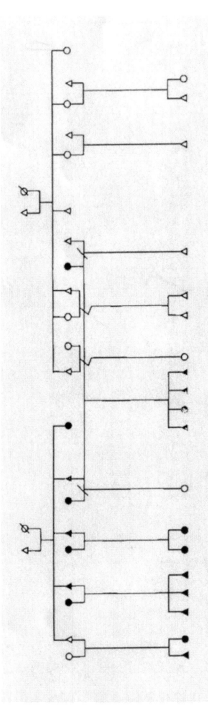

Deborah's family chart

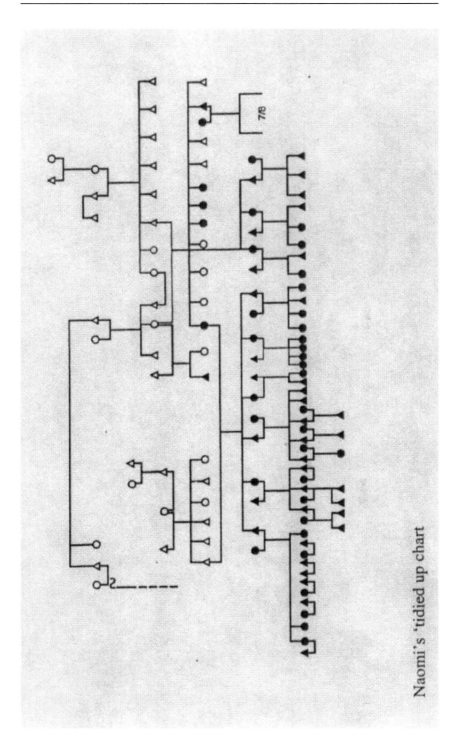

Naomi's 'tidied up chart

APPENDIX II

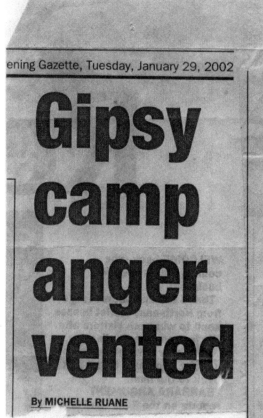

Gipsy camp anger vented

By MICHELLE RUANE

ANGRY opposition has been fired at a Teesside council over an illegal gipsy site.

Residents and firms want a reassurance from Redcar and Cleveland Council that the camp site, set up illegally by gipsies at Warrenby, near Redcar, will not become permanent.

The council's executive heard that gipsies had set up camp despite there being an official site at South Bank. Now residents and businesses have fired a protest letter to the council, along with a 280-signature petition, expressing their "absolute disagreement and total disgust" about the site.

"A properly constructed and wholly adequate site already exists in South Bank and the council

CALL: Cllr Tombe, pictured left, says they will asking them to be good neighbours

has therefore met its legal obligation," adds a letter accompanying the petition. Residents say they have heard "a suggestion" the site could be permanent.

A partner in one of the firms in the area, who asked not to be named for fear of reprisals, said they recently lost a contract due to the "condition" of surrounding land.

"This contract was worth approximately £300,000 per annum and it is unlikely we will be able to win it back, which may result in us having to lay off five staff," he added.

One resident, who asked not to be named, said: "Now the council has provided all amenities, including cleaning up the site, there is absolutely no reason for the travellers ever to leave."

But a Redcar and Cleveland Council spokesman said: "The official site at South Bank is full and there are a number of families who have set up at Warrenby. We are in dialogue with them and we will be providing water, toilets and organising refuse collection. In return they are signing an agreement on their behaviour."

He added if they fail to comply with the agreement, the authority would seek enforcement action against them.

The spokesman added: "It's not going to be a permanent site."

Councillors Sam Tombe, Lynne Pallister and Cliff Houlding are now planning to visit the site to meet the gipsies next week.

Cllr Tombe said councillors are trying to arrange a public meeting to discuss the situation.

"We will be asking them to be good neighbours," said Cllr Tombe.

Source: *Middlesbrough Evening Gazette*, Tuesday, January 29, 2002

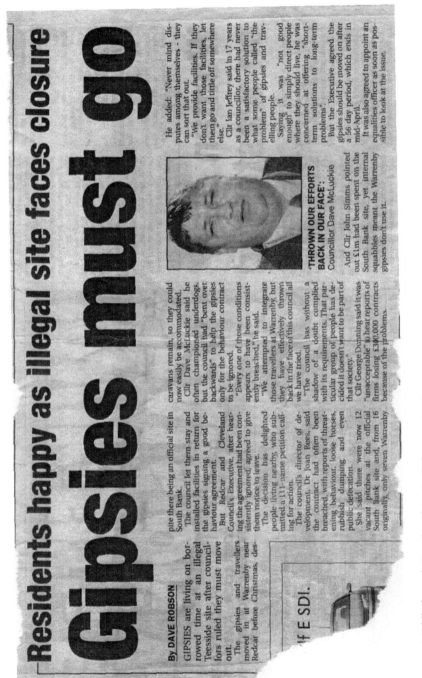

Residents happy as illegal site faces closure

Gipsies must go

By DAVE ROBSON

GIPSIES are living on borrowed time at an illegal Teesside site after councillors ruled they must move out.

The gipsies and travellers moved in at Warrenby near Redcar before Christmas, despite there being an official site in South Bank.

The council let them stay and installed facilities in return for the gipsies signing a good behaviour agreement.

But Redcar and Cleveland Council's Executive, after hearing the agreement had been consistently ignored, agreed to give them notice to leave.

The decision has delighted people living nearby who submitted a 111-name petition calling for action.

The council's director of development, Dr Joan Rees, said the contract had often been breached, with reports of threatening behaviour, loose horses, rubbish dumping and even public defecation.

She said there were now 12 vacant pitches at the official South Bank site and, from 16 originally, only seven Warrenby caravans remain, so they could now easily be accommodated.

Cllr Dave McLuckie said he often championed underdogs, but the council had "bent over backwards" to help the gipsies only for the behaviour contract to be ignored.

"Every one of these conditions appears to have been consistently breached," he said.

"We attempted to integrate those travellers at Warrenby, but they have effectively thrown back in the face of this council all we have tried.

"The council has without a shadow of a doubt complied with its requirements. That particular group of people has decided it doesn't want to be part of that society."

Cllr George Dunning said it was "unacceptable" to hear reports of firms losing £300,000 contracts because of the problems.

'THROWN OUR EFFORTS BACK IN OUR FACE': Councillor Dave McLuckie

And Cllr John Simms pointed out £1m had been spent on the South Bank site, yet internal squabbles meant the Warrenby gipsies don't use it.

He added: "Never mind disputes among themselves - they can sort that out.

"We provide facilities. If they don't want those facilities, let them go and tittle off somewhere else."

Cllr Ian Jeffrey said in 17 years as a councillor, there had never been a satisfactory solution to what some people called "the problem" of gipsies and travelling people.

Saying it was "not good enough" to simply direct people where they should live, he was concerned at offering "short-term solutions to long-term problems".

But the Executive agreed the gipsies should be moved on after a 56 day period, which ends in mid-April.

It was also agreed to appoint an equalities officer as soon as possible to look at the issue.

Source: Middlesbrough Evening Gazette, February 2002

Evening Gazette, Saturday, March 16, 2002   www.icteesside.co.uk

Gipsies' fury over site state

'NOT FIT FOR HUMANS': Joseph Farrow with some of the rubbish at the South Bank site which he says is a rat-infested disgrace and wishes his family had never moved there

Picture: **STEVEN BROUGH**

By KELLEY PRICE

A GIPSY family living on an official site is claiming their new home is a rat-infested disgrace.

The site at Station Road, South Bank, has been set up by Redcar and Cleveland Council in a bid to move travellers from unwanted camps.

But gipsies at the site say the area is over-run with vermin and rubbish. Toilet facilities have been vandalised and electricity boxes have been smashed.

Redcar and Cleveland Council is searching for another site, a special "toleration" site where families can stay - in return for signing a contract similar to that of council tenants.

The site would act as an over-flow for families when the South Bank site is full and would also have electricity, toilets and refuse collection.

But Joseph Farrow, who moved to the South Bank site on Tuesday with his family, claims the area is not fit for humans.

He says the place is full of vermin, there is human faeces on the ground and hanging wires from electricity boxes are posing a danger to children.

The Farrows moved from an illegal site at Warrenby at the request of the council.

He said: "The council is supposed to be looking after the site but it's a proper tip.

"It's scandalous, I've never

We've been dumped on

It's scandalous, I've never seen anything like it. The council asked us to move from Warrenby and we were told it was a lovely site but we were wrongly led - I wish we'd never moved

seen anything like it.

"The council asked us to move from Warrenby and we were told it was a lovely site but we were wrongly led - I wish we'd never moved now. We shouldn't have to live like that."

Mr Farrow has promised to sign a council contract but is pressing for the site to be cleared up: "We've done as they've asked and moved here but it's not fit for anyone to live here at the moment."

The council is in the process of appointing an equality officer to

help forge links with the gipsy community.

A council spokesman said the authority had to strike a balance between maintaining good relations and adhering to responsibilities as a landlord and public authority.

An officer has visited the site to see Mr Farrow and inspect any problems. But councillor Dave McLuckie said the South Bank site was far superior to the Warrenby site which the Farrows had left behind.

He said: "Where a clean-up is required, we will make such a clean-up. But considering the disgraceful state travellers left the Warrenby site in, for anyone to claim the council site is in a worse state beggars belief."

The spokesman said: "There are works to be done and a few areas to be cleaned over the next few days - the area isn't like a housing estate, it is fenced but there is access from outside for people to come in.

"We want good relationships with the gipsies but there's a balance to be struck and we also have to maintain our responsibilities as a landowner and as a council.

"We hope to liaise closely with the gipsy community to make sure we can develop policies which help us work together effectively."

Source: *Middlesbrough Evening Gazette*, Saturday, March 16, 2002

BIBLIOGRAPHY

Abu-Lughod, L. 1991. 'Writing Against Culture', in R.G. Fox (ed.) *Recapturing Anthropology: Working in the Present*. Santa Fe: School of American Research Press. 137–62.

Acton, T.A. 1994. 'Moral Panics, Modernisation, Globalisation and the Gypsies'. Article for *Sociology Review* posted on the Traveller-acad mailbase, April 2000.

––––– 1997. *Gypsy Politics and Traveller Identity*. Hatfield: University of Hertfordshire Press.

Acton, T.A. and G. Mundy (eds) 1997. *Romani Culture and Gypsy Identity*. Hatfield: University of Hertfordshire Press.

Acton, T.A., S. Caffrey and G. Mundy 1997. 'Theorizing Gypsy Law', *American Journal of Comparative Law* 45 (2): 237–49.

Ahearn, L.M. 2001. 'Language and Agency', *Annual Review of Anthropology* 30: 109–37.

Anderson, B. 1999 [1983]. *Imagined Communities*. London: Verso.

Austen, J. 1996 [1816]. *Emma*. St Ives: The Softback Preview.

Bakhtin, M. 1981. *The Dialogic Imagination: Four Essays by M.M. Bakhtin* (ed.) M. Holquist. Austin: University of Texas Press.

Bancroft, A. 1999. '"Gypsies to the Camps!": Exclusion and Marginalisation of Roma in the Czech Republic', *Sociological Research Online* 4 (3): U1–U18.

Bargach, J. 2001. 'Personalizing It: Adoption, Bastardy, Kinship and Family', in J.D. Faubion (ed.) *The Ethics of Kinship: Ethnographic Inquiries*. Oxford: Rowman and Littlefield. 71–97.

Barth, F. 1969. *Ethnic Groups and Boundaries: the Social Organisation of Culture Difference*. London: Allen and Unwin.

––––– 1973. 'Descent and Marriage Reconsidered', in J. Goody (ed.) *The Character of Kinship*. Cambridge: Cambridge University Press. 3–19.

––––– 2000. 'Boundaries and Connections', in A.P. Cohen (ed.) *Signifying Identities: Anthropological Perspectives on Boundaries and Contested Values*. London: Routledge. 17–36.

Bartlett, F.C. 1932. *Remembering: A Study in Experimental and Social Psychology*. New York: Macmillan.

Bauman, R. 1984 [1977]. *Verbal Art as Performance*. Prospect Heights, Illinois: Waveland Press.

————— 1986. *Story, Performance and Event: Contextual Studies of Oral Narrative*. Cambridge Studies in oral and literate culture. Cambridge: Cambridge University Press.

Bauman, R. and C.L. Briggs 1990. 'Poetics and Performance as Critical Perspectives on Language and Social Life', *Annual Review of Anthropology* 19: 59–88.

Bell, F. 1985 [1907]. *At the Works: a Study of a Manufacturing Town*. London: Virago.

Benedict, R. 1935. *Patterns of Culture*. London: Routledge.

Berdahl, D. 1999. *Where the World Ended: Re-unification and Identity in the German Borderland*. London: University of California Press.

Berger, H.M. and G.P. Del Negro 2002. 'Bauman's *Verbal Art* and the Social Organization of Attention: The Role of Reflexivity in the Aesthetics of Performance', *Journal of American Folklore* 115 (455): 62–91.

Berger, P and T. Luckman. 1966. *The Social Construction of Reality: A Treatise in the Sociology of Knowledge*. London: Penguin.

Bernstein, B. 1964. 'Elaborated and Restricted Codes: Their Social Origins and Some Consequences', *The Ethnography of Communication. American Anthropologist* special publication 66 (6) part2.

Besnier, Niko. 1995. *Literacy, Emotion and Authority: Reading and Writing on a Polynesian Atoll*. Cambridge: Cambridge University Press.

Beynon, H., R. Hudson and D. Sadler. 1994. *A Place Called Teesside: A Locality in a Global Economy*. Edinburgh: Edinburgh University Press.

Bhabha, H.K. 1994. *The Location of Culture*. London: Routledge.

Bird-David, N. 1995. '"Hunter-gatherers" Kinship Organisation: Implicit Roles and Rules', in E. Goody (ed.) *Social Intelligence and Interaction: Expressions and Implications of the Social Bias in Human Intelligence*. Cambridge: Cambridge University Press.

Blacking, John (ed.) 1977. *The Anthropology of the Body*. London: Academic Press.

Bluck, S. and T. Habermas 2000. 'The Life Story Schema', *Motivation and Emotion* 24 (2): 121–47.

Borneman, J. 1992. *Belonging in the Two Berlins: Kin, State, Nation*. Cambridge: Cambridge University Press.

————— 2001. 'Caring and Being Cared For', in Faubion, J.D. (ed.). *The Ethics of Kinship: Ethnographic Inquiries*. Oxford: Rowman and Littlefield. 29–46.

Bourdieu, P. 1977. *Outline of a Theory of Practice*, trans. R. Nice. Cambridge: Cambridge University Press.

————— 1979. *Distinction: A Social Critique of the Judgement of Taste*, trans. R. Nice. London: Routledge.

————— 1990. 'Social Space and Symbolic Power', in P. Bourdieu *In Other Words: Essays Towards a Reflexive Sociology*. Stanford, California: Stanford University Press.

Bourdieu, P. and L.J.D. Wacquant. 1992. *Invitation to Reflexive Sociology.* Chicago: University of Chicago Press.

Braid, D. 2002. *Scottish Traveller Tales: Lives Shaped Through Stories.* Jackson: University of Mississippi Press.

Brand, R.J., D.A. Baldwin, and L.A. Ashburn. 2002. 'Evidence for "Motionese": Modifications in Mothers' Infant Directed Action', *Developmental Science* 7 (1): 72–83.

Brown, Karen McCarthy. 1991. *Mama Lola; A Vodou Priestess in Brooklyn.* Oxford: University of California Press.

Bruner, J. 1986. *Actual Minds, Possible Worlds.* Cambridge, Masssachussetts: Harvard University Press.

——— 1990. *Acts of Meaning.* London: Harvard University Press.

Bush, J., S. Moffatt and C. Dunn. 2001. '"Even the Birds Around Here Cough": Stigma, Air Pollution and Health in Teesside', *Health and Place* 7 (1): 47–56.

Caffrey, S. and G. Mundy. 1997. 'Informal Systems of Justice: the Formation of Law within Gypsy Communities', *American Journal of Comparative Law* 45 (2): 251–67.

Carrithers, M. 1992. *Why Humans Have Cultures.* Oxford: Oxford University Press.

——— 2000. 'On Polytropy: Or the Natural Condition of Spiritual Cosmopolitanism in India: The Digambar Jain Case', *Modern Asian Studies* 34 (4): 831–61.

——— 2001. 'Hedgehogs, Foxes and Persons: Resistance and Moral Creativity in East Germany and South India', in N. Roughley (ed.) *Being Human: Anthropological Universality and Particularity in Transdisciplinary Perspectives.* New York: Walter de Gruyter.

——— 2003, 'Story Seeds and the Inchoate'. Unpublished manuscript.

Carsten, J. 1991. 'Children in Between: Fostering and the Process of Kinship on Pulau Langkawi, Malaysia', *Man* 26 (3): 425–43.

——— 2000. *Cultures of Relatedness: New Approaches to the Study of Kinship.* Cambridge: Cambridge University Press.

Cleveland and Teesside Local History Society. 1994. *Saints Alive! How It All Began in Middlesbrough.* Middlesbrough.

Clifford, J. 1997. 'Spatial Practices: Fieldwork, Travel and the Disciplining of Anthropology', in A. Gupta and J. Ferguson (eds) *Anthropological Locations: Boundaries and Grounds of a Field Science.* London: University of California Press: 185ff.

Clifford, J. and G. Marcus (eds) 1986. *Writing Culture: the Poetics and Politics of Ethnography.* Berkeley: University of California Press.

Cohen, A.P. 1985. *The Symbolic Construction of Community.* Chichester: Horwood.

Cohen, A.P. (ed.) 2000. *Signifying Identities: Anthropological Perspectives on Boundaries and Contested Values.* London: Routledge.

Collier, J., M.Z. Rosaldo and S. Yanagisako. 1982. 'Is There a Family? New Anthropological views', in B. Thorne and M. Yalom (eds) *Rethinking the Family: Some Feminist Questions*. London: Longman.

Cook, G. 1994. *Discourse and Literature*. Oxford: Oxford University Press.

Demeritt, D. 2002. 'What is the "Social Construction of Nature"? A Typology and Sympathetic Critique', *Advances in Human Geography* 26 (6): 767–90.

Desjarlais, Robert R. 1992. *Body and Emotion: the Aesthetics of Illness and Healing in the Nepal Himalayas*. Philadelphia: University of Pennsylvania Press.

Dixon, J. 2001. 'Contact and Boundaries: "Locating" the Social Psychology of Intergroup Relations', *Theory and Psychology* 11 (5): 587–608.

Dolgin, J., D.S. Kemnitzer and D.M. Schneider. 1977. *Symbolic Anthropology: A Reader in the Study of Symbols and Meanings*. New York: University of Columbia Press.

Drew, P. and J. Heritage, (eds) 1992. *Talk at Work: Interaction in Institutional Settings*. Cambridge: Cambridge University Press.

Drury, J. and S. Reicher. 2000. 'Collective Action and Psychological Change: The Emergence of New Social Identities', *British Journal of Social Psychology* 39 (4): 579–604

Durham University North East Area Study. 1975. *The Social Consequences of the Teesside Structure Plan*. Durham: Durham University

Edwards, David B. 1994. 'Afghanistan, Ethnography and the New World Order'. *Cultural Anthropology* 9 (3): 345–60.

Eliot, T.S. 1972 [1940]. *The Waste Land and Other Poems*. London: Faber and Faber.

Emerson, C. 1986. 'The Outer Word and Inner Speech: Bakhtin, Vygotsky, and the Internalization of Language', in Morson (ed.) *Bakhtin: Essays and Dialogues on His Work*. London: University of Chicago Press.

Erickson, F. 2002. 'Culture and Human Development', *Human Development* 45: 299–306.

Eschenbruch, N. 2002. 'Nursing Stories. A Narrative Ethnography of Life and Death in a Germany Hospice'. Unpublished Ph.D. Thesis, Institüt für Europäische Ethnologie, Humboldt University, Berlin.

Fabian, J. 1983. *Time and the Other: How Anthropology Makes its Object*. New York: University of Columbia Press.

Farnell, B. 1995. *Do You See What I Mean?* Austin: University of Texas Press.

——— 2000. 'Getting Out of the Habitus: An Alternative Model of Dynamically Embodied Serial Action', *Journal of the Royal Anthropological Institute* 6 (3): 397–418.

Faubion, J.D. (ed.) 2001. *The Ethics of Kinship: Ethnographic Inquiries*. Oxford: Rowman & Littlefield.

Feld, S. and A.A. Fox. 1994. 'Music and Language', *Annual Review of Anthropology* 23: 25–53.

Fernandez, J. 1986. *Persuasions and Performances: the Play of Tropes in Culture.* Bloomington: Indiana University Press.
—— (ed.) 1991. *Beyond Metaphor: the Theory of Tropes in Anthropology.* Stanford: Stanford University Press.
—— 2000. 'Peripheral Wisdom'. In Cohen (ed.) *Signifying Identities: Anthropological Perspectives on Boundaries and Contested Values.* London: Routledge.
Fernandez, J. and M. Huber, (eds) 2001. *Irony in Action: Anthropology, Practice, and the Moral Imagination.* London: University of Chicago Press.
Fonseca, I. 1995. *Bury Me Standing: the Gypsies and Their Journey.* London: Chatto & Windus.
Foucault, M. 1972. *Archaeology of Knowledge.* London: Tavistock.
—— 1977. *Discipline and Punish: the Birth of the Prison.* London: Allen Lane.
—— 1979. *The History of Sexuality Vol. 1: An Introduction.* London: Lane.
—— 1980. *Power/Knowledge: Selected Interviews and Other Writings 1972–1977.* Brighton: Harvester Press.
—— 1986. 'Of Other Spaces', *Diacritics* 16: 22–27.
Fox R.G. (ed.) 1991. *Recapturing Anthropology: Working in the Present.* Santa Fe: School of American Research Press.
Fraser, A. 1995. *The Gypsies.* Oxford: Blackwell.
Friedman, V. 1985. 'Problems in the Codification of a Standard Romani Literary Language', in J. Grumet (ed.) *Papers from the Fourth and Fifth Annual Meetings, Gypsy Lore Society.* New York: The Chapter.
—— 1991. 'Case in Romani: Old Grammar in New Affixes', *Journal of the Gypsy Lore Society* 1: 85–102.
—— 1995. 'Romani Standardization and Status in the Republic of Macedonia', in Y. Matras (ed.) *Romani in Contact: the History, Structure and Sociology of a Language.* Amsterdam: J. Benjamins.
Friedrich, P. 2001. 'Ironic Irony', in J. Fernandez and M. Huber (eds) *Irony in Action: Anthropology, Practice, and the Moral Imagination.* London: University of Chicago Press.
Gay-y-Blasco, P. 1997. 'A "Different" Body? Desire and Virginity among Gitanos', *Journal of the Royal Anthropological Institute* 3 (3).
—— 1999. *Gypsies in Madrid: Sex, Gender and the Performance of Identity.* Oxford: Berg.
—— 2000. 'Gitano Evangelism: the Emergence of a Politico-Religious Diaspora'. Paper presented at the 6th EASA Conference, Krakow, 26–29 July 2000.
—— 2001. '"We Don't Know Our Descent": How the Gitanos of Jarana Manage the Past', *Journal of the Royal Anthropological Institute* 7: 631–47.
Geertz, Clifford. 1988. *Works and Lives; The Anthropologist as Author.* Oxford: Polity Press.

Geertz, H. and C. Geertz. 1975. *Kinship in Bali.* Chicago: University of Chicago Press.

George, L. 2001. '"Like Family to Me": Families of Origin, Families of Choice, and Class Mobility', in J.D. Faubion (ed.) *The Ethics of Kinship: Ethnographic Inquiries.* Oxford: Rowman & Littlefield.

Gilligan, C. 1982. *In a Different Voice: Psychological Theory and Women's Development.* Cambridge, Massachussetts: Harvard University Press.

Glass, R. 1948. *The Social Background of a Plan.* London: Routledge & Kegan Paul.

Goffman, E. 1981 [1979]. 'Footing', in E. Goffman *Forms of Talk.* Philadelphia: University of Pennsylvania Press.

———— 1986 [1974]. *Frame Analysis: an Essay on the Organization of Experience.* Boston, Massachussetts: Northeastern University Press.

Goody, E. 1982. *Parenthood and Social Reproduction: Fostering and Occupational Roles in West Africa.* Cambridge: Cambridge University Press.

———— (ed.) 1995. *Social Intelligence and Interaction: Expressions and Implications of the Social Bias in Human Intelligence.* Cambridge: Cambridge University Press.

Goody, J. (ed.) 1973. *The Character of Kinship.* Cambridge: Cambridge University Press.

Greenfields, M. 2003. 'It's My Land and I'm Doing No Harm', paper presented to the Gypsy Lore Society Annual Conference, University of Michigan, June 2003.

Gropper, R.C. 1975. *Gypsies in the City: Culture Patterns and Survival.* Princeton, New Jersey: Darwin Press.

Gullestad, M. 2002. 'Invisible Fences: Egalitarianism, Nationalism and Racism', *Journal of the Royal Anthropological Institute* 8: 45–63.

Gumperz, J.J. 1992. 'Interviewing in Intercultural Situations', in Drew and Heritage (eds) *Talk at Work: Interaction in Institutional Settings.* Cambridge: Cambridge University Press.

Gupta, A. and J. Ferguson (eds) 1997. *Anthropological Locations: Boundaries and Grounds of a Field Science.* London: University of California Press.

Halbwachs, M. 1980 [1950]. *The Collective Memory.* London: Harper and Row.

Hancock, I. 1997. 'Duty and Beauty, Possession and Truth: Lexical Impoverishment as Control', in T. Acton and G. Mundy (eds) *Romani Culture and Gypsy Identity.* Hatfield: University of Hertfordshire Press: 182–89

Hancock, I., S. Dowd and R. Djuric (eds) 1998. *The Roads of the Roma.* Hatfield: University of Hertfordshire Press.

Harris, C.C. 1969. *The Family: An Introduction.* London: Allen and Unwin.

Harrison, J.K. 2001. 'The Impact of Industry', in *Historic Reflections Across the Tees.* Middlesbrough: Cleveland and Teesside Local History Society.

Hawes, D. and B. Perez. 1996. *The Gypsy and the State: the Ethnic Cleansing of British Society*. Bristol: Policy Press.

Hayden, C. 1995. 'Gender, Genetics and Generation: Reformulating Biology in Lesbian Kinship', *Cultural Anthropology* 10 (1): 41–63.

Heath, S.B. 1986. 'What No Bedtime Story Means: Narrative Skills at Home and School', in B. Schieffelin and E. Ochs (eds) *Language Socialization Across Cultures*. Studies in the Social and Cultural Foundations of Language 3. Cambridge: Cambridge University Press.

Helgason, A. and G. Palsson. 1997. 'Contested Commodities: The Moral Landscape of Modernist Regimes', *Journal of the Royal Anthropological Institute* 3: 451–71.

Highmore, B. 2004. 'Homework. Routine, Social Aesthetics and the Ambiguity of Everyday Life', *Cultural Studies* 18: 306–27.

Holland, D. and N. Quinn (eds) 1987. *Cultural Models in Language and Thought*. Cambridge: Cambridge University Press.

Howker, J. 1985. *The Nature of the Beast*. London: Lions Tracks.

Hyman, M. 1989. *Sites for Travellers: a Study in Five London Boroughs*. London: London Race and Housing Research Unit.

Ingold, T. 1993. 'The Art of Translation in a Continuous World', in G. Palsson (ed.) *Beyond Boundaries*. Oxford: Berg.

Jackson, M. 1983. 'Knowledge of the Body', *Man* 18: 327–45.

——— (ed.) 1996. *Things As They Are: New Directions in Phenomenological Anthropology*. Bloomington: Indiana University Press.

——— 1998. *Minima Ethnographica: Intersubjectivity and the Anthropological Project*. London: Chicago University Press.

Jarman, E. and A.O.H. Jarman. 1991. *The Welsh Gypsies: Children of Abram Wood*. Cardiff: University of Wales Press.

Járóka, L. 2000. '"If Madonna were a Romanian Gypsy ...": Anthropology (and Media) in Action', *Anthropology in Action* 7 (1 and 2): 42–50.

Karim, L. 2001. 'A Kinship of One's Own', in J.D. Faubion (ed.) *The Ethics of Kinship: Ethnographic Inquiries*. Oxford: Rowman & Littlefield. 98–124.

Kendall, S. 1997. 'Sites of Resistance: Places on the Margin – the Traveller "Homeplace"', in T.A. Acton (ed.) *Gypsy Politics and Traveller Identity*. Hatfield: University of Hertfordshire Press. 70–89

Kenrick, D. 1999. 'What is a Gypsy?', in R. Morris and L. Clements (eds) *Gaining Ground: Law Reform for Gypsies and Travellers*. Hatfield: University of Hertfordshire Press. 64–69

Kenrick, D. and C. Clark. 1999. *Moving On; the Gypsies and Travellers of Britain*. Hatfield: University of Hertfordshire Press.

Krumhansl, C.L., P. Toivanen, T. Eerola, P. Toiviainen, T. Jarvinen and J. Louhivuori. 2000. 'Cross-cultural Music Cognition: Cognitive Methodology Applied to North Sami Yoiks', *Cognition* 76 (1): 13–58.

Lapage, G. 1997. 'The English Folktale Corpus and Gypsy Oral Tradition', in T.A. Acton and G. Mundy (eds) *Romani Culture and Gypsy Identity.* Hatfield: University of Hertfordshire Press. 18–30.

Langellier, K.M. and E.E. Peterson. 1993. 'Family Storytelling as a Strategy of Social Control', in D.K. Mumby *Narrative and Social Control: Critical Perspectives.* London: Sage. 49–76

Larrabee, M.J. (ed.) 1993. *An Ethic of Care: Feminist and Interdisciplinary Perspectives.* London: Routledge.

Lawrence, D. and S. Low. 1990. 'The Built Environment and Spatial Form'. *Annual Review of Anthropology* 19: 453–505.

Lemon, A. 2000. *Between Two Fires: Gypsy Performance and Memory from Pushkin to Postsocialism.* London: Duke University Press.

Liegeois, J-P. 1986. *Gypsies: An Illustrated History.* London: Al Saqi Books.

Linde, C. 1993. *Life Stories: the Creation of Coherence.* Oxford: Oxford University Press.

Low, S.M. 1996. 'The Anthropology of Cities: Imagining and Theorizing the City'. *Annual Review of Anthropology* 25: 383–409.

Luria, A. 1994. 'The Problem of the Cultural Behaviour of the Child', in R. Van der Veer and J. Valsinger (eds) *The Vygotsky Reader.* Oxford: Basil Blackwell.

MacDougall, D. 1999. 'Social Aesthetics and the Doon School', *Visual Anthropology Review* 15: 3–20.

Machin, D. 1994. 'Community and the Production of Everyday Narratives: Newspaper Journalists and Their Readers in a Spanish City'. Unpublished Ph.D. thesis, Durham University.

Machin, D. and M. Carrithers. 1996. 'From "Interpretative Communities" to "Communities of Improvisation"', *Media, Culture and Society* 18 (2): 343–52.

Mackie, D. and E. Smith. 1998. 'Intergroup Relations: Insights from a Theoretically Integrative Approach', *Psychological Review* 105 (3): 499–529.

Matras, Y. (ed.) 1995. *Romani in Contact: the History, Structure and Sociology of a Language.* Amsterdam: Benjamins.

——— 2002. *Romani: A Linguistic Introduction.* Cambridge: Cambridge University Press.

Matras, Y., P. Bakker and H. Kyuchukov (eds) 1997. 'The Typology and Dialectology of Romani'. Amsterdam Studies in the Theory and History of Linguistic Science. Series IV, *Current Issues in Linguistic Theory* 156.

McKeough, A. and A. Sanderson. 1996. 'Teaching Storytelling: a Microgenetic Analysis of Developing Narrative Competency', *Journal of Narrative and Life History* 6 (2): 157–92

Mattingly, C. 1998. *Healing Dramas and Clinical Plots: The Narrative Structure of Experience.* Cambridge: Cambridge University Press.

Mauss, Marcel. 1979 [1950]. 'Body Techniques', in M. Mauss *Sociology and Psychology – Essays*. London: Routledge

Mead, M. 1931. *Growing Up in New Guinea: A Comparative Study of Primitive Education*. London: Routledge and Sons.

Mead, M. and F.C. Macgregor. 1951. *Growth and Culture: A Photographic Study of Balinese Childhood*. New York: Putnam.

Middlesbrough Evening Gazette, 29 January 2002.

Middlesbrough Evening Gazette, 16 March 2002.

Middleton, D. and D. Edwards (eds) 1990. *Collective Remembering*. London: Sage.

Morris, R. 2000. 'Gypsies, Travellers and the Media: Press Regulation and Racism in the UK'. Paper presented to the Annual Meeting and Conference on Gypsy Studies of the Gypsy Lore Society, Washington DC, USA, 12 August 2000.

Morris, R and L. Clements (eds) 1999. *Gaining Ground: Law Reform for Gypsies and Travellers*. Hatfield: University of Hertfordshire Press.

Morson, G.S. 1986. *Bakhtin: Essays and Dialogues on His Work*. London: University of Chicago Press.

Myerhof, B and J. Ruby (eds) 1982. *A Crack in the Mirror: Reflexive Perspectives in Anthropology*. Philadelphia: University of Pennsylvania Press.

Narayan, Kirin. 1993. 'How Native Is a "Native" Anthropologist?', *American Anthropologist* 95 (3): 19–34.

Narmour, E. 2000. 'Music Expectation by Cognitive Rule-mapping', *Music Perception* 17 (3): 329–98.

Ochs, E and L. Capps. 1996. 'Narrating the Self', *Annual Review of Anthropology* 25: 19–43.

——— 2001. *Living Narrative: Creating Lives in Everyday Storytelling*. London: Harvard University Press.

Okely, J. 1983. *The Traveller-Gypsies*. Cambridge: Cambridge University Press.

——— 1997. 'Cultural Ingenuity and Travelling Autonomy: Not Copying, Just Choosing', in T.A. Acton and G. Mundy (eds) *Romani Culture and Gypsy Identity*. Hatfield: University of Hertfordshire Press. 190–205.

Orde, A. 2000. *Religion, Business and Society in North East England*. Stamford: Shaun Tyas.

Paine, R. 2000. 'Aboriginality, Authenticity and the Settler World', in A. Cohen (ed.) *Signifying Identities: Anthropological Perspectives on Boundaries and Contested Values*. London: Routledge. 77–116.

Palgrave, F.T. (ed.) 1926 [1861]. *The Golden Treasury of the Best Songs and Lyrical Poems in the English Language*. Oxford: Oxford University Press.

Peirano, M.G.S. 1998. 'When Anthropology is at Home: the Different Contexts of a Single Discipline', *Annual Review of Anthropology* 27: 105–28.

Polanyi, M. 1958. *Personal Knowledge*. Chicago, University of Chicago Press.

—— 1969 [1965]. 'The Structure of Consciousness', in M. Grene (ed.) *Knowing and Being: Essays by Michael Polanyi*. London: Routledge & Kegan Paul. 211–23.

Pratt, M.L. 1986. 'Fieldwork in Common Places', in Clifford and Marcus (eds) *Writing Culture: the Poetics and Politics of Ethnography*. Berkeley: University of California Press. 27–50.

Premack, D. 1984. 'Pedagogy and Aesthetics as Sources of Culture', in M. Gazzagia (ed.) *Handbook of Cognitive Neuroscience*. London: Plenum Press.

Quinn, N. 1991. 'The Cultural Basis of Metaphor', in J. Fernandez (ed.) *Beyond Metaphor: the Theory of Tropes in Anthropology*. Stanford: Stanford University Press. 56–93.

Rabinow, P. (ed.) 1984. *The Foucault Reader*. London: Penguin.

Ramsey, J.L. and J.H. Langlois. 2002. 'Effects of the "Beauty Is Good" Stereotype on Children's Information Processing', *Journal of Experimental Child Psychology* 81.

Rapport, N. 2003. *I am Dynamite: an Alternative Anthropology of Power*. London: Routledge.

Riddington, R. 1990. *Little Bit Know Something: Stories in a Language of Anthropology*. Iowa City: University of Iowa Press.

Rosaldo, R. 1989. *Culture and Truth: the Remaking of Social Analysis*. Boston: Beacon Press.

Rose, D. 1990. *Living the Ethnographic Life*. Newberry Park, California: Sage.

Rose, N. 1996. *Inventing Ourselves: Psychology, Power, Personhood*. Cambridge: Cambridge University Press.

—— 1999. *Governing the Soul: the Shaping of the Private Self* (2nd edn.). London: Free Association Books.

Royal Anthropological Institute of Great Britain and Ireland, 1951[1874]. *Notes and Queries on Anthropology*. London: Routledge & Kegan Paul.

Rutherser, C. 1999. 'Making Place in the Nonplace Urban Realm: Notes on the Revitalization of Downtown Atlanta', in S. Low (ed.) *Theorizing the City: the New Urban Anthropology Reader*. London, Rutgers University Press: 317–41.

Said, E. 1978. *Orientalism: Western Conceptions of the Orient*. London: Penguin.

Sampson, J. 1923. 'On the Origin and Early Migrations of the Gypsies', *Journal of the Gypsy Lore Society*, 3rd series, 2 (4): 156–69.

Schieffelin, B. 1990. *The Give and Take of Everyday Life: Language Socialization of Kaluli Children*. Studies in the Social and Cultural Foundations of Language 9. Cambridge: Cambridge University Press.

Schieffelin, B. and E. Ochs (eds) 1986. *Language Socialization across Cultures*. Studies in the Social and Cultural Foundations of Language 3. Cambridge: Cambridge University Press.

Schieffelin, E. 1976. *The Sorrow of the Lonely and the Burning of the Dancers.* New York: St. Martin's Press.

Schneider, D. 1984. *A Critique of the Study of Kinship.* Ann Arbor: University of Michigan Press.

Schrøder, K.C. 1994. 'Audience Semiotics, Interpretive Communities and the "Ethnographic Turn" in Media Research', *Media, Culture and Society* 16 (2): 337–47.

Schutz, A. 1944. 'The Stranger: an Essay in Social Psychology', *American Journal of Sociology* 49 (6): 499–507.

———— 1951. 'Making Music Together: a Study in Social Relationship', *Social Research* 18 (1): 76–97.

———— 1970. *On Phenomenology and Social Relations: Selected Writings* (ed.) Helmut Wagner. London: University of Chicago Press.

———— 1972 [1932]. *The Phenomenology of the Social World.* trans. G. Walsh and F. Lehnert. London: Heinemann.

Scott, James C. 1998. *Seeing Like a State: How Certain Schemes to Improve the Human Condition Have Failed.* London: Yale University Press.

Shields, R. 1991. *Places on the Margin: Alternative Geographies of Modernity.* London: Routledge.

Sibley, D. 1981. *Outsiders in Urban Society.* Oxford: Blackwell.

———— 1995. *Geographies of Exclusion.* London: Routledge.

———— 2001. 'The Binary City', *Urban Studies* 38 (2): 239–50.

Simmel, G. 1950. *The Sociology of Georg Simmel*, ed. and trans. Kurt H. Wolff. New York: The Free Press.

Simpson, R. 1994. 'Bringing the "Unclear" Family into Focus: Divorce and Re-marriage in Contemporary Britain', *Man* 29 (4): 831–51.

———— 1997. 'On Gifts, Payments and Disputes: Divorce and Changing Family Structures in Contemporary Britain', *Journal of the Royal Anthropological Institute* 3 (4): 731–45.

———— 1998. *Changing Families.* Oxford: Berg.

Smith, J. 1991. *Gypsies and Travellers in England and Wales.* Bristol: Bristol Shelter Office.

Stewart, M. 1997(a). 'The Puzzle of Roma Persistence: Group Identity Without a Nation', in T.A. Acton and G. Mundy (eds) *Romani Culture and Gypsy Identity.* Hatfield: University of Hertfordshire Press. 84–98

———— 1997(b). *The Time of the Gypsies.* Oxford: Westview Press.

Strathern, M. 1992. *After Nature: English Kinship in the Late Twentieth Century.* Cambridge: Cambridge University Press.

Strauss, C. and N. Quinn (eds) 1997. *A Cognitive Theory of Cultural Meaning.* Cambridge: Cambridge University Press.

Sutherland, A. 1975. *Gypsies: the Hidden Americans.* London: Tavistock.

———— 1977. 'The Body as a Social Symbol Among the Rom', in J. Blacking (ed.) *The Anthropology of the Body.* London: Academic Press.

———— 1997. 'Complexities of US Law and Gypsy Identity', *American Journal of Comparative Law* 45 (2): 393–405.

Sway, M. 1988. *Familiar Strangers: Gypsy Life in America*. Urbana and Chicago: University of Illinois Press.

Tannen, D., ed. 1993. *Framing in Discourse*. Oxford: Oxford University Press.

Tannen, D and C. Wallat. 1993. 'Interactive Frames and Knowledge Schemas in Interaction: Examples from a Medical Examination/Interview', in D. Tannen (ed.) *Framing in Discourse*. Oxford: Oxford University Press.

Trevarthen, C. and K.J. Aitken. 2001. 'Infant Intersubjectivity: Research, Theory, and Clinical Applications', *Journal of Child Psychology and Psychiatry* 42 (1): 3–48.

Trigg, E.B. 1973. *Gypsy Demons and Divinities: the Magical and Supernatural Practices of the Gypsies*. London: Sheldon Press.

Turner, A. 2000. 'Embodied Ethnography. Doing Culture', *Social Anthropology* 8 (1): 51–60.

Ucko, Peter J.and R. Layton (eds) 1999. *The Archaeology and Anthropology of Landscape: Shaping Your Landscape*. London and New York: Routledge.

Vygotsky, L. 1994. 'The Problem of the Cultural Development of the Child', in R. Van der Veer and J. Valsinger (eds) *The Vygotsky Reader*. Oxford: Basil Blackwell.

Vygotsky, L. and Luria, A. 1994. 'Tool and Symbol in Child Development', in R. Van der Veer and J. Valsinger (eds) *The Vygotsky Reader*. Oxford: Basil Blackwell.

Watanabe, S. 1993. 'Cultural Differences in Framing: American and Japanese Group Discussions', in D. Tannen (ed.) *Framing in Discourse*. Oxford: Oxford University Press.

Wertsch, J. 1991. *Voices of the Mind: a Sociocultural Approach to Mediated Action*. London: Harvester Wheatsheaf.

http://clients.thisisthenortheast.co.uk/millennium/history/page76.htm

http://www.teesvalley-jsu.gov.uk/tvstats1body.htm

INDEX